Monetary Policy on the 75th Anniversary of the Federal Reserve System

Monetary Policy on the 75th Anniversary of the Federal Reserve System

Proceedings of the Fourteenth Annual Economic Policy Conference of the Federal Reserve Bank of St. Louis

edited by
Michael T. Belongia
Federal Reserve Bank of St. Louis

Springer Science+Business Media, LLC

Library of Congress Cataloging-in-Publication Data

Economic Policy Conference of the Federal Reserve Bank of St. Louis
(14th: 1989: Federal Reserve Bank of St. Louis)
Monetary policy on the 75th anniversary of the Federal Reserve
System: proceedings of the Fourteenth Annual Economic Policy
Conference of the Federal Reserve Bank of St. Louis/edited by
Michael T. Belongia.
p. cm.
Conference held 10/19/89.
Includes bibliographical references.
ISBN 978-94-010-5731-8 ISBN 978-94-011-3888-8 (eBook)
DOI 10.1007/978-94-011-3888-8
1. Monetary policy—United States—History—Congresses.
2. United States—Economic policy—History—Congresses.
3. Federal Reserve banks—History—Congresses. I. Belongia,
Michael T. II. Title.
HG501.E26 1990
332.4'973—dc20 90-38802
CIP

Printed on acid-free paper

Set in 10/12pt Times Roman
by Graphicraft Typesetters Ltd., Hong Kong

Contents

Contributing Authors

William A. Barnett
Department of Economics
Washington University
St. Louis, Missouri 63130

K. Alec Chrystal
Centre of Banking
The City University of London
Frobisher Crescent
Barbican Centre
England

Alex Cukierman
Tel Aviv University
Tel Aviv 69978
Israel

Michelle R. Garfinkel
Research Department
Federal Reserve Bank of St. Louis
P.O. Box 442
St. Louis, Missouri 63166

Melvin Hinich
Department of Government
University of Texas at Austin
Austin, Texas 78712

Donald L. Kohn
Board of Governors of the
Federal Reserve System
Washington, D.C. 20551

N. Gregory Mankiw
Department of Economics
Harvard University
Cambridge, Massachusetts 02138

Allan H. Meltzer
Graduate School of
Industrial Administration
Carnegie-Mellon University
220 Schenley Park
Pittsburgh, Pennsylvania 15213

Jeffrey A. Miron
Department of Economics
Boston University
Boston, Massachusetts 02215

Manfred J. M. Neumann
Institut fur Internationale
Wirtschaftspolitik
University of Bonn
Lennestrasse 37
5300 Bonn
West Germany

Edmund S. Phelps
Department of Economics
Columbia University
New York, New York 10027

Charles I. Plosser
Department of Economics
University of Rochester
Rochester, New York 14627

Julio J. Rotemberg
Sloan School of Management
Massachusetts Institute of Technology
E52–434
Cambridge, Massachusetts 02139

Piyu Yue
Research Department
Federal Reserve Bank of St. Louis
P.O. Box 442
St. Louis, Missouri 63166

Preface

When the 12 District Banks of the Federal Reserve System opened their doors for business on November 16, 1914, few observers could have foreseen the Fed's present role as a major, if not dominant, player in U.S. and world economic policymaking. After all, two previous attempts to create a central bank in this country had ended in failure. Moreover, much of the economic theory and institutional structure that have given rise to monetary policy's influence in recent years were not yet in place. Indeed, it would take the Fed more than 20 years to learn (by accident!) the power of open market operations. Clearly, the modern Federal Reserve System has found itself with powers and responsibilities that were not envisioned by its founders.

These proceedings from a conference held at the Federal Reserve Bank of St. Louis on October 19–20, 1989, examine U.S. monetary policy from a variety of perspectives: a historical review of how it has affected aggregate economic performance; a positive analysis of why the Federal Reserve has chosen particular policy strategies; a review of normative arguments about what the Fed should pursue as its policy objective; a critique of how the Fed's "output"—the flow of monetary services in the U.S. economy—is measured; and, finally, a debate over the Fed's ability to influence real economic activity by changing the nominal quantity of money in circulation. Throughout, the authors blend historical data, institutional detail, economic theory, and empirical testing to identify the strengths and weaknesses of monetary policy as it has been implemented in the United States. As a collection, these articles are perhaps best seen not as the end-product of a recent research agenda but as a roadmap for future research on unresolved issues in monetary theory and policy.

Session I

As a preliminary to the conference's discussion of the historical record of U.S. economic performance, Allan H. Meltzer undertakes the difficult task of reviewing the Federal Reserve's role in economic policymaking. Recognizing both that 75 years of history were too much for a single conference paper and that Friedman and Schwartz (1963) and Brunner and Meltzer (1964) had thoroughly examined the Fed's first 50 years, Meltzer focuses primarily on the conduct and performance of U.S. monetary policy since the early 1960s. Finally, rather than yield to the temptation to second-guess the Fed's actions on an episodic basis, Meltzer instead takes the constructive route of trying to identify *systematic* components of the policy process that have caused problems for monetary policy in the past and, unless changed, can be expected to cause problems in the future.

Meltzer's review of the policy process embodies the arguments that have become known as the "monetarist critique." Briefly, he argues that the Federal Reserve has looked at the wrong variables to evaluate the influence of its policy actions. As a consequence, the Fed, in his view, generally has misinterpreted both how the economy is performing at the moment and which policy actions will be consistent with the desired path of future economic activity. To many, his arguments are familiar: using free reserves to guide policy and interest rates as a gauge of its policy stance, the Fed would consistently view monetary policy to be restrictive (or expansive) and undertake actions to ease (or tighten) when, in fact, the truth was just the opposite. Thus, one should expect that an activist approach to monetary policy in the context of this policy process would exacerbate both the inflation at cycle peaks and the output and employment losses at cycle troughs.

Meltzer also argues that the Federal Open Market Committee's (FOMC's) reliance on staff forecasts to chart the course of future economic performance has given policymakers a false sense that policy mistakes now can be offset by timely policy changes in the future. But an examination of the staff's forecasting record shows that even its short-term errors are large enough to cover a variety of disparate outcomes so that basing policy decisions on forecasts may contribute still more volatility to the business cycle.

Of all the evidence Meltzer presents to support his policy critique, perhaps the most damning is his finding that the average growth rate of money has been higher in each recent business cycle expansion than in the one previous to it. Specifically, we have gone from 4% average M1 growth in the expansion of the 1960s to rates in excess of 6% and then 7% during the 1970s to nearly 9% during the expansion of the 1980s. In Meltzer's mind, these data indicate that fundamental problems with the policy process lead to procyclical patterns in money growth that have produced a higher underlying inflation rate without the benefit of greater economic stability.

Meltzer's analysis of the historical record naturally leads him to recommend that the Fed be held accountable for achieving announced money stock targets. His specific method of accomplishing this has shown promising results in simulation experiments for reducing both the average rate of inflation and the variability of output.

A presentation of Meltzer's scope called for several discussants to address the variety of issues that were raised. In his comments, Jeffrey A. Miron investigated whether the Federal Reserve has had a demonstrable effect on U.S. economic performance. By examining consistent data series since 1870 and dividing the data both into 10-year and longer periods (1870–1913; 1919–1940; 1947–1987), Miron first finds that real economic growth has been nearly a full percentage point lower in the postwar period relative to 1870–1913. He also finds, consistent with Meltzer's arguments, a slight decline in the price level between 1870–1913 contrasted with a 4.4% average inflation rate since 1947. Finally, he reports that the Fed's emphasis on smoothing interest rates has been associated with little change in the variability of output over time.

To assess whether the Federal Reserve's approach to monetary policy and the U.S. record of economic performance have deviated from that in other countries, K. Alec Chrystal reviews Meltzer's arguments relative to the experience abroad. He argues that Switzerland, Germany, and Japan largely have achieved price stability by pursuing money stock targets in their conduct of monetary policy. Moreover, when these foreign central banks abandoned their money stock targets to pursue other objectives, such as the exchange rate, a higher inflation rate later ensued. Finally, he directs attention to the tradeoff between the benefits of deregulation in the banking industry, which will increase the stability of the financial system, and the impact these changes will likely have on the macroeconomic relationships of monetary policy.

Donald L. Kohn discusses U.S. monetary policy from the viewpoint of someone involved in its day-to-day implementation. Although Kohn acknowledges that drawing distinctions between changes in real and nominal interest rates, among other factors, contributed to some undesirable monetary policy results in the 1960s and 1970s, he is quick to point out that the brief "monetarist experiment" of 1979–1982 also was fraught with problems. More important, the continuing instability in velocity leads Kohn to argue that none of the monetary aggregates is likely to be a useful guide to policy. In a direct criticism of Meltzer's proposal to target the growth of the monetary base, Kohn cites results from a simulation experiment that indicated base targeting would produce extremely large and destabilizing variations in the federal funds rate.

Kohn also describes the current approach to monetary policy as one in which the FOMC monitors a variety of indicators to evaluate how monetary actions are transmitted to the economy. Though interest rates and exchange rates are particularly being watched for signals about near-term economic developments, Kohn reports that the aggregates still receive attention in gauging the long-run consequences of policy actions. The current procedures, according to Kohn, lead to frequent, small adjustments in policy as the FOMC pursues its stated goal of promoting economic expansion through price stability.

Session II

Relatively recent research in monetary economics has attempted to offer positive explanations for the policy processes (or behaviors) adopted by a central bank. Although "the Fed smoothes interest rates" has become an axiom to many observers of U.S. monetary policy, the intriguing and obvious question is: Why? Developing a model to rationalize this behavior is the problem addressed by Alex Cukierman.

Cukierman begins by constructing a choice-theoretic model in which the Fed values both price and financial stability. But, because financial instability typically will call for expansionary monetary policy inconsistent with price stability, and efforts to reduce inflation can take place only in the presence of financial stability, the Fed's systematic switching between these competing goals will lead to a policy that produces both interest rate smoothing and an inflationary bias. Cukierman notes that his model is consistent with changes in interest rate behavior after the founding of the Fed reported by Mankiw and Miron (1986).

Michelle R. Garfinkel, while supporting efforts to model Federal Reserve behavior and generally agreeing with Cukierman's analysis, raises several issues that may affect the conclusions that are drawn from it. For example, she finds his definition of the "financial stability" pursued by the Fed to be vague and the maximization of bank profits to be an odd objective for monetary policy. She also believes that the Fed's choice between two competing goals might disappear if it has both reserve requirements and reserve growth as separate policy instruments. Finally, she discusses some of the strategic aspects of policy. In particular, she offers an alternative model to illustrate that the inflationary bias of Cukierman's model is simply a result of his focus on a one-shot Nash equilibrium.

While research on positive theories to explain why the Fed has chosen particular policies is relatively new, the normative debate over what the Fed *should* do certainly predates its founding. Especially in the context of recent legislative proposals that call for the Fed to pursue price stability as its primary objective and a flurry of research on policy rules that would limit the Fed's discretion, the normative debate has been both vocal and tightly focused in recent years. Edmund S. Phelps discusses whether the Fed *should* have price stability as its main policy goal and whether any of several discretion-limiting rules would be desirable in achieving that outcome.

In general, Phelps is uneasy with either proposition. On the one hand, defining price stability itself is tricky since it could be either a constant price level, a constant and fully anticipated inflation rate, or a low inflation rate that is stable within narrow bands. Each definition has advantages and disadvantages when it is applied to textbook models and real-world situations so that none is perfect or clearly preferable to another. Phelps' instinct is that taking the necessary policy actions to move from today's inflation rate of approximately 4% to the 0% to 2% range, which many would call price stability, would have output and employment costs far in excess of lower inflation's benefits.

Phelps also finds problems with each of the proposed rules to limit the Fed's discretion. For example, shocks to velocity may require the Fed to readjust its target ranges for money growth periodically; but, once one opens the door to this possibility, the central bank has a convenient mechanism (or excuse) to explain deviations from its money growth targets. Also, if following a policy rule produces more stable money growth, that is likely to be associated with greater fluctuation in other variables. Under various assumptions about exactly where the rigidities appeared in the economy's reaction to shocks, Phelps shows how a supply shock could be exacerbated when a rule prevented the Fed from making an accommodating change in policy.

Manfred J. M. Neumann criticizes Phelps for not offering a consistent framework to evaluate each policy rule's relationship both to operating characteristics and final goals. Looking at each rule's ability to respond to current shocks, output shocks, or changes in trend velocity, Neumann's evaluation of the proposals finds only Meltzer's (1984) strategy for targeting the monetary base to be consistent with each criterion.

At a more general level, however, Neumann questions the need for a coercive rule when better monetary policy might be achieved through the legislative creation of "the ultra-conservative central banker." His proposed monetary constitution would have a variety of elements, but its overall intent would be to make the central bank truly independent and price stability its only policy objective. In his view, creating a central bank in this mold is much more likely to achieve price stability than adopting a rule within the existing institutional structure.

Session III

The abrupt severing in the 1980s of the close link between the growth rates of M1 and nominal GNP has launched a broad research effort that to date has failed to offer a definitive explanation for the change. Because the severing of this link coincides closely with widespread changes in the variety of deposit accounts offered to the public, many analysts have tried to adjust for shifts in money demand or find other approaches to rediscover traditional relationships between money and spending. Others have argued that the Federal Reserve has been measuring the money stock incorrectly for some time, but that, until the financial innovations of the early 1980s, the associated measurement errors had been small. Now, with these measurement errors clearly too large to ignore, these analysts believe poorly constructed monetary aggregates may contribute to policy mistakes.

William A. Barnett (with Melvin Hinich and Piyu Yue) sets forth this case by extending his earlier research on the theoretical grounds for, and practical construction of, Divisia monetary aggregates. The innovation of this most recent work is the introduction of risk aversion by agents and tracing through the importance of this feature on the measurement of an economy's monetary service flow. One result of his analysis is the addition of an extra step in constructing an aggregate monetary variable; after checking which assets can be grouped, aggregating them by a suitable index number formula, and evaluating the resultant measure against its practical end-use, Barnett adds the step of monitoring how closely the constructed measure actually tracks the theoretically ideal measure. Barnett uses these guidelines to produce a measure called "Theoretic M2."

In comparisons with the Federal Reserve's official monetary aggregates and Divisia aggregates constructed under the assumption of risk-neutral agents, Barnett finds that Theoretic M2 performs best. Although differences between the Divisia measures are small, the empirical improvements of either measure (risk neutrality or risk aversion) over the current official aggregates are large. These marked improvements lead Barnett to conclude that the Federal Reserve should abandon its current simple-sum measures of the money stock and construct new measures following the statistical practices of the Bureau of Labor Statistics and other government agencies.

Julio J. Rotemberg expresses general agreement with most of Barnett's analysis but offers several suggestions that, in his mind, would lead to further improvements in measurement. For one, Rotemberg revises Barnett's measure of the user cost of a financial asset in a way that removes any sensitivity to choice of a base period and facilitates the addition of new assets to the measure, should that become necessary. Rotemberg also suggests using something like stock market returns to replace the interest rate on a long bond to measure the benchmark rate of return in the user cost formula. Finally, Rotemberg recommends a revised currency-equivalent measure (CE), which isolates errors introduced by estimates of expected returns to the period in which they occur, whereas Barnett's measure carries the error permanently. In a reply, Barnett offers a proof that Rotemberg's "intuitive" arguments about his currency-equivalent measure of the money stock are true and that the CE index is indeed a measure of the economic stock of money under the assumption of stationary expectations.

All of the foregoing presume or present evidence to show that changes in the nominal quantity of money have important effects on economic activity. While conceding that the money-inflation link is strong, economists from the real-business-cycle school of thought would argue that further discussion of money's effect on output cannot be supported by economic theory or past experience. In fact, when viewed from the right perspective, Charles I. Plosser offers the Federal Reserve an argument to absolve itself from responsibility for smoothing variations in output as it pursues its primary goal of price stability.

Plosser's article attacks the purported link between changes in the nominal stock of money and output from several angles. First, he reminds the reader that years of theoretical work attempting to make this link have failed to identify the transmission mechanism through which it might work; this omission persists until this day. Second, economists who have made the connection between changes in nominal money and real output have not been careful to distinguish very different types of change in monetary policy. Specifically, changes in reserve requirements, which are real changes that affect relative prices and resource allocation, are the changes most often associated with fluctuations in output. Conversely, episodes in which only the nominal stock of money changed often show little effect on output.

Plosser then reports the results of statistical tests that attempt to distinguish between the real and nominal components of monetary policy actions and changes in output. Although his tests do not support his thesis uniformly, the weight of the evidence supports Plosser's claim of money's neutrality even in the short run.

Although N. Gregory Mankiw is sympathetic to Plosser's critical point that it is difficult to find significant correlations between changes in the nominal stock of money and output, he disagrees with the thrust of Plosser's analysis. For example, even if fluctuations in output were the result of shocks to "tastes and technology" and not changes in nominal money, monetary policy actions still might be capable of accomodating these shocks so that further output losses are avoided as the economy adjusts to its new output path. Moreover, Mankiw thinks it is unfair to criticize theories that link money to output because they have failed to specify an explicit transmission mechanism. Instead, Mankiw argues that all theories have holes as well as elements of truth. Or, as he puts it, if the world is messy, perhaps economic theory cannot help but be messy as well.

Acknowledgments

The Bank's annual economic policy conference is organized by its Research and Public Information Department. Thanks are due to Ruth Bryant, Susan McCollum and Linda Moser, who coordinated all local arrangements, ranging from the mailing list to menus and hotel accommodations. Ruth, who retired in June 1990, will be sorely missed at future conferences for her good judgment and attention to detail. Daniel Brennan helped edit the proceedings and worked closely with Zachary Rolnik of Kluwer to produce this volume. Finally, special thanks are due to Peggy Dooley for typing all of the conference correspondence in her usual conscientious and timely manner.

SESSION I

1 THE FED AT SEVENTY FIVE

Allan H. Meltzer

On December 23, 1913, Congress approved the Federal Reserve Act. Passage came after lengthy dispute, many pages of testimony, and more than 30 volumes of reports containing the findings of the National Monetary Commission. Despite the detailed investigation of financial systems that preceded passage and the number of alternative bills drafted, considered, and dismissed, the Act says very little about the purposes of the legislation. Decisions about how the central bank was to operate, and the objectives to be served, were left in large part to the organizers.

Decisions were not taken quickly. The new system took nearly eight months to get started. It was not until August 10, 1914, that Charles Hamlin, Paul Warburg, Frederic Delano, W. P. G. Harding, and Adolph Miller took their oaths of office as the first appointive members of the Federal Reserve Board. The two remaining members of the seven-person Board, Secretary of the Treasury McAdoo and Comptroller Williams,

I am grateful to Anna Schwartz, William Poole, Tom Mayer, Raymond Lombra, and George Benston for comments on an earlier draft. Helpful assistance was received from Ezra Angrist, Chris Bryan, and Jeremy Fand.

were ex officio members who had taken office earlier. Reserve Banks opened later.

The system had an unusual organizational structure, reflecting both ambivalence about the desirability of a central bank and beliefs about its functions. Carter Glass, the Chairman of the House Banking Committee, accepted the argument that there were advantages to the centralization of banking resources, but he believed that, in a country as large as the United States, there was no need for a single money center. Hence, the House report on the Glass bill favored regional banks that were expected to function cooperatively, but independently, to achieve the advantages of a central bank without acquiring the monopoly powers of a single bank of issue.[1] Also prominent in the discussion was the desire to reduce the frequency and severity of banking crises. The main remedies were found in providing discounts for bills of exchange (and other instruments) at the regional reserve banks and issuing Federal Reserve notes. The development of a market for bills of exchange and the use of open market operations were considered helpful also.

Very little is said about inflation, deflation or price stability in the Act or in the Congressional reports that preceded it. Many of the framers understood that money had an effect on prices. Silver agitation and banking crises had made this relation familiar. The silver issue had been settled politically in 1900, following William Jennings Bryan's second failure to win the Presidency, by passage of the Gold Standard Act in 1900, and by the rise in the world gold stocks and country price levels earlier in the century. The drafters of the Federal Reserve Act may have presumed that the long-term movement of prices would be determined by gold flows.

Looking back after seventy-five years, one finds that many of the issues faced by the drafters and organizers return. Development of the Federal Reserve as an institution reflects not only the history in which it has played a part but also changing views about the principles by which the Federal Reserve should operate, the objectives to be served by monetary policy, centralization or decentralization of the system between the Board in Washington and the Reserve Banks, the problems of avoiding recessions and financial failure, and the shifting emphasis given to price and exchange rate stability as a goal of public policy.

A 75th anniversary, a diamond jubilee, suggests a comfortable settling into a secure niche with many of these issues resolved, a time to reflect on past accomplishments and problems surmounted. This is hardly the appropriate picture of the Federal Reserve at 75. Its history is not a record of continuous achievement of well-understood goals. The 75-year record shows only two periods of sustained non-inflationary economic growth or low inflation, from 1923 to the summer of 1929 and, with some exceptions, from 1952 to 1965. In addition to wartime inflations in 1917–1918, and 1941–1945 and 1951, the Federal Reserve record includes the most severe depression and the longest, most sustained, peacetime inflation in our history. If we date the period of below normal output as lasting from 1929 to the beginning of World War II in 1941, and the period of sustained inflation from 1966 or 1967 to 1989, these years and the years of wartime inflation include more than two-thirds of the period since 1914.

Surveying this history and much more that Federal Reserve has done, or failed to do, in its 75-year history is a daunting task for a book, an impossible task for a single article. Fortunately, Friedman and Schwartz (1963) have provided a landmark history of the years to 1960, and Brunner and Meltzer (1964/1989) have related some of the principal policy errors to the framework used to guide monetary policy from the 1920s to the end of the 1960s. The present article will concentrate on selected events since 1960. Extending earlier work is made easier by the availability of materials, including reports by insiders and the release of primary materials. Where once researchers had to reconstruct the decision process and some of the basic data, there is now abundant material describing that process in detail and its outcomes at various times. Where once the Federal Reserve could be described as operating secretly, there is now a wealth of information.

The first section picks up where the earlier discussion left off. I summarize some of the principal criticisms of the Federal Reserve by Friedman and Schwartz and Brunner and Meltzer in the 1960s, and discuss the extent to which the criticisms remained valid in the years that followed. Much of the attention is on the choice of operating procedures and domestic policy. These issues were important in earlier work and received much attention both within and outside the Federal Reserve in the years since 1960. Two other prominent issues during this period are the use of Regulation Q and its effects on the financial industry, financial structure, and the economy, and the international role of the dollar under Bretton Woods and fluctuating exchange rates. Neither of these issues was entirely the responsibility of the Federal Reserve, but the Federal Reserve had a major role in setting and implementing policies. Space and time permit only brief discussion of both issues. This is a serious omission that leaves the history incomplete.

In many places, I treat the growth rates of monetary base and M2 as main indicators of the thrust of monetary policy. Both the base and measures of money are endogenous variables under an interest rate control procedure. As is well known and extensively documented, the Federal Reserve used the federal funds rate as the main control variable throughout the period. The degree of control varied under the different experiments, or quasi-experiments, with operating procedures, but there was generally a funds rate target and usually the manager of the system open market account kept the funds rate close to the target. Often there were targets for M2 growth and other monetary aggregates also, but relatively large differences of actual from target growth were permitted under all control procedures.

The base and M2 growth permit comparison of rhetoric to reality about the Federal Reserve's aims. I do not doubt that those responsible at the Federal Reserve during these years were honest and sincere public officials. They did not desire many of the outcomes they caused, or to which they contributed, including a high and durable inflation, devaluation, the end of the Bretton Woods system, several deep recessions, historically high market interest rates, and weakening of the financial structure. Some of them understood that the goals which they accepted such as low inflation, growth of real output, a stable money market, a stable international value of the dollar, low unemployment, stable money market conditions, safety and soundness of financial institutions, and profitability of the housing industry could not be achieved simultaneously. At critical points, Federal Reserve decisionmakers gave greater weight to stable money market conditions and stable federal funds rate than to other, more distant goals, just as they had in the preceding 50-year period. With hindsight it seems clear, as it was to some at the time, that improved control of money and a lower growth rate of money would have lowered the rate of inflation and might have entirely avoided inflation and devaluation. Stable, non-inflationary monetary growth would have reduced the severity of recessions, many of which were induced by the monetary contractions introduced to lower inflation or slow its rise.

Figures 1–1 through 1–6 show the growth rate of the monetary base and the level of the federal funds rate monthly from 1960 to 1988. The base is the St. Louis measure, and the monthly growth rates are calculated from the preceding year to avoid short-term fluctuations. The federal funds rate is the principal indicator of monetary policy used by the Federal Reserve. The monetary base is the principal alternative, although other aggregates are introduced below.

If the Federal Reserve had controlled the monetary base, maintained price stability, and permitted more short-term variability in interest rates, inflation would have been lower, nominal and real interest rates would not have reached the levels of 1981–1982, and the Bretton Woods system would have survived longer. Banks and thrift institutions would not have experienced alternating effects of inflation and disinflation on their asset portfolios and their liabilities, so it seems likely that there would have been fewer failures. The world economy would not have experienced the rapid disinflation of the 1980s. The international debt problem would not have

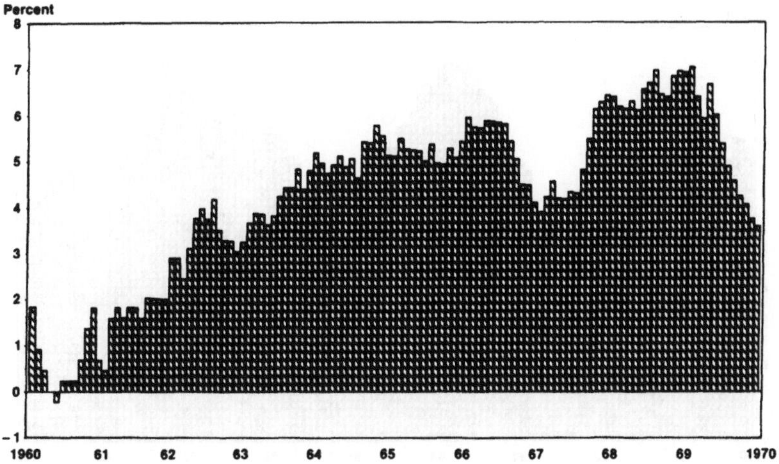

Figure 1–1. Annual growth of the monetary base during the sixties

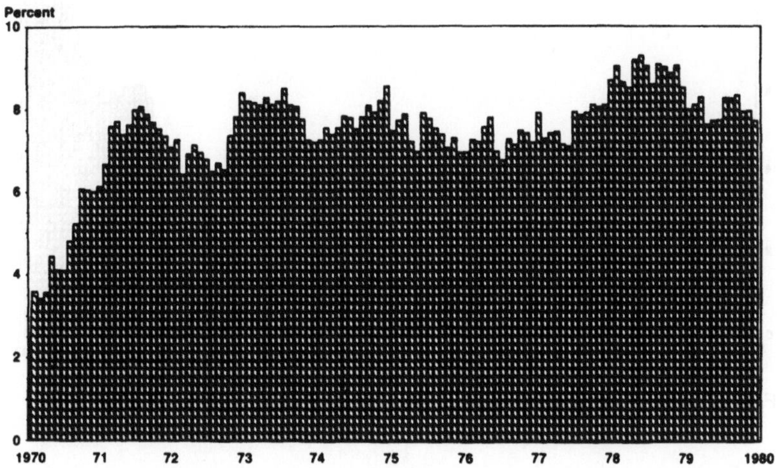

Figure 1–2. Annual growth of the monetary base during the seventies

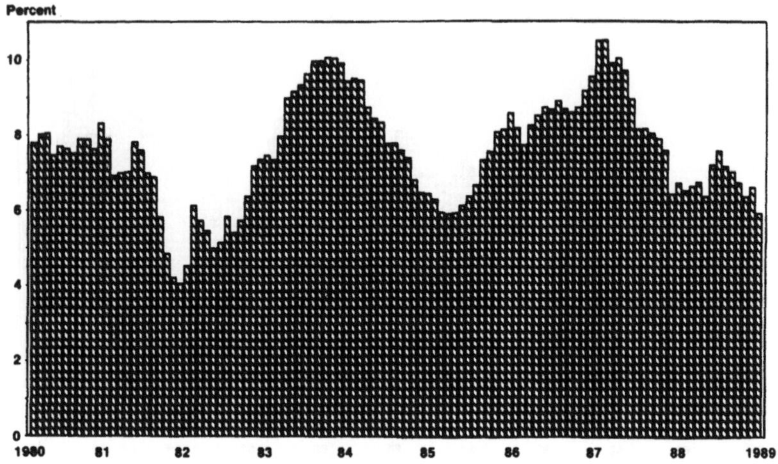

Figure 1–3. Annual growth of the monetary base during the eighties

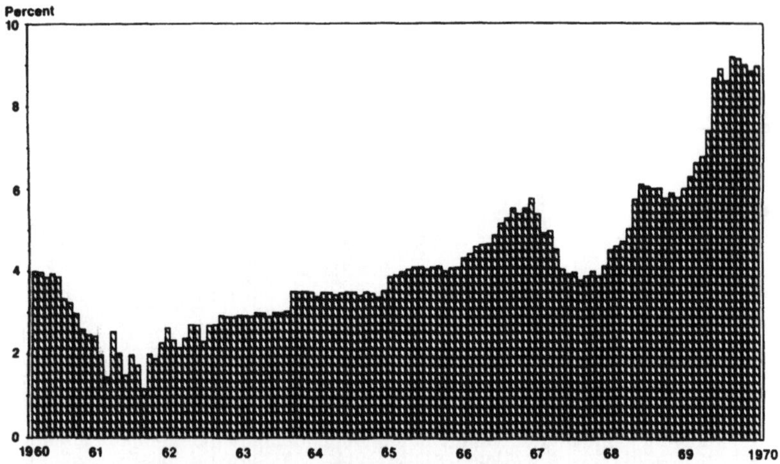

Figure 1–4. Federal funds rate during the sixties

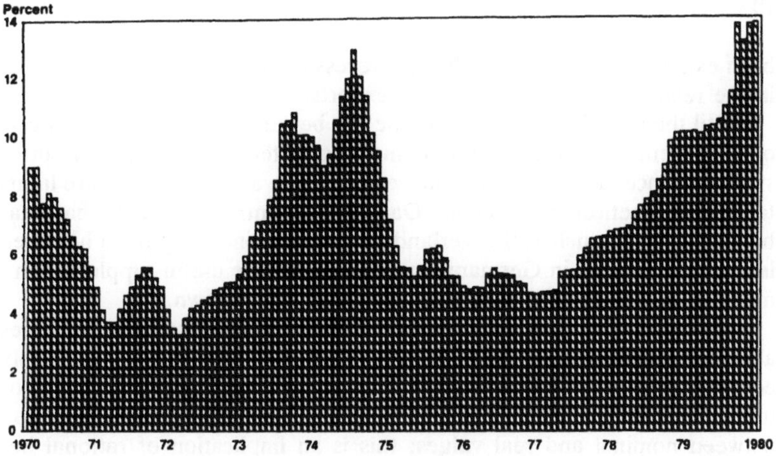

Figure 1–5. Federal funds rate during the seventies

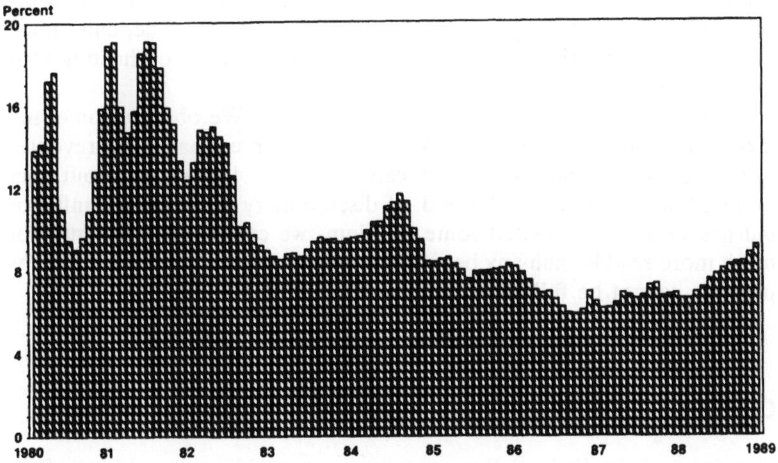

Figure 1–6. Federal funds rate during the eighties

been exacerbated by the disinflation, recession, and the attendant decline in the relative prices of commodity exports.

Until the experiment is run, no one can be certain about the full effects of a different operating procedure and a consistent effort to achieve price stability. Since identical circumstances cannot be achieved, there are limits to our hypothetical experiments. Data from countries where the base has been controlled, such as Switzerland, or where monetary growth has been less inflationary, as in Germany and Japan, provide useful supplementary information to support or modify the conclusions drawn.

The Lucas critique warns us about the difficulty of drawing inferences about the consequences of alternative policy rules, but it does not apply equally to all inferences. The response of prices to money and the effects of inflation on interest rates and exchange rates depend on the distinction between nominal and real values; this is an implication of rational behavior, not of a particular institutional arrangement or policy rule. The short-run non-neutrality of money is a result of costs of acquiring accurate information, the existence of contracts, and laws written with nominal values. These costs, contracts, and laws arise under many different policy rules. The timing of the principal responses to money may depend importantly on the institutional structure and policy rules; many of the long-term effects do not.

An historical discussion has an inevitable bias. We observe some mistakes and some achievements. We cannot observe what was prevented from happening. Our hypotheses can help draw inferences about such events, but their power is limited. If discretionary action raised inflation but prevented or mitigated some problem, we can observe the inflation much more readily than any benefit achieved by discretionary action. This problem cannot be fully overcome in a study of this kind.

Criticisms and Responses

Criticisms of the Federal Reserve vary over a wide range. Many of the critics seek either to achieve different explicit or implicit objectives or to shift the distribution of costs and benefits resulting from policy actions. These criticisms of the effects of policy are part of the political process in democratic countries.

The monetarist critique, as it came to be known, had some of these features, but it concentrated much more on the process by which policy is made and implemented. The outcomes of policy actions were less than optimal, according to these critics, because the procedures for making policy were not well designed to achieve the objectives of relatively stable growth, at stable prices and high or maximum employment. The focus was on the choice of policy targets, the framework used to interpret or assess events, and reliance on discretion instead of rules for policy. Specific criticisms included the Federal Reserve's reliance on interest rates, "tone and feel" of the credit market, and free reserves, the latter defined as member bank excess reserves minus member bank borrowing from the Federal Reserve.

The critics argued that reliance on these measures led to systematic misinterpretation of the thrust of monetary policy and to a procyclical monetary policy; money growth rose faster in periods of expansion than in recessions. The procyclical movements of money contributed to higher inflation and deeper or more protracted recessions. Further, some of the critics claimed that the Federal Reserve's instructions to the manager of the system open market account were often vague, so that the manager had considerable discretion about the thrust of policy.

Friedman and Schwartz's (1963) history documented the role of money in business cycles and provided evidence of the importance of money as a causal factor in fluctuations. These authors showed that the failure of the Federal Reserve to function as lender of last resort in 1929–1933 contributed to the widespread failures of banks and to the depth and severity of the depression. Brunner and Meltzer (1964) concentrated on the framework guiding policy, particularly the use of free reserves as a target of policy, an indicator of the current thrust of policy, and as a casual variable in the transmission of monetary policy. These authors pointed out that systematic misinterpretation of policy was inherent in the use of free reserves as an indicator of the policy thrust. A rise in member bank borrowing lowered the level of free reserves but increased the amount of total reserves. The Federal Reserve interpreted a decline in free reserves as contractive (and a rise in free reserves as expansive). An increase in total reserves is expansive for the monetary system, so the interpretation based on free reserves led to misinterpretation. The Federal Reserve attempted to accommodate the conflict by arguing that banks borrowed only for short periods and only in case of need.[2] This argument is flawed; it relies on the fallacy of composition. Even if individual banks are reluctant to borrow, as Riefler (1930) attempted to show, the repayment by one bank, with the demand for bank credit and total reserves otherwise unchanged, shifts the demand to borrow to another bank. Total borrowing and total reserves do not contract. On the contrary, member bank borrowing is procyclical.

A related issue involved the interpretation of interest rates. The dominant interpretation in the System has been that a rise in interest rates is contractive for the economy; "money" is "tighter." A decline in interest rates is expansive; money is "easier." The relatively low interest rates in the 1930s were interpreted as a sign of easy policy.

There are two major problems with the Federal Reserve's interpretation. First is the failure to distinguish between nominal and real interest rates. With deflation, as in the early 1930s, nominal rates could be low or falling while (deflation-adjusted) real rates were relatively high or rising. In the inflation of the 1960s and 1970s, the same problem arose again, but this time the problem was that historically high nominal rates were, in fact, associated with relatively low real rates. Second, reductions in the stock of base money raise interest rates and increases in the base initially lower interest rates. Interest rates rise also, with continued growth in base money, if the public's supply of earning assets to banks increases or if the banks increase required reserves to support a higher level of bank deposits and, simultaneously, the public increases its currency holdings.

The critics claimed that concentration on short-term interest rates and money market conditions gave a narrow focus to policy operations. Friedman and Schwartz interpreted the historical evidence as showing that changes in money operated with a lag that varied in length. The response to policy actions spreads from the money market to output, employment, and prices with a delay measured in quarters or years, whereas the effects on the money market occur quickly. Brunner and Meltzer presented evidence suggesting that the Federal Reserve recognized turning points in the economy with little delay. The focus on money market conditions and short-term interest rates misled them into believing that effective action to expand or contract the pace of economic activity had been implemented.

The Federal Reserve's response to the monetarist critique was defensive to a degree but not entirely. Some staff members wrote memos summarizing the arguments and accepting some of the main criticisms.[3] The Federal Open Market Committee (FOMC) appointed a three man subcommittee, in 1964, to study the directive that the FOMC used to instruct the manager about policy. The subcommittee concluded that "the directive was incomplete, sometimes internally inconsistent, often too vague, and that it failed to show what policy was intended in explicit enough terms for the manager to follow the Committee's wishes" (Maisel, 1973, p. 168).[4] These were some of the same criticisms that had been made by the so-called monetarists.

By a vote of 9 to 3, the FOMC rejected the subcommittee report. At the time, William McChesney Martin was Chairman of the Board of Governors. Martin was a banker and the son of a former president of a Reserve bank. As Assistant Secretary of the Treasury, he had taken a leading role in negotiations leading to the 1951 accord between the Federal Reserve and the Treasury. Martin was market oriented and a firm advocate of the traditional approach of relying on the tone and feel of the money market and the use of free reserves as a target of policy and an indicator of actions taken. Deficiencies in the conduct of monetary policy were, to him, unavoidable in a complex economy. They could best be handled by relying on the judgment of experienced people who respond flexibly to events as they unfold. In Martin's phrase, a flexible response leaned against the wind; see Maisel (1973, pp. 63, 81, 169–170) and Brimmer (1971, p. 32).[5] With Martin opposed, major changes were unlikely.

Throughout its history, the Board of Governors and the FOMC had shown little interest in money or monetary aggregates. Data on money (M1) were not collected and reported on a regular basis until monthly data appeared in the *Federal Reserve Bulletin* for February 1944. Daily average data began to be collected in 1947, but it was not until 1960 that the *Bulletin* began to publish data for the money stock based on daily averages. Further refinements to data on monetary aggregates were made periodically thereafter, and in February 1971 the *Bulletin* published data on M2 and M3 for the first time. In recent years, the data have been revised and the definitions changed to reflect innovations in banking and financial practices.

Maisel's report called for a break with past traditions that deemphasized or ignored money. A majority of the Board and many of the staff were opposed. Only one of the Reserve Banks, St. Louis, responded favorably. Under the leadership of Homer Jones, the St. Louis bank began to publish weekly and monthly releases showing growth rates of a number of monetary aggregates. Publishing these data in a form accessible to financial market participants helped to move the discussion into the public arena. Newspapers reported on the aggregates and the predictions of inflation or recession that gave considerable weight to changes in money. Further research at the bank (Andersen and Jordan, 1968) tested the influence of monetary and fiscal variables on nominal GNP and concluded that the effect of changes in money was larger and more reliable than the effects of fiscal variables. These and other activities, including a steady stream of research within parts of the system, helped to keep the criticisms from being shunted aside. Criticisms and discussion in the academic and semi-popular literature contributed also. Perhaps most important, however, were the rising rate of inflation, which gave substance to the criticisms, and the ineffectiveness of policies instituted to prevent inflation.

Response to Inflation

The Johnson administration's response to inflation relied heavily on the use of guideposts and guidelines. These were intended to limit price and wage increases in the private sector. Maisel (1973, p. 76) notes that the guidepost policy for wages and prices had been extended, de facto, to the prime lending rate. This encouraged borrowing and, in the opinion of several members of the Board, added to inflationary pressures. Maisel (1973, pp. 68–81) has a wide ranging discussion of the December 1965 decision to raise the discount rate from 4% to 4.5%. By raising the discount rate, the Board intended to give the banks an opportunity to raise the prime rate and "tighten" money. At the same time, the Board voted to raise ceiling rates for time deposits by one percentage point (to 5½%) under their authority to set Regulation Q ceiling rates. These actions touched off a dispute with President Johnson who interpreted the actions as a break with his policy.

The actions that followed the December decision raise some of the issues in the discussion of alternative policy procedures. Free reserves had been rising throughout the fall; they now reversed course and fell from $8 million in December to −$255 million by the following March. Member bank borrowing increased by a similar amount, and the federal funds rate rose. Judged by all of these measures, Federal Reserve policy had tightened. The seasonally adjusted monetary base continued to rise, however, and the stocks of money and credit rose also.

> To those who adhered to the traditional doctrine and saw money market conditions tightening, the Fed was doing its part to fight inflation. But to those of us who saw the fast growth of the monetary aggregates and the rapid creation of money and credit, it seemed that the Fed, far from combatting inflationary forces, might even be adding to the inflation (Maisel, 1973, p. 81).[6]

The result was another discussion of the directive that ended in a compromise the following June (1966). The Committee continued to use money market conditions as the principal guide, but a proviso clause was added to the directive. If required reserves rose more rapidly than anticipated, the Manager was to lower free reserves and raise money market rates.

Neither at the time nor at subsequent meetings did the proviso clause have much effect. For the rest of the decade of the 1960s, free reserves and money market conditions remained the principal indicators and targets of monetary policy. As a result, the Federal Reserve continued to misinterpret its actions. An example is the period following the 10% income tax

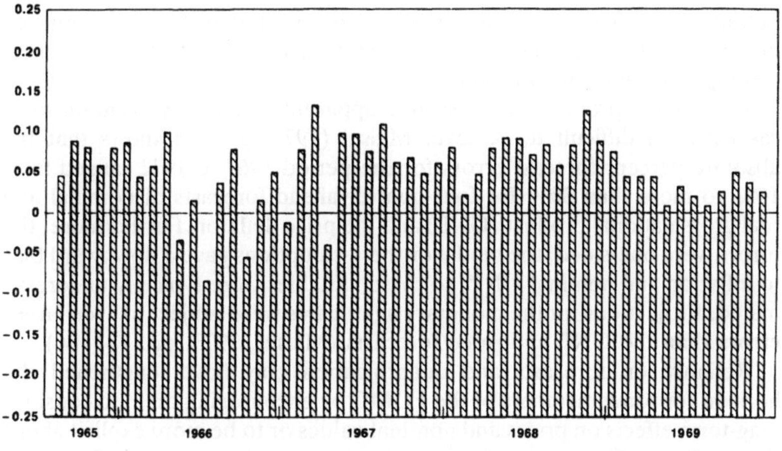

Figure 1–7. Monthly growth of M1 (S.A.), August 1965–December 1969

surcharge, passed in June 1968. The surcharge was intended to reduce the budget deficit, strengthen the dollar, and lower the inflation rate. The Federal Reserve responded to the surcharge by voting to ease monetary policy. From June to September, free reserves rose from −\$343 to −\$120 million; member bank borrowing declined, and federal funds moved down slightly (figure 1–4). The Federal Reserve believed that policy had eased. The growth of the monetary base shows a slight decline in its rate of growth for the 12 months ending in September, from the rate achieved in the 12 months ending in June (figure 1–1). The monthly growth rates of M1, shown in figure 1–7, show little change in the maintained average rate in the summer and fall of 1968 and a decline in 1969.

Partly in response to internal and external criticisms of this short-term focus, there was a change in policy procedures about this time. The staff began to make explicit forecasts of a number of variables and to include the forecasts as part of the information made available to the FOMC. The forecasts were obtained from a large-scale econometric model, developed by the Board's staff with the assistance of some academic economists. Among the advantages of model forecasts is that the staff had to make explicit some assumptions about response lags and directions of influence, and the members were confronted with estimates of the effects on large numbers of variables estimated simultaneously. The forecasts encouraged the members to recognize that their actions had consequences for prices, output, and inflation over a period much longer than the time between meetings. Also, the staff presented studies of the effects of different assumptions about policy actions.

A principal problem soon became apparent. Relatively accurate forecasts proved difficult to achieve. Maisel (1973, p. 185) shows that the absolute percent forecast errors for the period 1967 to 1972 ranged from 16% to more than 30% for four-quarter-ahead forecasts of nominal and real gross national product (GNP) and the price deflator. Furthermore, the errors were one-sided; the model or the assumptions gave a downward bias to inflation and nominal GNP, so these variables were typically underestimated. Projections for the monetary aggregates were subject to even larger errors than the GNP and price forecasts (Maisel, 1973, pp. 184–86).

Reliance on forecasts and quantification may have lengthened the horizon for some members of the FOMC by encouraging them to consider long-term effects on prices and nominal values or to be more explicit about these effects. The main effect was in the opposite direction. Forecasts helped to sustain the entrenched belief that policy actions could adjust the economy's near-term path. If a mistake was made, it could be corrected later. Thus, the new procedures did not remove, but rather strengthened, the pressure for activist policies directed at current and near-term events.

This short-term focus is reflected in the events of 1969–1970. Rising inflation, and rising public concern about inflation, precipitated a shift toward less expansive policy, a brief recession, and a turn back toward more expansive policy. A problem in this period, as in many others, was that policy was misinterpreted. The Federal Reserve had moved decisively toward restraint in the fall of 1968. From September 1968 to August–September 1969, free reserves fell by $800 million and the federal funds rate rose by more than three percentage points (figure 1–4), the most restrictive moves in the postwar period up to that time. However, through most of the period, the moving 12-month growth of the monetary base remained between 6% and 7% (figure 1–1). Judged by money market conditions, policy was contractive, but growth of the base indicated an expansive policy that added to inflationary pressures. In July 1969, growth of the base began to decline. At the start of the recession, in December, the moving 12-month growth of the base had fallen to 3.7%, half the growth rate reached in the previous December. Despite clear recognition by the FOMC in the winter of 1970 that a recession had started, and a decisive effort to reduce the funds rate and increase free reserves, annual growth of the monetary base remained about 4% until July 1970 (figure 1–2).[7]

The focus on financial market conditions and short-term interest rates remained. In the 1950s rates on federal funds had ranged between ½% and

4%. By the mid 1960s, federal funds reached 5½%, and by 1969, this rate was above 9% (figure 1–4). Much of the increase reflected the higher rate of inflation in the late 1960s. To many members of the FOMC, however, the connections between money growth, inflation, and interest rates were obscure, and the pressures for lower interest rates from government, homebuilders, and others were apparent. Also, there was considerable confusion or continued lack of clarity about the distinction between nominal and real interest rates. And, like many academicians, several members of the FOMC seem to have believed that expansive monetary policy could keep interest rates from rising at all maturities.

The Early 1970s

The events of the late 1960s, and the impending change of chairman, brought another reexamination of operating procedures. Beginning in 1969, a new committee on the directive, chaired by Governor Maisel, restudied the old issues.

Maisel's views differed from those of the monetarist critics in several respects. He wanted an activist policy based on forecasts of the future path of the economy, and he believed that guideposts and incomes policy would be required to lower inflation. But he accepted or shared many of the external criticisms of policy procedures. He recognized that the proviso clause, introduced to avoid excessive concentration on money market conditions, was ineffective because it was ignored. The Federal Reserve's public posture emphasized broad, wide-ranging consideration of many tendencies in the economy, as reflected in statements about looking at many different variables. In practice, the focus was much narrower. Much of the concern remained on money market conditions. These did not reflect very accurately either changes in the principal monetary aggregates or, more important, changes in real GNP, inflation, and other variables of principal concern to households and businesses.

At the start of the 1970s, principal measures of inflation had reached annual rates between 5% and 6%. Moreover, whether measured by interest rates, money wages, or unit labor costs, there was increased evidence that the public anticipated continued inflation; the nominal values of each of these measures increased relative to the real values, reflecting current and anticipated inflation. One result was greater skepticism about policymakers' commitments to price stability as shown by the response of inflation to policy changes. The brief slowing of the economy, following slower growth of money in 1966, had been followed by a sharp reduction in the rate of price increases. From a peak annual rate of increase of 7.2% in

February, the annualized monthly Consumer Price Index (CPI) declined to −1.2% in January 1967. The six-month moving average shows a similar but smaller decline from a peak of 4% (annual rate) in January 1966 to a trough of 1.3% (annual rate) in February 1967. In less than a year, inflation had been nearly eliminated without a recession. The 1969–1970 recession also produced disinflation, but only for a short time. The peak six-month moving average of the CPI reached 6.6% in November 1969. A trough at 3.5% in March and April 1971 was short-lived. By May this measure of inflation was back to 4%, the peak rate reached in the 1966–1967 experience.

The Nixon administration came into office in January 1969, promising to lower inflation without a recession. President Nixon's memory of his narrow defeat in the 1960 election in which recession was believed to have played a part, public memories of Republican policies from 1929 to 1933, and a desire to avoid incomes policies were important for this commitment. Alas, no one had a clear idea about how it was to be done (Stein, 1988, pp. 148–54).[8]

The FOMC shared the administration's goal of lower inflation but differed on both treatment and procedures. Some believed that anticipations had become firmly rooted and could be removed only by decisive action. Others thought, or hoped, that a moderate policy would work or believed it would work if accompanied by some informal system of price and wage controls or incomes policy that the administration opposed (Maisel, 1973, p. 232). In addition to this difference in beliefs, there were continuing differences about the relative importance to be given to monetary aggregates, interest rates, and money market conditions. To resolve some of these differences, the Board voted in April 1969 to raise reserve requirements, hoping to give a shock to expectations while leaving policy unchanged. The reserves removed by the change in the reserve requirement ratio were to be restored by open market operations. The effect of these changes was to leave the growth of the monetary base (St. Louis) unaffected, but to change the relative growth rates of money and bank credit (bank earnings assets). By August, it was clear from data published at the time that money growth was continuing to expand but bank credit had slowed (Maisel, 1973, p. 242). The difference in response is consistent with the expected effects of an increase in reserve requirement ratios on money and bank credit. Throughout the summer and fall, the FOMC continued to vote for "maintaining prevailing firm conditions." Free reserves of −$850 and −$1,000 million, and a monthly average federal funds rate of 8.6% to 9.2% show this policy (figure 1–4). As noted earlier, the monetary base shows a highly expansive policy until June followed by a shift toward contraction.

Regulation Q ceilings added to the problem of interpreting some principal monetary aggregates. With market rates far above the 5.5% ceiling rate on time deposits, banks and thrifts lost time deposits to competing instruments. Some of the deposits returned as demand deposits. The substitution of demand for time deposits raised the amount of reserves that banks were required to hold and appeared as an increase in M1, currency and demand deposits, relative to M2, which included time deposits. At the time, the ceiling on interest rates applied to all time deposits, irrespective of denomination, so large depositors held Euro-dollar deposits in foreign branches in place of negotiable certificates of deposit at domestic branches. This substitution lowered average reserve requirements at money center banks, so banks facilitated the substitution.

The January 15, 1970, meeting of the FOMC was the last meeting chaired by Martin. The directive prepared at that meeting, for the first time, mentioned monetary aggregates as a target of policy. The directive expressed a "desire to see a modest growth in money and bank credit," but the subsequent sentence called for the maintenance of firm conditions in the money market.

The directives for the rest of 1970 appear to give about equal weight to monetary aggregates and financial market conditions. A typical directive called for maintaining money market conditions consistent with moderate growth in money and bank credit. The directives did not specify what was meant by moderate growth and did not single out any particular monetary aggregate that the manager was supposed to monitor. Maisel (1973, p. 254) notes that the intention was to pay attention to a three-month average growth of money and credit, with main emphasis on M1. Between meetings the manager was to use money market conditions as an operating target. The staff was responsible for reconciling the operating target and the monetary indicator by relating the two empirically. At FOMC meetings, the members were to choose consistent targets based on staff estimates and other data. "[A] movement in money market conditions would not mean that monetary policy had changed. Policy was to be measured by movements in the monetary aggregates" (Maisel, 1973, p. 254).

The change in the directive to recognize monetary aggregates was not reversed. From 1970 on, with few exceptions, one or more monetary aggregates is mentioned in the directions to the manager. By the mid-1970s, the FOMC chose explicit numerical targets for one or more monetary aggregates at every meeting. There were also numerical targets for the federal funds rate, and these continued to serve as an operating target for the manager.

Three difficulties soon became apparent. First, the federal funds target specified a narrow band within which the manager was supposed to keep the funds rate. This was an operationally feasible task. If the rate was too high, the manager bought securities, and increased reserves; if it was too low, he sold securities, reducing reserves. The growth of the monetary aggregates became available only after a lag, and short-term changes were not easy to interpret. There were always two or more aggregates mentioned, and their monthly or quarterly changes would often go in different directions. Changes were subject to large seasonal and random variation. Hence, judgment often had to be used to decide whether to adjust the federal funds rate target or permit the growth rate of one or more of the monetary aggregates to remain above or below the specified range. Second, forecasts of the future path of the economy and of the monetary aggregates are subject to large errors. Adjusting policy in response to forecasts may add rather than reduce variability (Friedman, 1953). This difficulty does not arise from the use of monetary aggregates. It is inherent in any discretionary policy based on forecasts, if the absolute size of forecast errors is sufficiently large or if the forecasts are biased, as the inflation forecasts proved to be. The low reliability of the forecasts provided a reason for delaying or for making very small, cautious adjustments in the funds rate. Third, neither the FOMC, nor the Congress, nor successive administrations was clear about the goals of monetary (or economic) policy. There were frequent changes in the real and nominal variables of interest, and the weight given to a particular variable shifted. Prices, the balance of payments, interest rates, housing, unemployment, economic growth, and money market conditions are prominent in the discussion at different times. Neither the manager nor the FOMC had a clear vision about the interrelation of these goals or the precise way in which they could be affected by changes in money and interest rates. A short-run focus could account for the choice of real variables as targets, but there is not much recognition of the relation of the short-run changes to longer-term changes in prices and nominal values.

This uncertainty was not confined to the Federal Reserve. Academic economists and other outsiders who urged activist discretionary policies often minimized the longer-term consequences, perhaps because they thought inflation could be prevented "later" or because they expected to trade off unemployment for inflation. The Federal Reserve staff had to face the problem. The old procedures used judgments about tone, feel, and their relation to free reserves; the new procedures required the staff to supply estimates of the demand for money and the magnitude and timing of the responses of unemployment, output, prices, housing, balance of payments, and many other variables to policy actions.

There is no indication that the Fed considered an explicit policy rule.

Two options were available for discretionary policy. One, based on the supply function of money, would have controlled the monetary base, or total reserves, and allowed interest rates and later exchange rates to vary as required to keep some measure of money growth near the prescribed path. The second required estimates of the demand for money and the links between the money market interest rate that the Federal Reserve could control and interest rates on a broad spectrum of assets of different duration and risk.

The Fed chose the latter course and began to implement what is known as the two-stage procedure.[9] Under this procedure, there are short-term and long-term targets. Twice a year the FOMC chooses monetary targets that are thought to be consistent with its longer-term objectives, such as lower inflation or stable economic growth at relatively stable prices. Stage one is the choice of a strategy or path for the economy for the next four to six quarters and the set of monetary targets consistent with this path. The choice is based on information that each member brings to the meeting and on forecasts of the consequences of alternative policies prepared by the Board's staff. At each subsequent meeting, the FOMC chooses a short-term target, usually the federal funds rate, and the associated targets for various definitions of money (or monetary aggregates) that are believed to lie on the path leading to the longer-term monetary target. The choice of the short-term targets is the second stage of the procedure.

Prior to each meeting the staff uses the longer-term growth rates of money chosen by the FOMC, and assumptions about fiscal policy and other predetermined variables, as policy inputs to develop forecasts of the principal non-financial variables. These forecasts take the financial variables as givens. At the same time, other staff members at the Board, assisted by the staff of the New York bank, develop forecasts of financial variables taking the forecasts of real variables as givens. Short-term interaction, or simultaneity, between deviations of monetary and real variables from their anticipated paths are presumed to be small.

During the 1970s and 1980s, the Federal Reserve maintained the two-stage procedure but changed the implementation on two occasions. From 1970 through September 1979, implementation and control centered on the federal funds rate. From October 1979 to sometime in the summer or fall of 1982, non-borrowed reserves received increased emphasis, and the federal funds rate was changed more frequently and, at times, by larger amounts in response to deviations of non-borrowed reserves from the path believed to be consistent with short-term policy. Borrowed reserves replaced non-borrowed reserves in 1982 and have retained a role in the implementation of short-run policy since that time.

Problems with Federal Reserve Procedures

Many critics have concentrated on the inefficiency of the two-stage procedure. Benjamin Friedman (1975, 1977) develops these criticisms fully. The implicit or explicit suggestion in many of the criticisms is that a more efficient procedure for linking short-term and long-term forecasts would make a substantial difference. Many of the critics favored replacement of the two-stage procedure with a procedure that relied on a simultaneous solution for money, output, prices, and interest rates. Karamouzis and Lombra (1989) found, however, that neglect of simultaneity was not a major source of error. They report that the Federal Reserve reacted to the lagged deviations of money growth from target, but the response was relatively small and was delayed. A principal reason for the delayed reaction is that, typically, the Fed's initial interpretation of the deviation of money from target is that the demand for money shifted. They act on the assumption that the monetary deviation is largely transitory and can be ignored when setting the federal funds rate. Their interpretation is correct at times, incorrect at others. The problem is to distinguish the two. Simultaneous estimation procedures would not separate permanent and transitory deviations. The problem of interpretation would remain.

A more basic problem lies in the use of a money market rather than a monetary strategy. In the money market strategy the control process centers on the federal funds rate. This rate is considered a principal determinant of other interest rates and the prices of assets relative to the prices of corresponding outputs. The transmission of monetary policy spreads, after a lag, from the federal funds rate to other interest rates, to asset prices, output, and the demands for money and other assets (deLeeuw and Gramlich, 1969). Changes in the federal funds rate are thought to be significant policy actions; changes in money are often interpreted either as random changes in the demand for money or as lagged responses to prior changes in interest rates. In common with the older, Riefler-Burgess tradition, the Federal Reserve observes the demand for borrowed (or non-borrowed) reserves at the posted federal funds rate. If deposit growth increases, the demand for reserves rises. At first, the Federal Reserve satisfies demand by supplying reserves at the going federal funds rate. Persistent increases in the demand for reserves, to meet required reserves, may be followed by a decision to raise the federal funds rate. Following the decision, market interest rates would be expected to rise, slowing the growth of reserves relative to demand. The increase in the funds rate also increases member bank borrowing and, according to the hypothesis, subsequently reduces the quantity of money demanded.

As presented by Tinsely and associates (1982), the main features of the money market model can be reduced to a relation between the change in non-borrowed reserves, DNBR, and the change in the federal funds rate, DFF, given the discount rate (see also Karamouzis and Lombra, 1989, table 6). In simulations that study the longer-term consequences of various actions, the discount rate adjusts to the federal funds rate; in the short-term it is a policy variable that is fixed. Changes in the demand for money, time deposits, and reserves are determined, up to a stochastic component, by DFF. The effect of changes in relative prices, income, and wealth on the demand for these financial assets is shown as a shift in the intercept of the (linear) equations. This recursive model is not consistent with the best available theory and evidence.

A further deficiency of the money market model is the neglect of the broad spectrum of interest rates and asset prices that affect the demands for money and other financial assets. If changes in relative prices are tested one at a time, none may have a significant effect in a particular sample, yet the combined effect may influence the demand for money or change the supply of earning assets offered to banks. Anticipations change the relative yields on short-term and long-term securities, changing the term structure of interest rates, desired money balances, and the public's supply of earning assets to banks. These and other changes in relative prices are often a response to prior changes in money or to the anticipations of future changes or to the future effects of those changes. In the Board's short-term model, anticipations, relative prices, and real wealth affect desired financial asset holding only by shifting the demand for money (or a monetary aggregate). Typically, these shifts are accommodated at an unchanged federal funds rate by supplying or withdrawing reserves and money.[10] Furthermore, it is incorrect to assume that interest rate changes spread from the federal funds rate to other interest rates. Often, the opposite is true; the Federal Reserve may be slow to respond to the forces changing open market rates. Changes in the expected rate of inflation, the productivity of capital, the public's supply of earning assets to banks, or firms' desired leverage can change longer-term rates relative to the federal funds rate. As these examples suggest, the change in the term structure can have a real or nominal impulse. By fixing the federal funds rate and supplying or withdrawing base money, the Federal Reserve procedure assures that all real and nominal changes have a monetary effect.

To pursue one example, suppose the public, anticipating an increased return to captial or higher inflation, decides to borrow more. The public's supply of earning assets to banks increases, raising interest rates on the credit market. The Federal Reserve interprets the change as an increase in the demand for money. Typically, it treats the change in demand as transitory, so it holds the federal funds rate by supplying additional reserves and money, thereby reinforcing the initial anticipation and encouraging additional borrowing. Similarly, reductions in the public's supply of earning assets to banks are interpreted as unanticipated shifts in the demand for money and are matched by reductions in the stock of money at an unchanged federal funds rate.

Failure to distinguish changes in the demand for money and changes in the public's supply of earning assets to banks is a main reason that money typically has increased relatively faster during periods of economic expansion than during recessions. Money growth has been procyclical, often reinforcing recessions and inflations. Figures 1–8 and 1–9 show that, except for M2 in the 1980s, money growth is higher in each expansion than in the preceding recession. Also, from peak to peak, the rate of money growth increased, raising the average rate of inflation; the highest rates of growth occurred during expansions.

In principle, it is entirely possible to avoid procyclical money growth using an interest rate target. If the target is adjusted promptly in response to changed anticipations of inflation and changes in anticipated real returns, money growth responds less to procyclical changes in anticipated inflation and expansion. A central bank can, in principle, implement a stabilizing policy of this kind by giving greater weight to deviations of money growth from a non-inflationary path. In practice, it is difficult, but not impossible, to know how much the short-term interest rate should change. Evidence on inflation in Germany and Japan after the middle 1970s suggests that these countries have controlled inflation more successfully than the United States while implementing policy actions by setting short-term interest rates. Japan has achieved price stability or low inflation in recent years without experiencing a recession.

On Hitting the Targets

Figures 1–10 to 1–12 bring out the difference between the Federal Reserve's response to the federal funds target and the response to one of the money growth targets.[11] The federal funds (figure 1–10) rate is a monthly average. Figure 1–11 shows deviations of monthly growth of M2 from the target. The fluctuations are large and erratic. During much of the period, the Federal Reserve relied on two-month or three-month averages of money growth, so three-month moving averages of actual money growth in figure 1–12 give a better indication of the Federal Reserve's response to deviations of money growth from short-term targets during the period 1974–1978 than the monthly data in figure 1–11.

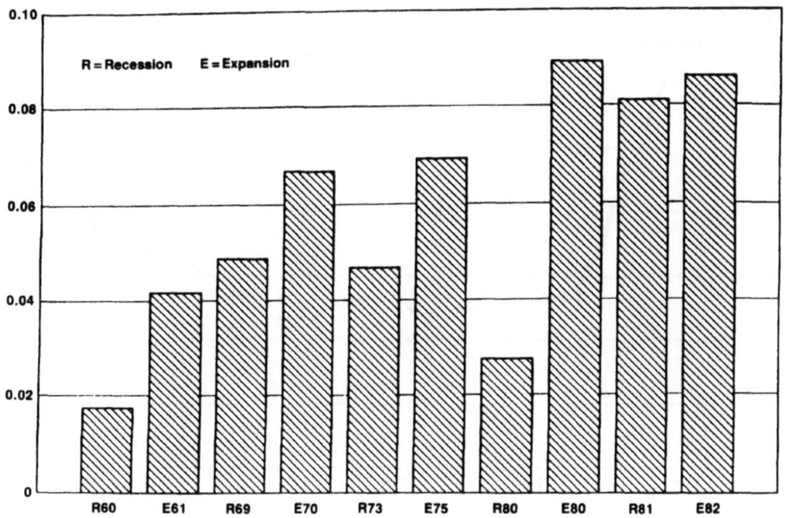

Figure 1–8. Mean growth rate of M1, 1960–1988

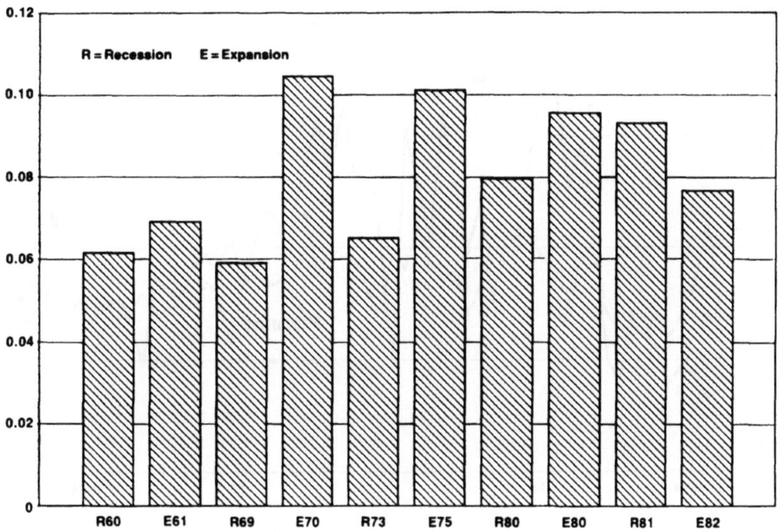

Figure 1–9. Mean growth rate of M2, 1960–1988

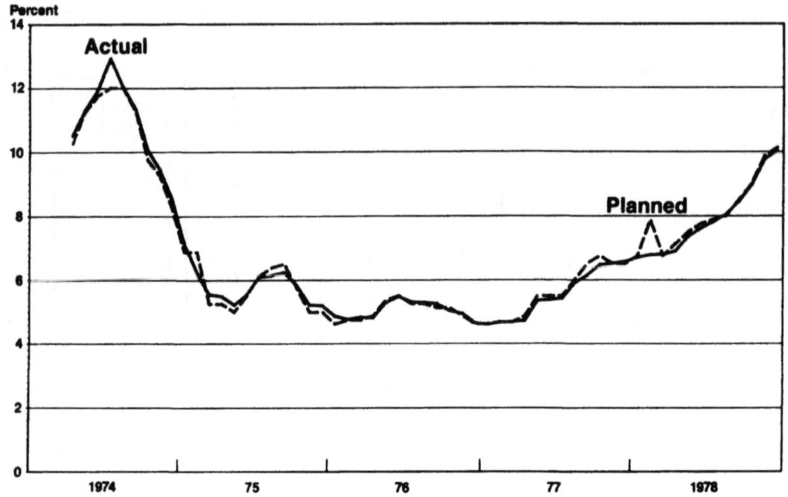

Figure 1–10. Actual vs. planned federal funds rate, March 1974–December 1978

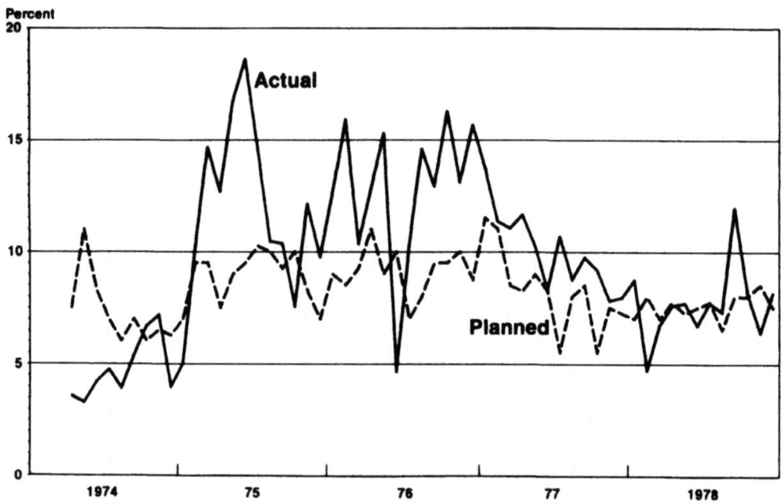

Figure 1–11. Actual vs. planned growth of M2, March 1974–December 1978

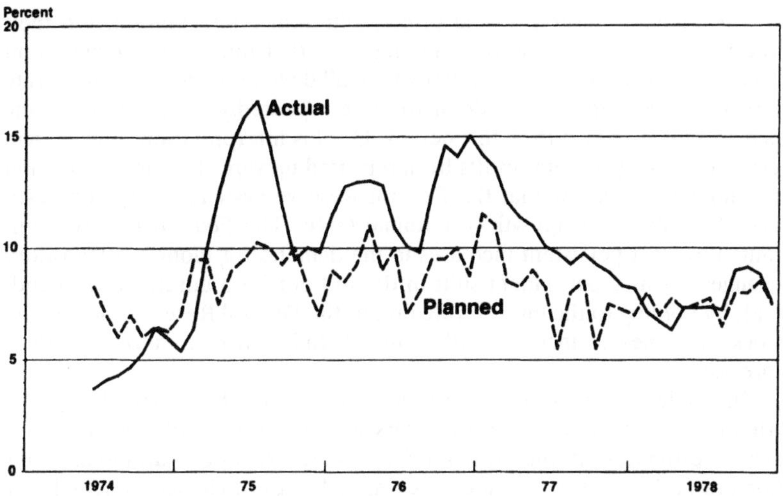

Figure 1–12. Actual vs. planned M2, three-month average, May 1974–December 1978

Two features stand out. First, almost all the deviations of money growth from target are positive during the period shown, and some are relatively large. Second, the Federal Reserve appears to have held to its federal funds rate targets and largely ignored the monetary targets throughout the period.

Why did the asymmetry in the responses of money and interest rates and the inflationary policy persist? The persistence of the deviations and their timing rule out unanticipated shocks, such as the oil embargo of 1973 or the oil price increases of 1974, as a full explanation. An obvious explanation is that the Federal Reserve ignored the targets for money growth and concentrated on the federal funds rate. This would explain the comparative size of the deviations from targets, but it does not explain the systematic excess supply of money (relative to the target). A likely reason is that the public's supply of earning assets to banks and government borrowing to finance deficits was satisfied at unchanged interest rates. The Federal Reserve's analysis neglects the public's supply of earning assets to banks, so these changes would be a surprise. Evidence in figures 1–19 and 1–20 (below) shows that the Federal Reserve financed a higher share of the federal debt in the 1970s than in earlier or later years.

The Federal Reserve would offer a different interpretation. On their interpretation of deviations of money growth from target, a persistent excess supply of money (and relatively small deviations from the funds rate target) suggests that the Federal Reserve repeatedly underestimated the demand for money during this period. On this interpretation, higher than expected money growth results from repeated upward shifts in the demand for money. We know that the Federal Reserve systematically underestimated inflation and growth of nominal GNP. The Federal Reserve continued to treat persistent increases in the demand for money as transitory changes (or as a permanent shift in desired portfolio unrelated to spending); by holding to the interest rate target, the Federal Reserve allowed the stock of money to increase with demand. Inflation rose more than their forecast.

The Federal Reserve hypothesis does not explain the errors adequately. Although the inflation forecast errors are consistent with the observed errors, estimates of the demand for money are not. Karamouzis and Lombra (1989, p. 43) computed the implied rates of change of actual and forecast values of output per unit of money, or monetary velocity, using staff forecasts of the demand for money. From 1973 to 1976, the Federal Reserve generally overestimated, and from 1976 to 1979 generally underestimated, velocity. This pattern of errors does not correspond to the errors in money growth, so neither unanticipated shifts in the demand for money (per unit of output) nor underestimation of the effects of inflation fully explain the errors in money growth. We note, however, that the share of the debt financed by issuing base money rose when velocity was overestimated and declined when velocity was underestimated. If the changes in debt were unanticipated, they would explain some of the underestimate of earning asset supply and a slowly adjusting federal funds rate.

The most remarkable feature of the errors in forecasts of inflation and control of money growth is their persistence. The Federal Reserve permitted errors in the same direction to continue from meeting to meeting for years without recognizing that their procedures were flawed. Their narrow focus on interest rates and money market conditions appears to have misled them in the great inflation of the 1960s and 1970s as in the great depression of the 1930s.

Contributions of Discretionary Policy

The forecast errors for velocity and money provide a check on the contributions made by Federal Reserve discretionary policy. A main argument for discretionary policy is that the Federal Reserve can offset shifts in the demand for money by changing the stock of money. We have seen that this analysis fails if there are unanticipated permanent and transitory shifts in the demand for money: for example, if the demand for money can be approximated by a random walk with drift. Karamouzis and Lombra (1989, pp. 41–42) computed the correlation between deviations of money and velocity from their respective target or anticipated paths to learn how serious the failure is. For the period 1973–1982 the correlation based on quarterly data is −0.65, so the percentage of the variance explained is about 42%. This overstates the effectiveness of policy. Part of the correlation is unrelated to efforts to offset shifts in the demand for money; it is a result of the gradual adjustment of desired money balances. Unanticipated increases in money growth temporarily increase money balances relative to output and lower velocity and its growth rate; unanticipated reductions in money growth temporarily increase velocity growth.

Like the changes in money, the combined effect of changes in money and velocity is procyclical. Unanticipated money growth has a positive effect on nominal GNP growth, as is well known from many studies. This suggests that tighter control of money would have avoided some of the procyclical and inflationary consequences of discretionary policy.

Brunner and Meltzer (1983, pp. 88–94) used ARIMA models for money (M1), base money (B) and their respective velocities (V_1 and V_B) to test whether Federal Reserve discretionary actions are stabilizing or destabilizing on average. The ARIMA models decompose measures of money and velocity into systematic and random components. The formula for the variance of a sum can be exploited.

$$\text{Var } y = \text{Var } m + \text{Var } v + 2 \text{ cov}(m, v)$$

where y, m, and v are first differences in the logarithms of nominal GNP, money, and velocity. Brunner and Meltzer (1983, table 1) report that for 1953–1980 and for the subperiod 1969–1980, the covariance of the systematic components of m and v is positive using both M1 and B as measures of money. A rule calling for constant money growth would have zero values for Var m and cov(m, v), so Federal Reserve actions appear to have increased variability in these periods relative to a rule calling for constant growth of M1 or B. If we assume that Var v would be unaffected by reliance on a rule, the data suggest that a rule requiring constant growth of the base would have eliminated three-fourths of the variance of the systematic components. The variance of actual nominal GNP would have been reduced, but the reduction would have been smaller. The reason is that the random (or unanticipated) changes in velocity must be added to the variability of the systematic component. That is,

Table 1–1. Quarterly Error Variances for Nominal GNP Growth

Source	*Period*	*Variance (%)*
Federal Reserve	1973–1982	4.2
Federal Reserve	1970–1973	2.0
Constant base rule	1953–1980	1.6
Constant base rule	1969–1980	2.1
Actual GNP growth	1969–1980	5.9

$$\text{Var } y = \text{Var } m^* + \text{Var } v^* + 2\text{ cov}(m^*, v^*) + \text{Var } \varepsilon + \text{Var } \gamma + 2\text{ cov}(\varepsilon, \gamma)$$

where ε and γ are the random components, and m^* and v^* are the systematic components.

Under a rule requiring constant growth of the base, unavoidable variability in nominal GNP growth would be the sum of the systematic and random components of base velocity. We cannot be certain how the variability of base velocity growth would change under a monetary rule. The evidence in the cited study suggests that, under the assumptions made, a rule for constant base growth would have produced an error variance of 1.6% to 2.1% during the period 1953–1980.[12]

Federal Reserve Forecasts

An obvious comparison is between a hypothetical rule that has an error variance of 1.6% to 2.1% and the errors in Federal Reserve forecasts. Unfortunately, the time periods that have been studied are not identical, so the comparison is at best suggestive. The difference in the variances or root mean square errors is sufficiently large, and the time periods overlap sufficiently to make the comparisons useful, however. Table 1–1 compares the variances of the hypothetical, constant base rule to the root mean square errors of Federal Reserve forecasts reported by Lombra and Moran (1980) and Karamouzis and Lombra (1989). The variance of actual GNP growth shown in the table is computed as the sum of the variances and covariances estimated by the ARIMA model used in Brunner and Meltzer (1983).

The data suggest that the variance of Federal Reserve forecast errors is lower than the variance of GNP growth but generally higher than the variance produced by a rule for constant base growth. Although one comparison cannot be decisive, the data provide no evidence that discretionary policy is more stabilizing than a rule.

Additional evidence supporting this conclusion is reported by McCallum (1988). McCallum compared adaptive rules that achieved price stability. His rule adjusts monetary base growth in response to past changes in velocity growth and past deviations of real output growth from a 3% trend. For the period 1954–1985 (quarterly), the rule had a root mean square error of 2% while holding inflation close to zero. For comparison, McCallum reports that the variance of deviations of actual GNP growth from trend is 8.5% for this period.

Two possible sources of Federal Reserve errors are the model used to generate forecasts and the judgments used to adjust the model forecasts. Federal Reserve forecasting models have retained the IS-LM framework. The models have not incorporated rational expectations, open economy dynamics, and other recent developments. Nor has the model incorporated a credit market. Comparison suggests, however, that Fed forecasts of GNP are as accurate as the forecasts from other models, including time series models that do not have any structure, IS-LM or otherwise (Karamouzis and Lombra, 1989; Meltzer, 1987). Alternative models that incorporate recent developments may produce smaller errors, but it is not clear how much room exists for improvement in the quality of forecasts. The similarity of mean absolute errors from different models suggests that much of the remaining average error may be random variation. Some tests of the forecast errors support the conclusion that most of the remaining errors are random. Random variation is more likely to be reduced by a change in the policy rule that reduces variability by changing the variances and covariances of money and other variables than by improvements in forecasting.[13]

Real GNP grows at an annual rate of 2½% to 3% on average. During the years 1970–1973 and 1973–1982, the GNP deflator rose at average rates of 5.7% and 8.1%. Table 1–2 shows the mean and mean absolute error (MAE) and the root mean square error (RMSE) for the Fed's quarterly forecasts for these periods. Forecast errors for the current quarter, the following quarter, and the next four quarters are large relative to the average rates of change. It seems clear that the Federal Reserve forecast errors, like those of other forecasters, are large relative to the changes they attempt to forecast. Moreover, the forecasts appear to be biased. This is particularly true of the inflation forecasts; the mean error and the mean absolute error are similar, again indicating that the Federal Reserve persistently underestimated inflation durıng the period of rising inflation. The errors in the forecasts of real GNP suggest, as does Meltzer

Table 1–2. Forecast Errors 1970–1982

	Mean		MAE		RMSE	
1970–1973	*y*	*p*	*y*	*p*	*y*	*p*
Current quarter	0.4	−0.9	1.6	1.2	2.1	1.4
Next quarter	0.8	−1.2	2.2	1.6	2.9	1.9
Four quarters	1.6	−3.9	2.5	4.0	3.4	4.8
1973–1982						
Current quarter	0.0	0.5	3.1	1.4	3.7	1.9
Next quarter	−0.5	0.9	3.5	1.7	4.4	2.3
Four quarters*	−0.7	0.9	2.0	1.6	2.5	2.0

Note: y are p are real GNP growth and inflation as measured by the GNP deflator.
* For 1973–1982, the errors are for the full four quarters ahead; for 1970–1973, the error is for the particular quarter.
Source: Lombra and Moran (1980); Karamouzis and Lombra (1989).

(1987), that on average the Federal Reserve cannot distinguish in the current quarter whether the economy is in a boom or recession in that quarter. With a mean absolute error of 3.1% and a mean long-term growth rate of 3%, on average forecasts would not be able to detect differences between zero and 6%.[14] Much the same is true for forecasts four quarters ahead, a period more relevant for Federal Reserve discretionary action.

Errors in forecasting nominal GNP growth lie in the same range as the errors for real GNP growth. For 1973–1982, Karamouzis and Lombra (1989, p. 21) show a mean absolute error for current quarter nominal GNP growth of 3.3% and a RMSE of 4.2%. The latter is more than twice the RMSE obtained for a similar period using a monetary rule that keeps the base rising at a constant rate.

The quality of the staff inflation forecast is shown in figure 1–13. The figure shows the persistent bias in the forecast that was discussed earlier. During the period of rising inflation, inflation was underestimated, and during the period of disinflation, inflation was overestimated.

Forecasts of Money Growth

Each month the Federal Reserve staff forecasts the money stock using their model of the demand for nominal money. Evidence is now available on the quality of these forecasts and the quality of alternative forecasts based on the money supply model of Brunner and Meltzer (1964a, 1989) as developed by Rasche and Johannes (1987). Forecasts by the Board's staff

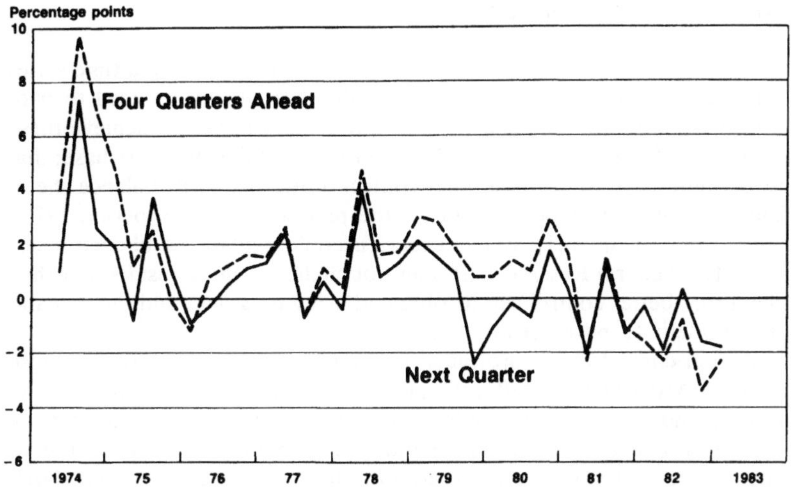

Figure 1–13. Forecast errors for GNP deflator
Source: Karamouzis and Lombra (1989) based on Federal Reserve green books.

and by Rasche and Johannes are actual forecasts made in advance of the events.

The principal conclusions to be drawn from this work are summarized by Rasche and Johannes (1987) and by Brunner and Meltzer (1983). First, monetary control is technically feasible for one-quarter or two-quarter periods. An acceptable degree of control can be achieved using either the Board's procedure or the Rasche-Johannes procedure. Second, during much of the period, lagged reserve requirements increased the difficulty of controlling money growth. This conclusion is accepted by the Board's staff (Lindsey et al., 1981). Lagged reserve requirements have been all but abandoned. Third, traditional operation of the discount window lowers the degree of monetary control. A penalty rate system for discounting would enhance control. Fourth, long-run control can be achieved about as well by controlling either the monetary base or bank reserves. Control of the monetary base increases control of money in the short run (relative to control of bank reserves). Fifth, forecast errors are not substantially different following the 1979 and 1982 changes in control procedures or before and after deregulation. The Rasche-Johannes procedure appears to be robust to these changes (Rasche and Johannes, 1987, p. 12).

Why Is Monetary Control So Poor?

Rasche and Johannes (1987, p. 187) conclude that, by using a time series forecasting procedure, errors in controlling M1 can be reduced to two-thirds of 1% per annum and for M2 to one-half of 1%. To achieve these results, the Federal Reserve would have to control the monetary base; that is, it would have to maintain tight control of the size of its balance sheet. These results are based on data for the relatively variable period 1979–1985, when the financial system experienced deregulation and deep recession. The Federal Reserve staff does not challenge these results, but they claim that better control can be obtained using judgment and the demand side model[15] (Lindsey et al., 1981).

Actual control errors are much larger than the errors shown in these studies. According to staff estimates by Lindsey and associates and to Rasche and Johannes, the Federal Reserve could achieve better control of money growth. Two complementary explanations of their failure to improve control have been offered. One focuses on the perceived short-term cost. The other raises broader issues about the use of discretionary policy. I discuss each in turn.

Figures 1–10 to 1–12 (above) show that the Federal Reserve kept the actual level of the federal funds rate close to the target level but tolerated relatively large deviations from the money growth target. The degree of control of interest rates and money differ in other periods, but the general pattern repeats. There is considerable evidence that this pattern reflects the Fed's reluctance to permit relatively short-term changes in credit market interest rates. Lombra and Moran (1980) report that, at times, the FOMC chose targets for money and the federal funds rate that were inconsistent with the staff's forecasting model. A principal reason appears to be that the members were reluctant to allow interest rates to rise as much as required by staff forecasts. They hoped to achieve lower inflation by reducing money growth but were reluctant to let interest rates rise by relatively large steps.

This is an example of money market myopia. With hindsight there is little doubt that neither long-term nor short-term nominal rates of interest would have reached the levels experienced in 1981–1982—15% to 20%—if the Federal Reserve had prevented inflation. The same is true of ex post real rates, since the first effects of the monetary contraction of the early 1980s raised real rates of interest. During the early 1980s, ex post real rates of interest reached the highest levels in this century. Failing to permit market rates to rise sufficiently in the 1960s and 1970s required larger increases in nominal and real rates later. The levels reached by these rates could not have been predicted at the time, but it must have become clear that the level of interest rates increased with inflation. Yet, the Federal Reserve continued its policy procedure until 1979.

A second reason for continued use of inefficient control procedures and imprecise announcements has been suggested by Cukierman and Meltzer (1986) and by Stein (1989). These authors show analytically that, at times, central banks prefer arrangements that obscure current or planned actions. The reason is that the central bank may wish to change policy without announcing or revealing the change. This is particularly true when the central bank desires an expansion of real activity. Unanticipated changes in money can be made larger and more potent for real variables if the public has difficulty interpreting central bank actions and announcements. If the public can accurately forecast policy or readily distinguish between permanent and transitory changes in money growth, opportunities to affect the pace of real activity would be severly limited. However, there are limits to the central bank's ability to exploit its opportunity to mislead the public. When the central bank chooses to reduce inflation, costs of disinflation depend on past performance and on the credibility of its statements. The more skeptical the public is about the central bank's commitment to disinflation, the higher the cost of disinflation. Hence, maintaining a stock of credibility for the future restricts the tolerable inefficiency of control procedures and the imprecision of announcements today.

The Inflation Problem

The decade of the 1970s was a period of unprecedented inflation for the (mainly) peacetime U.S. economy. The average rate of increase of the GNP deflator from 1969 to 1979, 7.0%, is above the 6.1% average for the 1940s that includes a major war. Growth of money remained high, on average, for the decade. The monetary base rose at a compound annual rate of 7.7%, and M2 rose at a compound rate of 9.3% from December 1969 to December 1979.

In Martin's last year as chairman, the GNP deflator rose by 5.5%. Arthur Burns' public statements before taking office as chairman showed him to be not only opposed to inflation but opposed to policies that produced inflation. In office, he behaved very differently. The inflation rate averaged 7.0% during his seven years as chairman. As a professor, he had criticized the Kennedy and Johnson administrations' reliance on wage-price guidelines. In office, he became a leading advocate of informal controls on prices and wages (Stein, 1988, p. 155).

In the 1968 campaign, President Nixon had promised to reduce inflation with only a moderate rise in unemployment. Since economists are far from certain about how to deliver that result, the administration was unable to announce and follow a coherent policy. At the Fed, Burns preached against inflation and the problem of inflationary anticipations while conducting a monetary policy that increased inflation and sustained the anticipation that inflation would increase. As we have seen, the Federal Reserve raised the growth rates of the base and money within a few months of Burns' appointment as chairman (February 1970), so at the time monetary policy did not contribute to the administration's desired reduction in inflation. Figure 1–2 shows that, during Burns' term in office, the annual growth rate of the monetary base remained above 7% most of the time. Burns' (1978) speeches show a clear understanding of the critical role of price and wage anticipations in the inflation process, but he attributed the failure of anticipations to decline in periods of unemployment to recent changes in the wage-price process and ignored inflationary monetary policy. To counter these changes, Burns (and many others) believed government had to intervene with guidance or control of wages and prices.

Burns' study of the business cycle at the National Bureau of Economic Research (NBER) gave him an eclectic view of economic processes that fits harmoniously with the eclectic view at the Federal Reserve. He found it easy to argue publicly that fiscal policy, full employment, the spread of unemployment compensation, cost-push, a general inflationary bias in the economy, and other forces were the main causes of inflation. He seemed to find no inconsistency in warning about the dangers of inflation, while claiming that "monetary policy has provided the funds needed for a good expansion of production and employment" (1978, p. 152). His speeches from his years as chairman are filled with discussions of the various causes of inflation and warnings about the costs of inflation. If he believed that the Federal Reserve had an important influence on inflation, he was reluctant to say so.[16]

A further problem in the early 1970s was that Burns had accepted the chairmanship of the Committee on Interest Rates and Dividends and membership on the Cost of Living Council. Both had been established under the wage and price control program. The Committee was supposed to monitor interest rates and dividends but had no authority to control them, whereas the Council had authority to control wages and prices. If interest rates rose, Congress was likely to press for more binding controls. Burns (1978, p. 139) opposed mandatory controls on interest rates. One way to avoid controls was to restore the policy followed during the early Johnson administration—keep interest rates from rising, at least for a time, by a combination of monetary growth and direct pressure on banks. That may explain why the Federal Reserve increased the growth rate of money during the price control period in 1972 and early 1973. Since the expansive monetary policy was in accord with the administration's desire to lower unemployment in an election year, no criticism came from that side (Stein, 1988, p. 184). The growth rate of money in the second half of 1972 was the highest in the postwar period up to that time.

The experiment with controls failed to lower inflation. By hiding the inflation, it may have encouraged the Federal Reserve to follow more expansive monetary policies, adding to subsequent inflation. What is certain is that after controls were removed, broad based measures of inflation were higher in every year from 1974 through 1982 than before controls were in place. Countries that followed less expansive monetary policies and avoided price controls—notably Japan, Germany, and Switzerland—did not share this fate. In these countries inflation rates declined in the late 1970s and, by the end of the decade, were below the rates at the start. These foreign economies were subject to many of the same shocks that affected the U.S. economy, particularly the rise in oil and food prices in the 1970s that were often blamed for U.S. inflation. They experienced currency revaluation, not devaluation, at the start of the fluctuating exchange rate period. This difference was a consequence of the inflation, not as is often suggested, the cause of a change in relative prices and country price levels.

The oil embargo in the fall of 1973, and the subsequent oil price increases in 1974, struck an economy that had been stimulated by rapid expansion of the monetary aggregates in earlier years. In the winter of 1973, prior to the oil shock, the FOMC directives called for slower growth in the monetary aggregates. M2 growth fell from a peak rate of 12.2% for the 12 months ending in January 1973 to 6.2% for the 12 months ending January 1974. M2 growth continued to fall slowly in 1974 until it reached a trough of 5.25% in January 1975. Twelve-month growth of the monetary base shows a small decline at the end of 1973 and a rise in 1974 (see figure 1–2). The movement of the base is more consistent with the intent of Federal Reserve policy, as expressed in the minutes of the period. By the fall of 1974, the Fed was seeking faster growth of the monetary aggregates despite the high rate of price increase for the year.

One problem with the conduct of policy in 1974 arose from confusion between levels and rates of change of prices and output. An increase in oil prices raises costs of production and lowers the efficient level of output. Once the price level increase is absorbed, the measured rate of price change returns to the path consistent with monetary growth and the growth rate of output. The shock reduces the level of output; since the decline in output (and rise in prices) does not occur instantly, measured rates of change are affected temporarily. The loss of output is a permanent change in level, but there should be no lasting effect on the growth rate of output.

Most policy discussions ignored the difference between inflation—defined as the maintained rate of price change—and the one-time increase in the price level that caused a temporary increase in reported measures of monthly or annual rates of price change. Also ignored was the distinction between a cyclical recession and a permanent reduction in the level of output.[17] Those who were most concerned about "recession" favored a more expansive monetary policy, although they failed to explain how the creation of money to increase nominal aggregate demand could offset the effects on output and employment of a reduction in the supply of oil. Those who were most concerned about the "inflation" induced by the rise in oil prices favored a reduction in money growth. They failed to explain why one-time changes in the price level—up or down—should not be permitted to stand. The change in price level is part of the means by which the community adjusted money wages, money balances, and other nominal values to the wealth transfer that society had to bear. By shifting aggregate demand, changes in money growth made the adjustment to the supply shock more difficult to interpret. The reason is that, in the present state of knowledge, the effects of the change in aggregate demand on prices and output are difficult to separate from the responses to the supply shock.

Judged by the growth rate of nominal M2, money growth first reinforced the shock, then tried to offset it. The Fed kept on the brakes in 1974, then stepped on the accelerator in 1975. Between January 1975 and January 1976, the 12-month rate of increase in money rose from 5.25% to 12.5%. The NBER dates the recession from November 1973 to March 1975. Using these dates, seasonally adjusted monthly M2 growth falls during the recession until December 1974, then rises two months before the trough (figures 1–11 and 1–12).

Burns' tenure at the Federal Reserve ended with inflation higher than when he assumed office. For the eight years of 1970–1977 inclusive, the GNP deflator rose at a compound rate of 6.8% and the Consumer Price Index by 6.5%. In his last speech as Chairman, Burns (1978, pp. 255–256) recognized the failure to control inflation, but he placed the blame on the policies of the 1960s and the lack of political will.

Burns' replacement as chairman was a successful businessman, G. William Miller. Miller lacked Burns' command of economic data and its interpretation, and he also lacked any clear view about what monetary policy should do or how it should be conducted. During Miller's relatively brief tenure—February 1978 to August 1979—the Federal Reserve maintained an expansive policy, perhaps reflecting administration policy. The Carter administration was anxious to avoid recession and to reduce unemployment. It tried a number of informal controls on wages and prices and maintained controls on energy prices to control "inflation." Its major policy initiative was an effort to achieve a coordinated increase in aggregate demand by major industrial countries. At first, this initiative was not accepted by foreign governments; the rate of inflation rose in the United States relative to inflation rate abroad, and the dollar declined on the currency markets. By the last year of the Carter administration, 1980, broad-based measures of inflation in the United States were at least twice the rates in Germany and Japan.

The decline in the dollar, rising inflation, and rising criticism at home and abroad brought a change in policy at the end of the decade. In August 1979, with the measured rate of consumer price increase between 13% and 15% for the year, Miller became Secretary of the Treasury and Paul Volcker became chairman of the Board of Governors.

The 1979–1982 Experiment

On October 6, 1979, after a Saturday meeting, the Federal Reserve announced a change in the method used to conduct monetary policy. The new procedure was intended to be a better means of achieving previously announced growth rates of monetary aggregates. Greater emphasis was given to "the supply of bank reserves" and less emphasis to "confining short-term fluctuations in the federal funds rate" (Federal Reserve, 1979, p. 1). At the same time, the discount rate was increased by a full percentage point, and some technical adjustments in reserve requirements were introduced.

The announcement was widely interpreted as the beginning of a "monetarist" experiment. In fact, the change in procedure was intended to be relatively modest, as the announcement hinted. Control of market interest rates was not abandoned, nor was tight control of total reserves or the monetary base considered. Two principal changes were made. A relatively large, one-time increase in market interest rates followed the announcement. The federal funds rate was raised from a mean of 11.5% at the September meeting to a range of 11.5% to 15.5% on October 6 (figure 1–5). Greater emphasis was given to the growth of non-borrowed reserves and less emphasis to tight control of the federal funds rate, as suggested by the wider range for federal funds agreed to at the meeting.

The experiment ended late in the summer of 1982. Figure 1–14 shows absolute deviations of actual from the planned or target federal funds rate and absolute deviations of actual from planned growth of M2 for the period of the experiment. Federal funds rate deviations are measured as the difference between the average monthly rate and the mean target reported in the minutes for the same month. Deviations of M2 growth are differences between a three-month moving average and the mean of the high and low targets selected at each meeting. For comparison, figure 1–15 shows the same two measures for the period preceding the policy shift.

Comparison of the two figures shows the change in policy. In the earlier period, departures of the federal funds rate from its target, shown by the solid line, are much smaller and less frequent than in the subsequent period. Deviations of M2 growth from target are not noticeably different under the new policy regime. The change in procedures appears to have increased the variability of the federal funds rate without reducing the variability of money growth (as measured by M2). Large deviations from the planned targets for M2 growth are common during the 1979–1982 period. A considerable body of research suggests that these findings hold using other measures of interest rates and money. Table 1–3 reports comparative values of mean absolute deviations and standard deviations of the difference between the series shown in the two figures for several periods.

The table makes clear what the figures suggest. The new procedure was inefficient. Variability of the federal funds rate increased, but variability of money growth increased also. At least partly attributable to the change in policy procedures, the variability of ex post real rates of interest rates rose at all maturities. Table 1–4 shows one-year and ten-year real rates computed by subtracting the rate of change of the GNP deflator.

The similarity of the standard deviations of real rates for one-year and ten-year securities is puzzling. The similarity persists during each subperiod. In part, the similarity reflects the use of a common measure of inflation, but this is far from a complete explanation.[18]

Several studies of the experiment are now available: see, among others, Cook (1989), and Karamouzis and Lombra (1989). From them, we learn that the experiment did not involve any major change in the staff's analysis of money and interest rates. To accommodate the change, the staff reversed the direction of causality between money and interest rates. Where the staff previously chose the desired change in the federal funds rate and accepted the associated change in money, they now specified the target change in money and, in principle, accepted the associated change in the federal funds rate. Using the change in the federal funds rate obtained

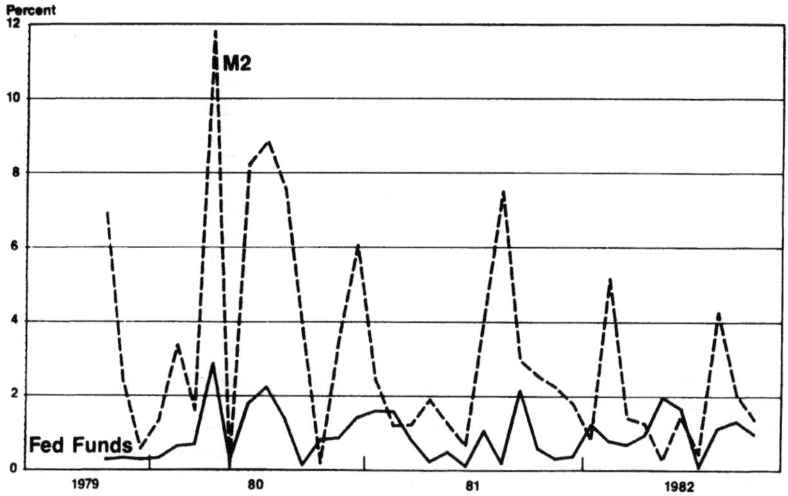

Figure 1–14. M2 vs. federal funds deviations, October 1979–October 1982

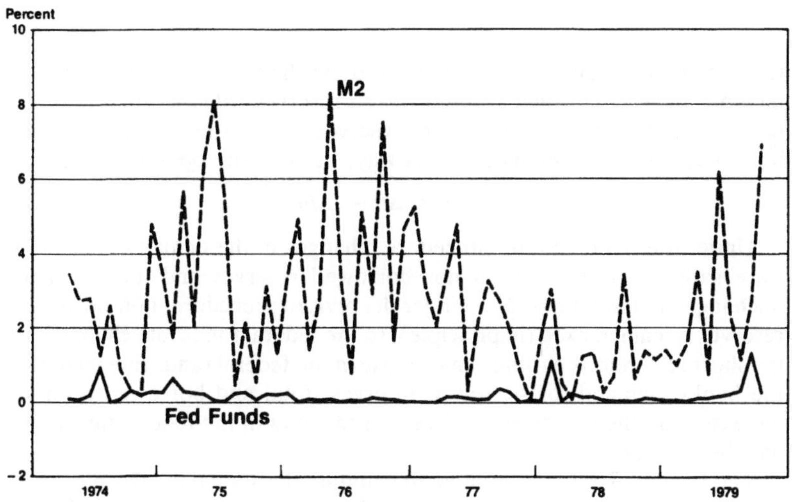

Figure 1–15. M2 vs. federal funds deviations, March 1974–October 1979

Table 1–3. Deviations from Monthly Targets

Period	*Mean Absolute Difference* Fed Funds	M2 Growth[a]	*Standard Deviation* Fed Funds	M2 Growth[a]
1/74–10/79	0.2	2.7	0.2	2.0
10/79–10/82	0.9	3.1	0.7	2.9
10/82–11/88	0.7	2.6	0.5	3.1
All months	0.6	2.7	0.6	2.7

[a] Actual growth is a three-month average.

Table 1–4. Mean and Standard Deviation (Quarterly) Ex Post Real Rates of Interest (Percent)

Period	*Mean* One Year	Ten Year	*Standard Deviation* One Year	Ten Year
1960/1–1973/1	1.8	2.2	1.2	1.2
1973/2–1979/3	−0.8	−0.5	2.2	2.8
1979/4–1982/3	4.2	3.7	4.3	4.8
1982/4–1988/3	5.0	6.5	2.5	2.6

from their money model, the staff derived the changes in total reserves and member bank borrowing. Non-borrowed reserves (*nbr*) is the difference between total (*tr*) and borrowed reserves (*br*). The change in non-borrowed reserves, obtained in this way, became the operating target.

$$\Delta nbr \equiv \Delta tr - \Delta br$$

Under the old operating procedure, changes in the demand for money were satisfied by changes in non-borrowed reserves and money at an unchanged federal funds rate. Under the revised procedure, non-borrowed reserves remained fixed (in principle), so the federal funds rate changed. In the short run, ceteris paribus, an increase in the federal funds rate increases the banks' demand for borrowed reserves; total and borrowed reserves increase, and the money stock rises. A reduction in the federal funds rate has the opposite effect.

The Federal Reserve continued to maintain the system of lagged reserve requirements under which banks used deposits held two weeks earlier as the base for computing required reserves on settlement dates. Given the stock of non-borrowed reserves, banks could obtain additional required reserves only by borrowing. Since the discount rate was often considerably lower than the federal funds rate and other market rates, banks had an incentive to delay adjustment of assets and deposits.[19]

In practice, the new control method proved to be a relatively modest change from past procedure. At each meeting, the Federal Reserve chose an average growth of *nbr* between meetings to meet the target for money growth. However, the federal funds rate did not vary to continually adjust the demand for reserves to the *nbr* target; the supply of non-borrowed reserves was not held at the level consistent with the target for money. Instead, the federal funds rate was allowed to rise or fall only when the Federal Reserve decided not to modify its *nbr* target, and *nbr* was allowed to deviate from target when the Federal Reserve did not choose to accept the required change in the federal funds rate. Cook (1989) notes that there were two types of discretionary change in the funds rate. One type of adjustment changed the distribution of Δnbr within the period without changing the average; the second adjusted the average growth of *nbr* to allow for unanticipated changes in reserves that occurred independently of money growth.[20]

Cook (1989) estimates that approximately two-thirds of the changes in the federal funds rate were discretionary during the 1979–1982 period. This estimate is based on the average relation between changes in the federal funds rate and changes in borrowing, so the point estimate may be misleading. However, Cook shows that his model predicts movements of the federal fund rate during the period. If we accept his estimate, it follows that the change in control procedure was a smaller departure from previous practice than many observers believed at the time.

The new procedure added to uncertainty about what the Federal Reserve was doing. As noted earlier, variability of money, reserves, and interest rates increased in part as a result of the uncertain and inefficient control procedure. Karamouzis and Lombra (1989, p. 51) report that "several members of the FOMC (in private communications) have indicated that the details and full ramifications of the changes in procedures . . . were not clear to them nor, in their judgment, to most FOMC members at the time [October 1979] or for months thereafter." A usual source of information, the speeches and writing of officials, did not function or, worse, was unintentionally misleading.

One technical reason for the heightened variability and uncertainty was that the relation of borrowed reserves to interest rates is relatively unstable. Increases in borrowing were often difficult to interpret, so it was easy for the FOMC members and the staff to be skeptical of recommendations for action that depended on the borrowing equation. Under the federal funds targetting procedure, shifts in borrowing were accommodated most or all of the time; under the *nbr* procedure, shifts in borrowing were accommodated much of the time. This meant that the money target was an unreliable guide to desired Federal Reserve policy.

It should not be surprising that interest rates showed substantial response to deviations of money supply from target during the *nbr* targetting period. Market participants could not know, because the Federal Reserve did not usually know, how much of an observed change in money was a permanent change. The announced targets for money had generally not been achieved prior to 1979, and they were not generally achieved during the period 1979 to 1982. Hence, the information content of recent movements was high relative to the information in announcements or past averages. Rational behavior implies that current changes would have great influence on market participants' anticipations under the circumstances (Cukierman and Meltzer, 1986).

At first, the experiment had little effect on the maintained rate of increase in the monetary base. The 12-month growth rate of the monetary base remained in the 7% to 8% range until 1981 (figure 1–3). By October 1981, the 12-month growth rate had fallen to 3.8%. The decline in base money growth, and a sharp fall in the growth of velocity for all monetary aggregates, was followed by a decline in inflation. From the peak rate of 9.7% in 1981, inflation, as measured by the GNP deflator, fell to 6.4% in 1982 and 3.9% in 1983.

The Federal Reserve's experiment succeeded in lowering the inflation rate. Inflation (GNP deflator) fell from an average rate of 8.7% for the five years ending in 1981 to 3.2% for the five years ending in 1988. The costs of the reduction were larger than necessary. The 1981–1982 recession is often described as the most severe in 50 years. This is an overstatement. The increase in unemployment and the decline in real growth are both smaller than in the 1973–1975 decline. Nevertheless, for the year 1982 industrial production was below the level reached in 1978, and payroll employment was below the 1979 level. Unemployment rose 3.2 percentage points and real GNP fell 3.2% from the NBER expansion peak, in third-quarter 1981, to the recession trough in fourth-quarter 1982. Some of the cost of disinflation was a consequence of the uncertainty surrounding the policy rule, but much of the cost probably reflected prevailing skepticism about administration, congressional, and public tolerance for unemployment rates above 10%.

Although the recession receives most of the attention, it is not the only cost of the disinflation. Inflation and disinflation interacted with institutional arrangements such as ceilings on saving and time deposit interest rates, prohibition of interest payments on demand deposits, income tax rates based on nominal values, and other restrictions to permanently alter the financial system. Sustained losses by financial firms and government intermediaries imposed large costs on taxpayers and solvent firms. The disinflation was worldwide, so it resulted in a marked fall in commodity prices (including petroleum prices), thereby contributing to the problem of developing country debt. As is often the case, a robust recovery in the U.S. followed the steep decline. By 1984, employment and production were above their previous peaks. The consequences of changes in asset values proved more durable. It seems likely that, absent the 20-year cycle of inflation and disinflation, the problems of the thrift industry, of international debt of developed countries, and of government intermediaries in agricultural and mortgage lending would have been smaller or largely avoided.

After 1982

Although inflation remained well above the rate of the early 1960s and was high by historical standards, the disinflation policy ended in the fall of 1982. The Federal Reserve did not announce the shift in policy. The initial announcement referred to some technical difficulties in interpreting monetary aggregates arising from the expiration of special tax exempt accounts at financial institutions. Money growth surged. Figure 1–16 shows the extraordinary increase in M2 growth late in 1982.

The Federal Reserve abandoned the efforts to implement control by means of the non-borrowed reserves procedure. The new procedure exploits the relation between the level of member bank borrowing (*br*) and the difference between the federal funds rate and the discount rate (*d*). If *br* is a linear function of *d*, we can write

$$br = a_0 + a_1 d + u$$

where u is a random variable. Changes in a_0 represent permanent shifts in the relation of *br* to *d*, and changes in u are presumed to be transitory. Thornton (1988) suggests that the federal funds rate is assumed to depend on the volume of non-borrowed reserves (*nbr*). This relation also is subject to permanent and transitory changes. If the *br* and *nbr* functions remain stable—particularly if there are no permanent shifts in the relations—the Federal Reserve can control the federal funds rate and *br* by varying *nbr* and the discount rate. Since $br + nbr$ equal total reserves, the volume of total reserves is determined by supplying *nbr* up to the point at which the

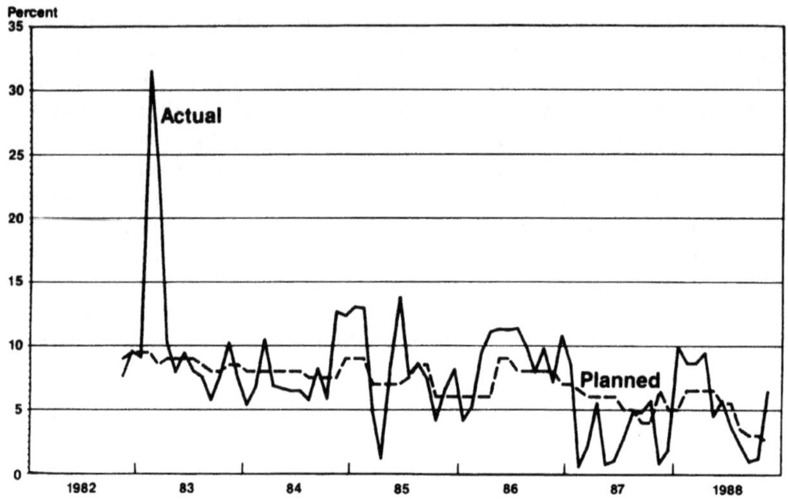

Figure 1–16. Actual vs. planned growth of M2, October 1982–November 1988

federal funds rate determines a level of *br* consistent with the Federal Reserve's choice of total reserves.

The central role assigned to borrowing in the control procedure represents a partial return to the Riefler-Burgess framework. Earlier work, Brunner and Meltzer (1964/1989), and more recent work, Thornton (1988), suggest that changes in member bank borrowings are not closely related to changes in money. The borrowing relation is subject to permanent and transitory changes that are difficult to identify when they occur.[21] Hence, the Federal Reserve faces the same problem as under the *nbr* procedure; it must decide whether to hold the level of borrowing and let the funds rate adjust or to stabilize interest rates and permit total reserves and the money stock to deviate from their target. Figure 1–16 shows that there were frequent, large deviations of M2 growth from target.

Figure 1–17 shows corresponding data for the federal funds rate. These data suggest that until late 1984, the Federal Reserve allowed relatively large deviations from the monthly funds rate target. After 1984, the deviations decline. They remain larger in absolute value than was true before 1979. Table 1–3 above confirms this impression.

Not all of the variability in measures of monetary policy arise from the control procedure. The FOMC continues to shift the goal of policy. Table

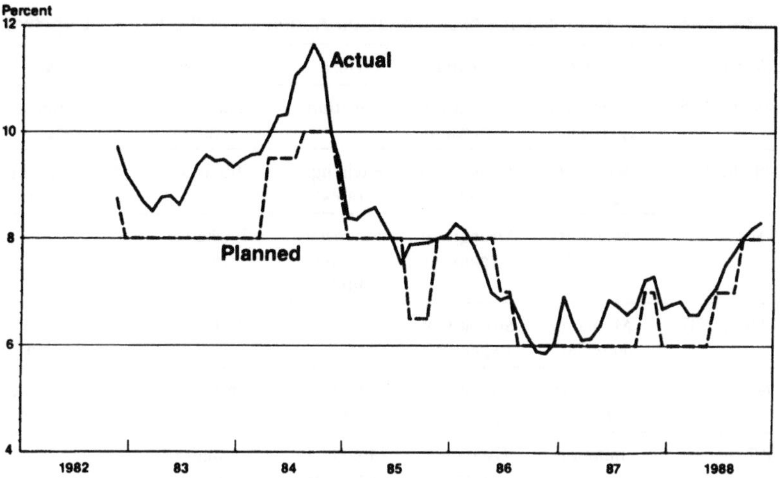

Figure 1–17. Actual vs. planned federal funds rate, October 1982–November 1988

1–5 shows that there were 12 reorderings of policy goals in three and one-half years. One occured after the stock market crash in October 1987. This shift in objectives recognized the Fed's role as lender of last resort. Other changes are more difficult to interpret. We know very little about what the changes mean in practice. It may be that the changes in objective have no content. Analysis is difficult, given the relatively imprecise control of reserves and monetary aggregates. Reluctance to permit sufficient variability of the federal funds rate casts doubt on the importance the Federal Reserve attaches to the stated objectives or their ordering. Furthermore, it is difficult to relate current actions to inflation, the pace of economic activity, or the exchange rate.

Comparison of periods in which monetary aggregates were placed first with other periods in which they were placed fourth or fifth shows no clear evidence of a change in the degree of control. In figure 1–16, the deviations of M2 growth from target early in 1985 are not much different from the deviations from target in 1987–1988. Nor are the latter very different from the deviations from July 1986 to July 1987 when monetary aggregates were placed first or second.

The years 1982 to 1988 show no major break from the past in the conduct of monetary policy. Statements of intention to use monetary

Table 1–5. Order in which Policy Variables Appeared in the FOMC Directive

Meeting	*First*	*Second*	*Third*	*Fourth*	*Fifth*
3/85 to 7/85	Monetary aggregate	Strength of expansion	Inflation	Credit market conditions	Exchange rates
8/85 to 4/86	Monetary aggregate	Strength of expansion	Exchange rates	Inflation	Credit market conditions
5/86	Monetary aggregate	Strength of expansion	Financial market conditions	Exchange rates	—
7/86 to 2/87	Monetary aggregate	Strength of expansion	Exchange rates	Inflation	Credit market conditions
3/87	Exchange rates	Monetary aggregate	Strength of expansion	Inflation	Credit market conditions
5/87	Inflation	Exchange rates	Monetary aggregate	Strength of Expansion	—
7/87	Inflation	Monetary aggregate	Strength of expansion	—	—
8/87 to 9/87	Inflation	Strength of expansion	Exchange rates	Monetary aggregate	—
11/87	Financial market conditions	Strength of expansion	Inflation	Exchange rates	Monetary aggregate
12/87 to 5/88	Financial market conditions	Strength of expansion	Inflation	Exchange rates	Monetary aggregate
7/88	Monetary aggregate	Strength of expansion	Inflation	Financial markets	Exchange rates
8/88 to 11/88	Inflation	Strength of expansion	Monetary aggregate	Exchange rates	Financial markets

Source: *Economic Review*, Federal Reserve Bank of San Francisco, Spring 1989, p. 11.

policy to control monetary aggregates or inflation seem unrelated to the actual growth rates of the monetary base, M2, or other monetary aggregates. Announced targets for monetary growth were missed more often than they were achieved. The Federal Reserve announced multiple targets but typically gave little attention to any of them. Control of the federal funds rate remained the principal short-term focus of policy action, although larger deviations from target were permitted than in the 1960s and 1970s.

In August 1987, Alan Greenspan replaced Paul Volcker as chairman of the Board of Governors. Greenspan has reduced the growth of the monetary aggregates. His public statements emphasize the importance of restoring and maintaining price stability. He responded promptly to the stock market crash by providing reserves for a brief period, and he made clear that the Federal Reserve would serve as lender of last resort to the financial system. When the risk of an increased demand for money appeared to subside, the growth rate of money was reduced, and the policy of disinflation resumed.

What Has Changed?

At the end of the 1980s, the Federal Reserve was still searching for a reliable method of control that would stabilize the domestic money market without sacrificing longer-term control of the price level. The most recent effort to limit inflation depends on a construct known as p^* that was developed at the urging of Chairman Greenspan. Increases in p^* relative to p indicate that inflation and deflation will rise, and a reduction in p^* relative to p signals disinflation. The computation of p^* starts from the quantity equation and the assumption that the velocity of M2 is trend stationary (Hallman, Porter, and Small, 1989).[22] The assumption that velocity is trend stationary runs counter to a large body of recent work suggesting that measures of monetary velocity are subject to permanent shocks and that velocity is well modeled as a random walk. If velocity is (approximately) a random walk, the actual price level will not return to p^*, as required for the model to be a reliable guide to inflation control. The reason is that permanent deviations of velocity from a fixed trend will be mirrored by deviations of p from p^* in the same direction.

Nevertheless, the introduction of p^* marks a new effort to consider the longer-term implications of policy. Also, the computation of p^* does not depend on forecasts from a large-scale model. The problem is the Federal Reserve has announced, and subsequently ignored, many indicators of inflation that are as reliable as p^*. It remains to be seen whether this new effort to find a price anchor will be another in the line of indicators that the Fed announced and subsequently ignored, starting with reserves against private deposits (RPDs) in the 1960s and including various monetary aggregates, measures of debt, borrowed reserves, non-borrowed reserves, and others. The answer will depend much more on the decision to allow

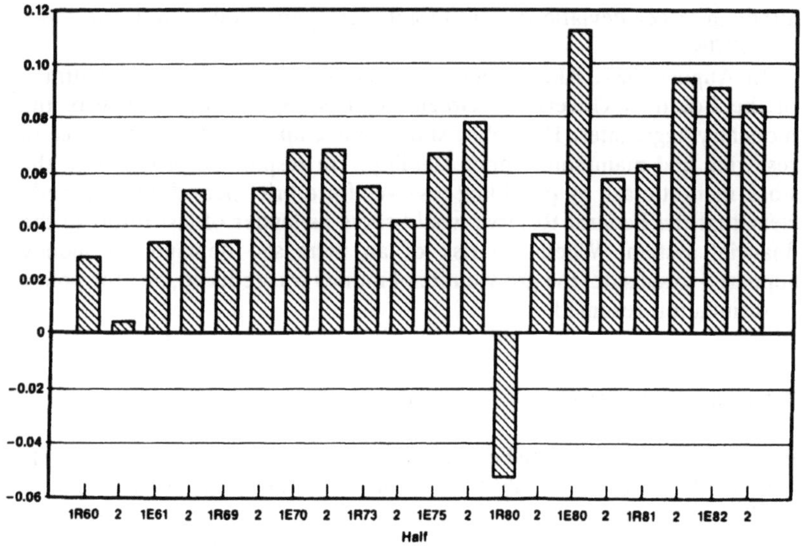

Figure 1–18. Mean growth rate of M1 by half recession and half expansion

sufficient flexibility of short-term interest rates (and other money market targets) than on the choice of a particular indicator of inflation.

Figure 1–17 above shows that the Federal Reserve permitted increased interest rate flexibility in the 1980s. This change enabled the Fed to lower money growth after mid 1987. Experience is too brief to draw any general conclusion about whether this policy will remain in effect.

One of the main criticisms of past Federal Reserve policy is that money growth has been procyclical. Recent experience suggests that this, too, may have changed. Figures 1–8 and 1–9 above showed that for the 1980s, there is some evidence that this pattern no longer holds for M2. Figure 1–18 shows more detail about the cyclical pattern of monthly M1 growth. Each half cycle is divided into two equal parts. During the 1960s and 1970s, the data show that M1 growth on average rises in the latter part of an expansion and falls in the latter part of a recession; M1 growth is not only lower in the depth of the recession than at the peak of the expansion but it falls during the recession and rises during the expansion. In the 1980s, this pattern vanishes. M1 growth is highest late in the 1981–1982 recession and declines, slightly, late in the 1982 recovery.[23]

The problem is to decide whether the recent pattern reflects a change in disintermediation, a change in Federal Reserve behavior, or is mainly a chance event. The mean monthly growth of the monetary base is higher in the current expansion than in the preceding recession. This is consistent with past Federal Reserve policy; it suggests that no change in behavior has occured. Working in the opposite direction is the slower growth of the monetary base and other monetary aggregates after the summer of 1987 (figure 1–3). Typically, late in an expansion, growth of principal monetary aggregates would be higher than in the preceding recession. A further complication in interpreting M1 is that the end of regulation Q ceilings changed the pattern of disintermediation. In previous postwar expansions, the rise in market rates induced the public to shift from commercial bank time deposits to open market paper and other, less regulated instruments, thereby reducing time deposits relative to demand deposits. The change in disintermediation lowers the growth of M1 late in the expansion relative to its previous norm. It is, therefore, difficult to draw a firm conclusion from the available data on M1 about whether Federal Reserve actions remain procyclical.

One change in Federal Reserve policy actions, or perhaps an outcome of its actions, is the decline in the share of debt financed by issuing base money. In Brunner and Meltzer (1976), the role of monetary policy in the financing of the government budget is summarized by the ratio of the stock of base money to the sum of the base plus the debt. In a closed economy, the denominator of the ratio is the cumulated value of past government deficits. In an open economy, the base includes the cumulated sum of foreign exchange (and gold) purchases. For the United States, the foreign component is a relatively minor sum, so I use the ratio to summarize the role of monetary policy in financing deficits contemporaneously or by subsequent open market operations. Figures 1–19 and 1–20 show the ratio for the years 1960 to 1988. There is a transition quarter in 1976 when the fiscal year changed; the 1976 data are for the fiscal year ending in June. The St. Louis version of the monetary base is used throughout.

A deficit financed by issuing debt lowers, and debt retirement raises, the ratio. Open market purchases increase, and open market sales reduce, the ratio. A rise in the ratio indicates that relatively more of the cumulated deficit has been financed by the monetary authority.

Figure 1–20 makes clear that the ratio has been falling during the years of relatively high budget deficits. If the ratio had remained at the average value for the 1970s (.158) in the 1980s, the stock of base money would have been more than 30% higher for the decade. The resulting increase in average base growth would have produced higher inflation. The Federal Reserve avoided the inflationary potential of a large deficit by slowing base

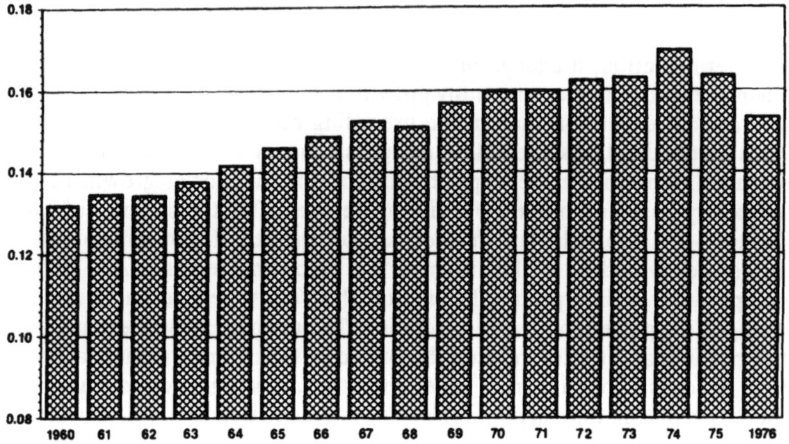

Figure 1–19. Base/(debt + base), 1960-2Q 1976

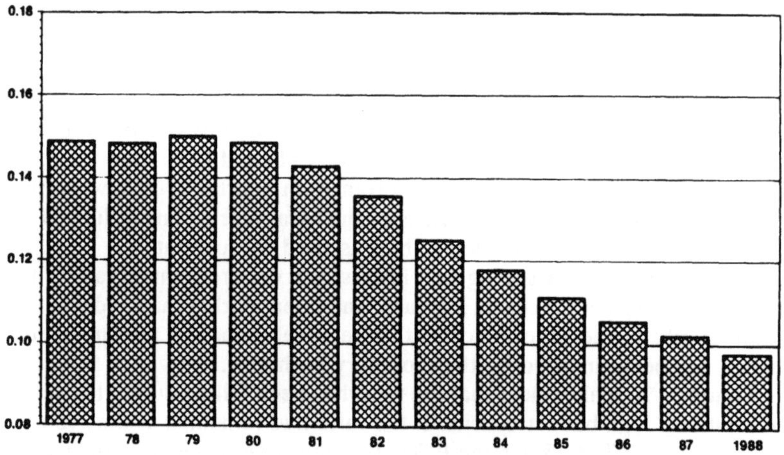

Figure 1–20. Base/(debt + base), 1977-3Q 1988

money growth absolutely and relative to the growth of the cumulated deficit.

In the recent years, careful analysis of the relation of monetary to fiscal policy in an intertemporal context shows that fiscal policy has implications for monetary policy. Some of this work implies that continued deficits necessarily induce inflation (Sargent and Wallace, 1981). In analyses where money, debt, and capital are distinct assets, the long-run response of the price level to fiscal deficits depends on the ratio of base money to the cumulated deficit. In a closed economy (or in an open economy with a fluctuating exchange rate), the monetary authority can influence the long-term result.[24] The data for the 1980s suggest that the numerator of the ratio declined and the denominator increased. Within the ranges observed, the monetary authority has been able to lower inflation by lowering the growth rate of the base despite the continuation of relatively large measured budget deficits.

In addition to the changed relation of fiscal to monetary policy, there have been major changes in the relation of the Board in Washington to the Reserve Banks and changes in the Federal Reserve's understanding of its role as lender of last resort. From the start of the system through the 1930s, much of the authority for decisions resided in the Reserve Banks, as Friedman and Schwartz (1963) note. In the postwar period, and particularly in the 1970s and 1980s, the Board has held the dominant role. In the early years, the governor (later president) of the New York Federal Reserve Bank had a major role in the formulation of monetary policy; now, his power is limited by the tighter control exercised by the Board and its staff.

Friedman and Schwartz (1963) document the failure of the Federal Reserve System to serve as lender of last resort to the banking system in the 1930s. The Fed responded differently in the 1970s and 1980s. Following the failure of the Penn Central Railroad in June 1970, the Federal Reserve notified banks that it was prepared to lend in an emergency. Similar actions were taken in other periods of financial distress that followed the failures of several large banks in the 1970s and 1980s. Following the October 1987 stock market decline, the Federal Reserve again recognized that it is the lender of last resort to the entire financial system; it provided reserves and expanded the monetary base promptly and maintained growth of money until the risk of a forced contraction subsided.

So great is the change that a new problem has arisen: the Fed often fails to distinguish between its responsibility toward the financial system and the failure of an individual bank. The Federal Reserve made loans, or encouraged bankers to lend, directly, to First Pennsylvania, Continental Illinois,

Table 1–6. Shocks to the Base and Base Velocity at Cyclical Turning Points in the United States

Quarter of NBER Turning Point[a]	*Forecast Error in Percent per Annum* — *Shock to Real GNP*	*Shock to Base*	*Shock to Base Velocity*	*Comment*
1960/4		−0.20	−1.16	*B* leads
1961/1 T		+1.05	−0.76	*VB* contemp.
1961/2	+1.80	−0.44	+2.52	
1969/2		−0.95	+0.66	*B* leads
1969/3		−0.80	+0.59	*VB* contemp.
1969/4 P	−1.26	+0.51	−1.43	
1970/1		−0.14	−0.69	
1970/3		+0.63	−0.13	*B* leads
1970/4 T		+0.31	−1.11	*VB* contemp.
1971/1	+2.52	+0.34	+2.07	
1973/2		−0.26	−0.86	*B* lags (weak)
1973/3		−0.29	−0.46	*VB* leads (weak)
1973/4 P		−0.38	+0.71	*VB* contemp.
1974/1	−1.85	+0.56	−2.14	
1974/4		−0.01	−0.50	*B* contemp. (weak)
1975/1 T		−0.48	−1.11	*VB* contemp.
1975/2	+2.48	0.12	0.91	
1975/3		0.26	2.32	
1979/3		−1.25	+1.82	*B* leads (weak)
1979/4		+1.42	−1.41	*VB* contemp.
1980/1 P		−0.10	+0.20	
1980/2	−3.17	−0.26	−2.70	
1980/3 T		+0.85	−0.49	*B* leads
1980/4	+0.71	+0.88	+0.75	*VB* contemp.
1981/2		0	−0.79	*VB* leads (weak)
1981/3 P		+0.49	+0.41	*B* + *VB* contemp.
1981/4	−1.61	−0.60	−1.05	
1982/2		+0.12	−0.44	*B* leads
1982/3 T		+0.30	−0.88	
1982/4	+0.87	+0.98	−0.23	
Mean absolute error (percent) 1960/2–1984/4	0.8	0.4	1.0	

[a] P = peak, T = trough.
Source: Meltzer (1986).

and other failing banks. This pattern of behavior encourages banks to undertake risks that they could have avoided.

Recently the Federal Reserve has recognized in its public statements that the principal goal of a central bank is to achieve and maintain price stability. Central banks in Europe and Japan took a similar position earlier. Central bankers in developed countries appear to be much less confident that they can adjust aggregate demand, output, and employment or that attempts to do so contribute to economic stability. If this change persists, it will be a significant departure from past belief and practice.

One result of the change would be a more stable monetary policy. In earlier work, I estimated the effect of unanticipated changes in base money, base velocity, and real GNP using a multistate Kalman filter on each of these series separately (Meltzer, 1986).[25] The unanticipated changes in each variable are obtained as the difference between actual values and the values predicted by the multistate filter. Bomhoff (1983) describes the filter process. The time series are quarterly data from 1960 through 1984. The shocks to real GNP at or near business cycle turning points, chosen by the National Bureau of Economic Research, show the size and direction of change near the start of an expansion or contraction. The mean absolute value of the shocks at turning points is 2.25 times larger than the mean absolute error for the period as a whole. These data are shown in table 1–6.

The table shows that unanticipated changes in the base typically lead shocks to real output by one to three quarters—three to nine months. This is consistent with several studies using different methods to measure changes and their timing. Shocks to base velocity are, most often, contemporaneous with the shock to real GNP.

Table 1–6 characterizes shocks to base money and velocity as weak or strong. This characterization is based on a comparison to the mean absolute error (or unanticipated change) for the period as a whole. The mean absolute errors are shown in the last row of the table.

Shocks to the monetary base lead the shock to output at six of the nine turning points, but one of the leads is relatively weak. The base lags at the turning point only in one case, 1973–1974 recession. Unanticipated changes in base velocity are usually contemporaneous with the shock to output and often follow a prior shock to the base. The principal exceptions are the declines following the oil shock of 1973–1974, when velocity has a weak lead over output, and following the introduction of credit controls in March 1980, when the prior unanticipated change in the base is small. In 1973–1974, the shock to the base and to base velocity were in the same direction; Federal Reserve actions augmented the real shock. This finding, using a very different procedure, reinforces the conclusion reached in the discussion of table 1–1 above; monetary policy was destabilizing. In the 1980s, prior unanticipated movements in the base and base velocity are offsetting; the decisive shock is the shock to base velocity resulting from the imposition of credit controls.

The shocks to money are, by construction, impulses that cannot be anticipated using the past history of the series. The lead of the base at turning points may, therefore, suggest causation running from the unanticipated change in the base to the subsequent change in output. Many of the largest shocks to output in this period are preceded by relatively large unanticipated changes in the base that are in the same direction. Furthermore, the nine business cycle turning points include six of the ten largest shocks to output during the period and the preceding shocks to the base are relatively large or cumulative. However, the interaction between money and output is almost certainly more complex than suggested by the lag structure used to construct the table, so I regard the evidence as a supplement to the evidence in earlier studies. Stock and Watson (1987) summarize this literature and contribute evidence of an effect of past changes in money on output (industrial production).

The conclusion to be drawn from table 1–6 and other past and recent evidence is not that all fluctuations are monetary in origin. Unanticipated changes can be real or nominal. Presumably, institutional changes could reduce the size of unanticipated changes in both series, say, by changing patent policy or increasing mobility of labor and capital in one case and by instituting a monetary rule (or changing the rule) in the other. A monetary rule that reduces variability, uncertainty, and fluctuations would be socially beneficial even if, as seems likely, real shocks would remain.

Conclusion: Was the Experiment Successful?

This lengthy examination of the Federal Reserve's operations and actions has pursued two main themes. One reconsiders the criticisms of Federal Reserve operations, actions, and policies made at about the time of the 50th anniversary and the Federal Reserve's responses. The other brings the analytic history of domestic policy operations up to the present. In the past 25 years there have been intermittent changes in operating techniques and frequent changes in objectives. After 75 years, the Federal Reserve System still has not formulated coherent attainable long-term objectives or developed efficient operating procedures related to those objectives. The focus remains principally on short-term considerations, principally those affecting the money market.

The 75th anniversary of an institution is a time for assessing its contributions to wealth and welfare. For the Federal Reserve, issues of this kind, though related to the themes of the article, are broader. They include an assessment of international operations, regulatory arrangements affecting the financial system, its safety and efficiency, and the Federal Reserve's contribution to economic stability, price stability, and perhaps to the level or growth of output.

Advocates of a central bank early in this century argued that British exporters had a competitive advantage because they were able to discount bills that could be rediscounted at the Bank of England. Access to central bank rediscounts was expected to supplement the market, create a broader, more liquid market for bills of exchange, and reduce risk for individual holders and for the market. If we interpret the mandate to provide an elastic currency as more than Federal Reserve note issuance, bill purchases and discount operations are part of that mandate. In the early years, these operations were a major activity, but their importance declined in the 1930s. Few would now rest the case for a central bank or assign much significance for welfare to the existence and operations of the discount mechanism. Markets developed to provide these services.

The Federal Reserve got under way slowly in 1914, and it has been slow to change. It was slow to permit interest rates to adjust enough to prevent inflation. It was slow to recognize that Regulation Q did not protect existing financial institutions. The United Kingdom, Canada, and other countries learned to avoid financial panics much earlier than the United States (Schwartz, 1986). The Federal Reserve was slow to recognize its responsibilities as lender of last resort in periods of panic, and its policies were at times a factor contributing to panics. Friedman and Schwartz (1963) note that, prior to the establishment of the Federal Reserve, the clearinghouses and banks performed some of the functions of a lender of last resort that the Federal Reserve failed to provide in the 1930s. Until the 1970s, and perhaps after, it was not clear when or whether the Federal Reserve would perform these functions. The existence of the Federal Reserve may have deterred the market from finding alternative solutions.

The costs of the 1930s mistakes did not end with the wartime recovery. The depression left a residue of legislation and regulation affecting banks, financial institutions, and financial markets. Banking problems of the 1930s were wrongly interpreted as a consequence of interest payments on deposits, so interest payments were prohibited on demand deposits and restricted on time deposits (Benston, 1964). Failures were also blamed on speculation, so investment and commercial banking were separated and mandatory margin requirements were introduced (Benston, 1989). Some of these restrictions were removed slowly; others remain nearly 60 years later.

The Federal Reserve was slow to urge Congress to remove the restrictions on interest payments and slow to raise the ceilings so that the restrictions were not binding. In the 1960s, the Fed acquiesced in, or perhaps encouraged, the extension of the ceilings to other financial instruments including deposits at thrift institutions. During the years of high inflation, the real losses suffered by depositors at banks and thrift institutions and by the institutions eventually led to repeal of most of the restrictions. But the losses also contributed to a weakening of the financial structure and to the failure of more than one-third of the thrift institutions and many banks.

Many of the losses and many of the continuing problems of financial fragility are the result of the Federal Reserve's failure to control inflation in the 1960s and 1970s and to the rapid disinflation of the early 1980s. By the 1980s prices of land and other inflation hedges had risen to anticipate continued U.S. inflation of 8% or 9%. Disinflation lowered the values of these assets, in some cases below the value of the loans or mortgages which they supported. Absent the inflation and disinflation, much of the variability and many of the losses would have been avoided.

The inflation of the 1960s and 1970s and non-indexation of tax rates financed expansion of the welfare state and a burdensome system of income redistribution. Research has not established that these transfer programs would have been smaller or less costly if their costs had been financed by explicit taxes. Casual, but persuasive, evidence from the elections of the 1980s, however, suggests that the voters would have opposed increased taxes to pay for these programs. Hence, some of the programs may not have been approved or extended in the 1960s and 1970s absent the tax revenues from inflation.

Under the Bretton Woods agreement, U.S. inflation spread to much of the rest of the world, just as U.S. deflation had spread under the fixed exchange rates of the early 1930s. The spread of inflation under fixed exchange rates lowered the real wealth of foreign oil producers by reducing the value of their holdings of dollars. Research has not established that losses arising from world inflation strengthened the producer's cartel and encouraged them to respond by raising the relative price of oil. Again, it would not be surprising if inflation contributed to the oil shocks in this way.

Offsetting these actual or potential burdens is the increased stability of

U.S. real output in the postwar period. Meltzer (1986a) shows a substantial reduction in the size of unanticipated shocks to output and inflation in the postwar years under fixed and fluctuating exchange rates. Federal Reserve actions may have contributed to the increased stability. Similar reductions in unanticipated variability are found for other countries (Bomhoff, 1983; Meltzer, 1986). DeLong and Summers (1986) suggest that the the reasons for the increased stability of postwar output are not well understood, however, so the relative contributions of the Federal Reserve and other institutions or their policies remain an open issue.

These comments suggest that the losses resulting from Federal Reserve actions, slow responses, and inaction outweigh the benefits. The Great Depression, the great inflation, and the costs of interest rate regulation imposed large losses, social as well as private. Since many of the benefits of Federal Reserve actions—recessions prevented, inflation avoided—are unobservable, summarizing benefits is more difficult. These benefits would have to be large, however, to offset the more easily observed costs. It seems unlikely that benefits comparable to the losses can be found.

The losses arising from the Great Depression, the great inflation, and other actions were not malicious or willful acts. Many were the result of mistaken beliefs about the way policy works, or reliance on forecasts and judgments that were faulty. Some were the result of deliberate attempts to trade higher inflation for lower unemployment, attempts that continued long after research had established that there was no long-term tradeoff. Some, particularly in the postwar period, were the result of the slow response characteristic of a government organization pressured by farmers, homebuilders, congressmen, and others who wanted interest rates to remain low or to rise, if they must, slowly. The Federal Reserve's status as an independent agency does not remove pressures of this kind. The pressures can be reduced only, if at all, by reducing opportunities for discretionary action or by strengthening incentives to maintain price stability.

Not all of the problems and errors were the result of pressures to pursue multiple goals or to change objectives. Some were the result of incorrect forecasts. Federal Reserve forecasts of output appear to be neither worse, nor demonstrably better, than other forecasts. Federal Reserve forecasts of inflation were consistently biased downward throughout the 1970s, however. On average for the postwar period, the non-forecastable variability in U.S. real growth and inflation is a relatively large fraction of the average quarterly or annual change. Hence, policies based on forecasts are necessarily subject to large errors, even if the forecasts are up to the highest standard that economists can provide. Some evidence (Brunner and Meltzer, 1983; McCallum, 1988) suggests that variability would be reduced and stability enhanced by following an adaptive rule that does not rely on forecasts.

The Federal Reserve has experimented with alternative control procedures and has shifted the weight on explicit forecasts and implicit judgments about the future many times. As far as we know, the Fed has never tested an explicit rule that relies only on past information. In public statements, rules have been rejected as inflexible and inefficient because they do not use available information. This criticism does not apply to adaptive rules. Further, it is disingenuous. The Federal Reserve does not behave haphazardly; it follows some, possibly complex, rule to implement its free reserves or interest rate policy procedure. The strategy and perhaps the rule change periodically. The rejection of "rules" should be seen as an attempt to maintain opportunities for shifting the weights in its objective function, which is to say pursuing more variable policies. These shifting objectives produce higher inflation and increase variability (Cukierman and Meltzer, 1986).

I have suggested that the costs of Federal Reserve policy have outweighed the benefits in the first 75 years of Federal Reserve history. In the 1960s many economists believed that the future of discretionary policy was much better than its past. They expected that an explicit econometric model, with a well-specified structure, would provide useful forecasts, improve policy operations, and increase policymakers' contributions to the stability of real and nominal values. This has not happened. Economists have not been successful in identifying stable structural parameters within broad ranges, and we have not discovered in any precise way how the structure responds to anticipations, taxes, age distribution, regulation, and other institutional changes. Efforts to identify the length of response lags have been unsuccessful. Partly as a result, forecast errors have been large relative to average changes, and the results of discretionary policy action, based on forecasts, have disappointed central bankers. Yet, the Federal Reserve has continued to rely on forecasts and to undertake discretionary actions based on forecasts.

One reason for continued reliance on forecasts and suboptimal procedures may be the low level of accountability. The major errors made in the 1930s, 1960s, and 1970s did not lead to major reforms that increase accountability. To improve accountability, while retaining independence of the Federal Reserve within government, incentives must be changed. In New Zealand, the governor's salary is now tied to his performance. In the past, I have urged a different system for the United States. The Federal Reserve would be allowed to choose policies and procedures. It would announce explicit targets for money growth as at present. Since research at the Federal Reserve and elsewhere shows that annual targets can be achieved with relatively small errors, the Federal Reserve would be required to explain failures to keep money growth within (say) 1% of the target annually. The President would have the option of accepting the explanation or requiring the resignation of the Board.

This proposal may not be ideal. Perhaps more effective or more attractive proposals will be forthcoming. Without institutional change that increases incentives for achieving price stability and reducing variability, there is no reason to be confident that at the 100th or 150th anniversary, future writers will have an empirical basis for believing that the experiment has been successful—that the Federal Reserve has contributed positively to wealth and welfare.

Notes

1. For the report on the Glass bill, see House Report 1593, 62nd Congress, 3rd sess. (February 28, 1913) in Krooss (1969, vol. 3, pp. 2143–95).

2. The interpretation was based on work done in the 1920s and reported in W. R. Burgess (1927) and W. W. Riefler (1930). Burgess and Riefler were economists in the Federal Reserve System at the time they wrote.

3. Examples are internal memos by Davis (1964) at the New York Federal Reserve Bank and Sigel (1964) at the Board of Governors.

4. Sherman J. Maisel served as a member of the Board of Governors from 1965 to 1973.

5. Andrew F. Brimmer served as a member of the Board of Governors from 1966 to 1974.

6. "As I gained more insight into the way monetary policy was being made, I began to suspect that the Fed might be committing some of the errors our critics accused us of" (Maisel, 1973, p. 82). See also Brimmer (1971, pp. 48–50).

7. Figure 1–7 shows that growth of M1 showed beginning in January 1969.

8. Herbert Stein was a member of the Council of Economic Advisers at the time. He became chairman in 1971 following the resignation of Paul McCracken.

9. There are many descriptions of this procedure. I follow Lombra and Moran (1980). See also Karamouzis and Lombra (1989). The two-stage procedure has been criticized not only by those who wanted to control money but also by those who favored discretionary policy based on forecasts. See especially Friedman (1975) who used a Poole (1970)-type analysis to show that the choice between use of targets for reserves or interest rates depends on the variance of errors in equations relating each of these variables to nominal output. Analysis of this kind assumes more reliable knowledge of structure than economists have been able to provide. Friedman criticized the two-stage procedure on several grounds, including dependence on tight control of money and the assumption that current output is independent of current monetary policy action. See also Friedman (1977).

10. Some governors now regard changes in the term structure as an indicator of inflation, contrary to the staff model where long rates depend only on short rates. I do not believe that this conflict has been resolved or that real and nominal changes in the term structure have been recognized in either the staff's or the governors' interpretation.

11. Targets were chosen for M1, M2, and M3, and other aggregates at various times. I have used M2. The detail would change, but the main conclusions here would be unchanged if I used M1. In months when the Federal Reserve did not meet, the targets were unchanged;

targets for these months are reported at the value for the previous month. Some of the data for actual values differ from data observed at the time because of revisions to the data. Data for the targets are taken from periodic Federal Reserve reports of its decisions.

12. Three caveats should be mentioned. First, the Lucas critique applies. We cannot know how much the variance of velocity would change with a change in the monetary rule, but there is no reason to presume it would increase. Second, a constant growth rule may not be optimal. There is some evidence that an adaptive rule is superior (McCallum, 1988). Third, ex post separation into random and systematic components may be more reliable than could be done at the time. If so, the procedure overstates what can be achieved by discretion.

13. This should not suggest that all forecasts have the same errors. Robinson (1989) studied the properties of forecasting models for the demand for money, including models similar to the Fed staff model. She found significant differences, but none of the models produced errors that are small relative to the variance of nominal GNP.

14. Actual growth 1973–1982 is estimated to have been 1.6% compounded annually.

15. The Board staff criticizes the Rasche-Johannes procedure for using an endogenous variable, the base, as the control variable. They do not establish a bias but limit their criticism to a potential bias. Rasche and Johannes carry out detailed tests that suggest that any bias is trivial.

16. Stein (1988, p. 154) states that Burns believed that monetary policy could facilitate expansion if other conditions were "right."

17. One exception is a group of non-government economists known as the Shadow Open Market Committee. At its meeting on September 12, 1975, the Committee pointed out that the supply shock was not a recession so the losses could not be avoided by expansive policy.

18. The relatively high average value of the ex post rates reflects some extreme values during the disinflation. For third quarter 1988, the values are 2.0% and 2.9%.

19. In February 1984, after the experiment ended, the lag was reduced from two weeks to a few days.

20. Examples are an increase in required reserves against liabilities not included in the money stock or an increase in excess reserves.

21. Thornton (1988, p. 37) used a variable coefficients model to estimate the *br* relation. He found that there was considerable variability in the intercept. The Federal Reserve usually responded by reducing the size of the change in the funds rate.

22. The discussion of the p^* model in this paragraph is based on Rasche (1989).

23. All data end in November 1988.

24. Some qualifications are required. As shown in Brunner and Meltzer (1976) at low values of the ratio, stability of the model is not assured.

25. This section follows Meltzer (1986, pp. 175–176). Table 1–6 is taken from that source. Additional evidence on monetary policy as a cause of fluctuations is given in Romer and Romer (1989) using historical data and Fair (1989) using a structural model. See also Stock and Watson (1987) for recent evidence on the relation of money to income and a brief summary of some of the issues in that large literature.

References

Andersen, L., and Jordan, J. L. 1968. "Monetary and Fiscal Actions: A Test of their Relative Importance in Economic Stabilization." *Review*, Federal Reserve Bank of St. Louis (November):11–24.

Benston, G. 1964. "Interest Payments on Demand Deposits and Bank Investment Behavior." *Journal of Political Economy* 72 (October):431–49.

Benston, G. 1989. *The Separation of Investment and Commercial Banking: The Glass-Steagall Act Revisited and Reconsidered*. London: Macmillan.

Bomhoff, E. J. 1983. *Monetary Uncertainty*. Amsterdam: North-Holland.

Brimmer, A. F. 1971. "The Political Economy of Money," Washington, D.C.: Board of Governors (multilithed).

Brunner, K., and Meltzer, A. H. 1964/1989. *The Federal Reserve's Attachment to the Free Reserve Concept*. Washington, D.C.: House Committee on Banking and Currency. Reprinted in K. Brunner and A. H. Meltzer (Eds.), *Monetary Economics*. London: Basil Blackwell.

Brunner, K., and Meltzer, A. H. 1964a. "Some Further Investigations of Demand and Supply Functions for Money." *Journal of Finance* 19 (May):240–83.

Brunner, K., and Meltzer, A. H. 1976. "An Aggregative Theory for a Closed Economy." In J. Stein (Ed.), *Monetarism*. Amsterdam: North-Holland, pp. 69–103.

Brunner, K., and Meltzer, A. H. 1983. "Strategies and Tactics for Monetary Control." *Carnegie-Rochester Conference Series on Public Policy* 18:59–103.

Brunner, K., and Meltzer, A. H. 1989. "Money Supply Theory." In B. M. Friedman and F. H. Hahn (Eds.), *Handbook of Monetary Economics*. Amsterdam: Elsevier (forthcoming).

Burgess, W. R. 1927. *The Reserve Banks and the Money Market*. New York: Harper.

Burns, A. F. 1978. *Reflections of an Economic Policymaker*. Washington, D.C.: American Enterprise Institute.

Cook, T. 1989. "Determinants of the Federal Funds Rate: 1979–1982." *Economic Review*, Federal Reserve Bank of Richmond, 75 (January-February):3–19.

Cukierman, A., and Meltzer, A. H. 1986. "A Theory of Ambiguity, Credibility and Inflation under Discretion and Asymmetric Information." *Econometrica* 54 (September):1099–1128.

Davis, R. 1964. "Research Memorandum: An Alternative Approach to the Monetary Mechanism." Federal Reserve Bank of New York, unpublished memo, November 30, 1964.

deLeeuw, F., and Gramlich, E. 1969. "The Channels of Monetary Policy: A Further Report on the Federal Reserve-MIT Model." *Journal of Finance* 24 (May):265–290.

deLong, J. B., and Summers, L. H. 1986. "The Changing Cyclical Variability of Economic Activity in the United States." In R. J. Gordon (Ed.), *The American Business Cycle: Continuity and Change*. Chicago: University of Chicago Press for the National Bureau of Economic Research, pp. 679–734.

Fair, R. C. 1989. "Does Monetary Policy Matter? Narrative versus Structural Approaches." NBER Working Paper 3045.

Federal Reserve. 1979. Press release, October 6, 1979.

Friedman, B. M. 1975. "Targets, Instruments and Indicators of Monetary Policy." *Journal of Monetary Economics* 1 (October):443–473.

Friedman, B. M. 1977. "The Inefficiency of Short-run Monetary Targets for Monetary Policy." *Brookings Papers on Economic Activity* 2: 293–335.

Friedman, M. 1953. "The Effects of Full Employment Policy on Economic Stability: A Formal Analysis." In M. Friedman (Ed.), *Essays in Positive Economics*. Chicago: University of Chicago Press.

Friedman, M., and Schwartz, A. J. 1963. *A Monetary History of the United States, 1867–1960*. Princeton, N.J.: Princeton University Press for the National Bureau of Economic Research.

Hallman, J., Porter, R. D., and Small, D. H. 1989. "M2 per Unit of Potential GNP as an Anchor for the Price Level." Staff Study. Board of Governors, Washington, D.C.

Karamouzis, N., and Lombra, R. 1989. "Federal Reserve Policymaking: An Overview and Analysis of the Policy Process." *Carnegie-Rochester Conference Series on Public Policy* 30:9–68.

Krooss, H. 1969. *Documentary History of Banking and Currency in the United States*. New York: Chelsia House in association with McGraw-Hill.

Lindsey, T., et al. 1981. "Monetary Control Experience Under the New Operating Procedures." *New Monetary Control Procedures II*. Washington, D.C.: Board of Governors.

Lombra, R., and Moran, M. 1980. "Policy Advice and Policymaking at the Federal Reserve." *Carnegie-Rochester Conference Series on Public Policy* 13:7–62.

Maisel, S. J. 1973. *Managing the Dollar*. New York: Norton.

McCallum, B. 1988. "Robustness Properties of a Rule for Monetary Policy." *Carnegie-Rochester Conference Series on Public Policy* 29:173–203.

Meltzer, A. H. 1986. "Size, Persistence and Interrelation of Nominal and Real Shocks." *Journal of Monetary Economics*, 17 (January):161–94.

Meltzer, A. H. 1986a. "Some Evidence on the Comparative Uncertainty Experienced under Different Monetary Regimes." In C. D. Campbell and W. R. Dougan (Eds.), *Alternative Monetary Regimes*. Baltimore, Maryland: The Johns Hopkins University Press, pp. 122–153.

Meltzer, A. H. 1987. "Limits of Short-Run Stabilization Policy. *Economic Inquiry* 25 (January):1–14.

Poole, W. 1970. "Optimal Choice of Monetary Policy Instruments in a Simple Stochastic Macro Model." *Quarterly Journal of Economics* 84 (May):197–216.

Rasche, R. 1989. "p* Type Models: Evaluation and Forecasts." Background paper prepared for Shadow Open Market Committee meeting, September 18 and 19.

Rasche, R. H., and Johannes, J. M. 1987. *Controlling the Growth of Monetary Aggregates*. Boston: Kluwer.

Riefler, W. W. 1930. *Money Rates and Money Markets in the United States*. New York: Harper.

Robinson, S. 1989. "Empirical Evidence on the Accuracy of Money Demand Forecasts and Their Importance to the Success of Discretionary Monetary Policy." Unpublished dissertation, Carnegie-Mellon University.

Romer, C., and Romer, D. 1989. "Does Monetary Policy Matter? A New Test in the Spirit of Friedman and Schwartz." NBER Working Paper 2966 (May).

Sargent, T., and Wallace, N. 1981. "Some Unpleasant Monetarist Arithmetic." *Quarterly Review*, Federal Reserve Bank of Minneapolis 5 (Fall):1–17.

Schwartz, A. J. 1986. "Real and Pseudo-Financial Crises." In F. Capie and G. E. Wood (Eds.), *Financial Crises and the World Banking System*. London: Macmillan, pp. 11–31.

Sigel, S. 1964. "Brunner and Meltzer's Alternative Approach to the Monetary Mechanism." Unpublished memorandum, Washington, D.C.: Board of Governors.

Stein, H. 1988. *Presidential Economics*, 2nd ed. Washington, D.C.: American Enterprise Institute.

Stein, J. C. 1989. "Cheap Talk and the Fed." *American Economic Review* 79 (March):32–42.

Stock, J. H., and Watson, M. W. 1987. "Interpreting the Evidence on Money-Income Causality," NBER Working Paper 2228 (April).

Thornton, D. 1988. "The Borrowed Reserves Operating Procedure: Theory and Evidence." *Review*, Federal Reserve Bank of St. Louis, 70 (January–February):30–54.

Tinsley, P., Farr, H., Fried, G., Garrett, B., and von zur Muehlen, P. 1982. "Policy Robustness: Specificiation and Simulation of a Monthly Money Market Model." *Journal of Money, Credit and Banking* 14 (November):829–856.

Commentary: Has the Fed Made a Difference? A Comparison of Pre- and Post-1914 Conditions

by Jeffrey A. Miron

1. Introduction

The goal of this commentary is to evaluate the role of the Federal Reserve System in determining changes in economic stability over time.[1] Previous papers have considered a number of hypotheses to explain the changes in variability, and most have given considerable attention to the possible effects of macroeconomic policies. None of these papers, however, has focused explicitly on the role of the Federal Reserve. I argue here that the Fed has played a crucial role in determining the changing variability of the economy. In particular, I suggest that the Fed has probably made output much *more* volatile than it otherwise would have been.

In section 2 of this article I provide a quantitative evaluation of the performance of the U.S. economy before and after 1914, the year in which the Federal Reserve System began operation. I find that during the interwar period, economic instability increased drastically relative to the pre-Fed period. After World War II, volatility decreased dramatically relative to the interwar period, but this decrease led to an economy that was, on the whole, only slightly less volatile than during the pre-Fed period. This conclusion holds using both the Balke and Gordon (1989) and the Romer (1989) data on real GNP.

The key difference between my analysis of output stability and the analyses in earlier papers is that I divide the sample period into three regimes, rather than only two. Almost all previous work compares the post-WWII period to the pre-1930 period, whereas my analysis examines three periods: pre-1914, interwar, and post-WWII. The crucial fact documented in this article is that output is much less stable during the interwar period than during the pre-1914 period; it then becomes more stable again

---

I am grateful to Todd Clark for research assistance. Financial support from NSF Grant SES-8710140 and a John M. Olin Fellowship at the National Bureau of Economic Research is gratefully acknowledged. This article was completed while I was a Visiting Associate Professor at the Sloan School, Massachusetts Institute of Technology, and a Visiting Scholar at the Department of Economics, Boston University.

after WWII. This fact makes a number of often proposed explanations for the changes in volatility hard to support since the relevant forces are unlikely to have increased and then decreased again.

Section 3 considers explicitly the role of a number of factors mentioned in the literature in potentially determining the amount of economic instability. These factors include possible effects of changes in the exchange rate regime, the degree of price rigidity, the composition of output, the nature of fiscal policy, and the structure of financial markets. I argue that most of these factors suggest there should have been a much greater stabilization betwen the pre-1914 and post-WWII periods than actually occurred.

The point of section 4 is to argue that the Fed contributed directly to the increase in variability during the interwar period and could have produced lower volatility than actually occurred during the post-WWII period. In making this argument, I do not offer any new evidence on whether or how monetary policy affects the economy. Instead, I simply summarize the existing evidence that supports an important Fed role. The section first provides some general background on the original motivation for the founding of the Fed and explains that it was not created to stabilize output. It then reviews the specifics of Fed performance during the interwar and post-WWII periods.

Section 5 concludes the article by discussing possible qualifications to my interpretation of the facts presented below.

2. Stylized Facts

I begin by presenting a set of basic stylized facts about the behavior of output and the inflation rate over the past century. The output and price level data employed for the pre-1929 period are those in Romer (1989). I use these data, rather than those in Balke and Gordon (1989), because Balke and Gordon's procedure for constructing their data makes a strong, problematic assumption about the appropriate deflator, and this assumption has a significant effect on the results. Nothing of importance, however, hinges on the use of the Romer data. All of the qualitative conclusions presented below and most of the quantitative ones follow almost as strongly using the Balke and Gordon data as using the Romer data. I comment further on this issue below.

Figures 1 and 2 show the rate of growth of real output and the rate of growth of the implicit price deflator for the period 1870–1987. Tables 1 and 2 present the mean and standard deviation of these two series for the three key sample periods of interest, as well as for a number of subsamples of

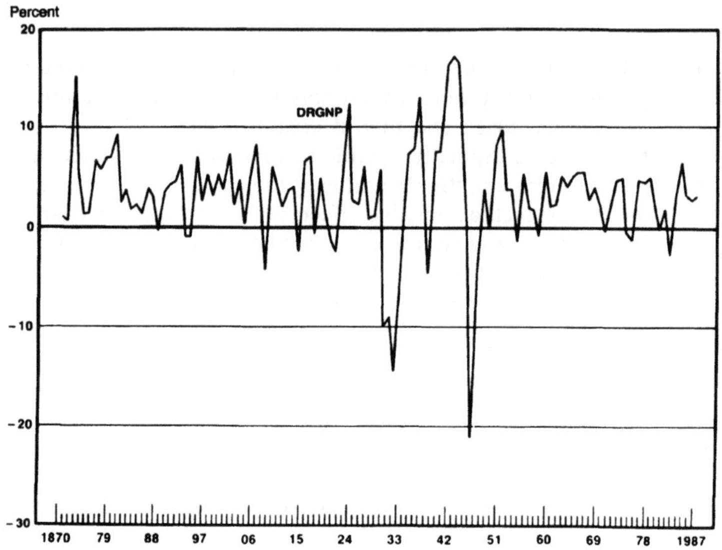

Figure 1. Real GNP, log growth rate

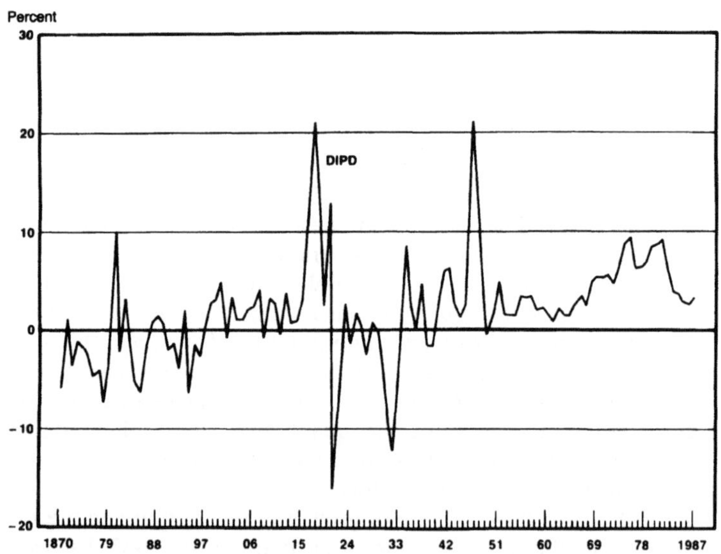

Figure 2. Implicit deflator, log growth rate

Table 1. Summary Statistics, Real GNP Annual Data, Log Growth Rates

Sample Period	*Mean*	*Standard Deviation*
1870–1913	3.92	3.24
1891–1913	3.66	2.97
1870–1890	4.21	3.57
1880–1913	3.53	2.77
1919–1940	1.99	7.03
1919–1928	2.95	4.28
1922–1928	4.56	4.04
1929–1940	1.20	8.82
1929–1933	−5.89	7.90
1934–1940	6.26	5.40
1947–1987	3.06	2.78
1947–1971	3.27	2.91
1947–1973	3.40	2.83
1972–1987	2.73	2.62
1974–1987	2.41	2.66

Table 2. Summary Statistics, Implicit Deflator Annual Data, Log Growth Rates

Sample Period	*Mean*	*Standard Deviation*
1870–1913	−.29	3.56
1891–1913	.94	2.80
1870–1890	−1.64	3.87
1880–1913	.59	3.38
1919–1940	−.71	6.27
1919–1928	−.41	7.30
1922–1928	−.51	2.85
1929–1940	−.96	5.59
1929–1933	−5.29	5.07
1934–1940	2.13	3.64
1947–1987	4.40	2.87
1947–1971	3.31	2.65
1947–1973	3.47	2.62
1972–1987	6.09	2.37
1974–1987	6.19	2.51

each of the three longer periods. Throughout the article I compare the pre-1914 period to two separate later periods, namely, the interwar period and post-WWII period.

As seen in table 1, the average rate of growth of real GNP was highest in the pre-Fed period; it exceeded 3.5% in every subsample. The second highest growth rate period was the postwar, in which real growth averaged just over 3.0%. The lowest growth period was the interwar, in which overall growth averaged only about 2.0%. Within both the prewar and postwar periods, the average growth rate was not particularly sensitive across subsamples; in the interwar period, however, there were periods of substantial negative growth combined with periods of highly positive growth.

Turning to the question of variability per se, the second column of table 1 shows that the postwar period was, as is commonly believed, the most stable, with a standard deviation of the growth rate of 2.78%. The postwar period was, however, only slightly less volatile than the pre-1914 period, and both periods were much more stable than the interwar period. During both the prewar and postwar periods, the standard deviation of the growth rate of real GNP was between 2.5% and 3.5% per year. During the interwar period, the standard deviation of the growth rate exceeded 5.5% in most subperiods. In all three cases, the conclusions about stability are not especially sensitive to breakdowns into finer subsamples. In particular, while the presence of the Great Depression in the interwar period is unquestionably part of the explanation for its increased volatility (and its lower average growth), the variability of output growth is higher even during the (relatively) stable 1920s than during the pre-1914 or post-WWII samples.[2]

It is useful to contrast these results to those in recent papers that present comparisons of output volatility over long periods (e.g., Romer, 1986a, 1986b, 1987, 1989; Balke and Gordon, 1989; De Long and Summers, 1988). All of these papers compare volatility between a post-WWII sample and a pre-1930 sample, rather than separating the 1920s from the pre-1914 period as done here.[3] To a significant degree they all find that the early period was more volatile than the later period because they include the volatile 1920s in their early sample. In particular, even the Balke and Gordon (1989) data show only a moderate reduction in volatility between the pre-1914 and post-WWII periods.[4]

I look next at the behavior of the inflation rate, shown in figure 2 and table 2. The average rate of inflation was clearly much higher in the postwar period than during either the pre-1914 or interwar periods, averaging 4.40% over the 1947–1987 period. By comparison, the inflation rate was slightly negative during both the pre-1914 and interwar periods. The variability of the inflation rate, on the other hand, was actually slightly lower during the postwar period than during the pre-1914 period, despite the large increase in the average inflation rate; and both periods displayed considerably less volatility than the interwar period. As with real output, these conclusions are robust across subsamples of the relevant three periods.

The picture that emerges is, therefore, as follows. During the 25-year period immediately following the founding of the Fed, economic performance was unambiguously worse than during the pre-Fed era. In comparison to the pre-1914 period, real growth was lower on average and more volatile, while the inflation rate was slightly higher on average and displayed much greater variance. The postwar period has been markedly better than the interwar period, but it has not overall been a clear improvement over the pre-Fed period. Real growth has been lower, although slightly more stable, and the inflation rate has increased significantly, albeit with a smaller standard deviation.

Of the facts presented above, it is the changes over time in the variability of output that are the most interesting and important to explain. On the one hand, it is reasonable to attribute the increase in the average inflation rate to the Federal Reserve; had it produced systematically lower money growth, there would almost certainly have been lower inflation. Likewise, there is little doubt that the Fed could have made the variation in inflation rates quite small if it had single-mindedly pursued that goal. On the other hand, most textbook and academic discussions adopt the perspective that monetary policy can potentially affect the variation of output around its natural rate of growth but cannot affect the natural rate of growth per se.[5] I therefore now concentrate on explaining the changes documented above in the variability of output over time.

3. Explanations for the Change in Output Volatility over Time

In this section I discuss factors other than the Fed that might have contributed to the differences in output variability between the three sample periods discussed above. The general conclusion is that none of the factors discussed can plausibly explain the changes in output variability. Instead, most of the factors imply that output should have become gradually more stable over time, making the factual results presented above all the more surprising. The next section, therefore, discusses what I consider the main remaining possible explanation, namely, the actions of the Federal Reserve.

3.1 The Exchange Rate Regime

Casual examination of the results displayed above might suggest that the exchange rate system is crucial in determining the volatility of output. The United States operated on fixed rates during most of the pre-Fed period (the Classical Gold Standard, 1879–1914) and much of the post-WWII period (the Bretton Woods System, 1944–1971), while during most of the interwar period there was no general system of fixed rates established between countries (Eichengreen, 1985). To a first approximation, therefore, the variability of output is low during fixed rate periods and high during flexible rate periods. Baxter and Stockman (1989) find for a sample of 14 OECD (Organization for Economic Cooperation and Development) countries that the volatility of industrial production generally increases from the Bretton Woods period to the flexible rate period.

There are a number of reasons to question the role of the exchange rate regime in explaining the facts above, however. On theoretical grounds, there is no clear presumption that a fixed rate system should be more stable than a flexible rate system. The two kinds of systems insulate the economy from different kinds of shocks, so the behavior of output depends on the general economic environment, not just the exchange rate regime. Thus, it is not clear why the change in the exchange rate system would, in and of itself, have altered the performance of the economy.

A closely related point is that a country's and the world's choice of exchange rate system are both endogenous. One possibility, therefore, is that during stable periods the world is able to maintain a system of fixed rates, whereas when underlying events become more volatile, fixed exchange rate systems break down. This interpretation is certainly the standard one with respect to both the breakdown of the classical gold standard and the breakdown of Bretton Woods. Under this interpretation, the change in the exchange rate system is mainly a reflection of changes in the behavior of the economy rather than an independent determinant of that behavior.

Finally, more detailed examination of the results in table 1 provides ambiguous evidence on the correlation between the exchange rate regime and the volatility of output. In the post-WWII period the variability of real GNP was higher during the Bretton Woods period than in the subsequent flexible rate period, a result confirmed using quarterly industrial production by Baxter and Stockman (1989). In the pre-1914 period, output volatility was higher in the flexible rate part of the period (1870–1879), but not by much. Thus, the U.S. experience does not provide any firm evidence that the exchange rate regime is crucial.

3.2 Price Flexibility

In a set of provocative recent papers, De Long and Summers (1986a, 1986b) suggest that the degree of aggregate price rigidity is an important determinant of output variability. They argue that the Keynes effect on real interest rates is empirically important and that the U.S. economy has become less Walrasian (i.e., prices have become more rigid) over time, so that output variability should have decreased. They offer the price flexibility hypothesis as an important factor in explaining the decrease in volatility from the pre-1930 to the post-WWII period.

The De Long and Summers hypothesis seems unlikely to be an important factor in explaining the results presented here. All of their arguments suggest there has been gradually decreasing price flexibility over the past 100-plus years. This characterization is difficult to reconcile with the facts because output variability increases dramatically and then decreases, contrary to their characterization of price flexibility. In addition, the changes in output variability occur rapidly whereas the changes in price flexibility have probably occurred more gradually.

3.3 Composition of Output

One important change in the economy over the past 100 years is a significant restructuring in the composition of output. As with the price flexibility hypothesis, changes in the composition of output cannot be first order effects in understanding the facts presented above. These changes are unlikely to have occurred sufficiently rapidly to produce the striking changes in output variability discussed above, and it is implausible that the changes in output shares could have changed in such a way as to first increase and then decrease output variability. Examination of the data shows both that actual output shares change slowly and that the changes are generally monotonic.

To the extent that changes in the composition of output have produced changes in output variability, they probably go in the direction of gradually decreasing volatility. The most dramatic changes have occurred in two industries, agriculture and government. The share of agriculture has fallen steadily from about 20% of GNP in the late 1800s to less than 3% in the 1970s. Conversely, government accounted for only about 5% of output at the end of the 19th century but more than 15% recently. Since agriculture is a relatively volatile sector and government a relatively stable one, these changes in output composition suggest that the post-WWII economy should have become more stable, perhaps significantly more, than the pre-1914 economy.

3.4 Automatic Stabilizers and Discretionary Fiscal Policy

Another important difference between the pre-1914 and post-WWII economies is the nature of fiscal policy. The progressivity of the income tax system provides an automatic stabilizing effect on disposable income, and government transfer programs such as unemployment insurance provide a similar effect on the expenditure side. As De Long and Summers (1986a) correctly emphasize, these forces lead to smoother consumption expenditures only if there are significant liquidity constraints. Otherwise, consumers can borrow and lend to offset transitory variations in income, making the timing of the government's tax and transfer schemes irrelevant. Since there is strong evidence that liquidity constraints are important in determining consumption (Zeldes, 1989), however, it is plausible that the introduction of automatic stabilizers has, other things being equal, contributed to a decline in output volatility.

A second aspect of fiscal policy that could potentially explain differences in output performance over time is the deliberate use of fiscal policy to stabilize output. It is not necessarily the case, of course, that discretionary policy has in fact helped stabilize the economy. Indeed, Eckstein and Sinai (1986) find a relatively small impact of fiscal policy in reducing the variability of output, so the net effect of this factor is perhaps not large.

3.5 Financial Markets

The final important change in the economy that may have contributed to changes in output stability is the introduction of deposit insurance in 1934. Since 1933, bank runs have not been an important feature of the U.S. economy, whereas before 1933 bank failures exerted a contractionary effect on the money stock, exacerbating the effects of other negative shocks. The absence of this effect has undoubtedly contributed to improved economic stability since 1933.

4. The Fed and Economic Stability

The discussion so far suggests that on a priori grounds one should have expected the interwar and particularly the post-WWII periods to have displayed less volatility than the pre-Fed period. In fact, volatility was much greater during the interwar period and only slightly reduced during the postwar period. This section argues that the actions of the Federal Reserve were responsible for a substantial fraction of the changes in the behavior of output documented above. There are three parts to the argument. The first provides a general perspective on Fed policy by suggesting that the Fed was not originally created to maintain output stability. Instead, it was designed to promote the "stability" of financial markets, which in some cases meant destabilizing output (and inflation). The second and third parts review specific aspects of Fed policy during the interwar and post-WWII periods, respectively.

4.1 General Background

In order to understand why the Fed might have carried out policies that destabilized the economy, it is necessary to review the motivation for the founding of the Fed. The distinctive feature of the monetary system before 1914 was the absence of a central bank, and one of the most significant economic problems was financial panics. These panics were thought to result from the inelasticity of the money stock, which occurred because there was no central bank to provide funds in times of high demand.

The inelasticity of the money stock was particularly a problem with respect to *seasonal* shifts in asset demands. In the spring and fall of each year, seasonal increases in loan demand were accompanied by seasonal increases in the demand for currency relative to deposits. With the reserves of the banking system held fixed, these shifts in asset demands meant that interest rates rose sharply and reserve/deposit ratios fell. The likelihood that an event such as a large loan default precipitated a panic, therefore, increased systematically in the seasons with high loan and currency demand, since the probability that any given size shock caused banks to fail increased when reserve/deposit ratios were low. As Miron (1986) documents, the probability of a panic was much higher in the fall than it was during the rest of the year, consistent with the high interest rates and low reserve/deposit ratios that prevailed during this season.

The problem of recurring financial panics, and their seasonal nature in particular, were important factors in the decision to found the Federal Reserve System and in the thinking of the original practitioners of central banking in the United States (Miron, 1986).[6] The strong desire to prevent financial panics led to the two main, but potentially contradictory, tenets of interwar monetary policy. On the one hand, much Fed thinking was determined by the real bills doctrine, which argued that central bank lending should make the money stock elastic with respect to shifts in the level of economic activity, thereby smoothing nominal interest rates. The belief in real bills stemmed mainly from the Fed's concern over seasonal movements in interest rates. An additional concern of contemporary bankers and academics, however, was the high incidence of stock market speculation during the pre-1914 period, especially since there were significant stock market crashes associated with the major financial panics. Since most stock was purchased on credit, central bankers worried that a policy of increased lending in response to higher interest rates fueled speculation. This meant they did not believe in adhering strictly to the real bills doctrine but instead thought it important to restrain the provision of credit if they believed it was being used for speculative purposes.

Thus, the founders of the Federal Reserve System believed that the overall objective of monetary policy was the stabilization of asset markets, particularly the elimination of financial panics. At a practical level, this meant that monetary policy was supposed to eliminate the transitory variation in nominal interest rates and reduce the major swings in stock prices.

4.2 Interwar Period

With this general perspective as background, I turn to reviewing the record of Fed policy in the interwar period. The first point to make is that the Fed was indeed successful in eliminating the seasonal and other transitory variation in short-term nominal interest rates. Figure 3 plots monthly data on the six-month commercial paper rate for the period 1890–1987, while table 3 shows the autocorrelation function for the level of the short rate. What the figure suggests and the table confirms is that the short rate exhibited significant seasonal and other mean reverting variation before 1914 but essentially none thereafter. Apparently the Fed did accomplish one of its important objectives.[7]

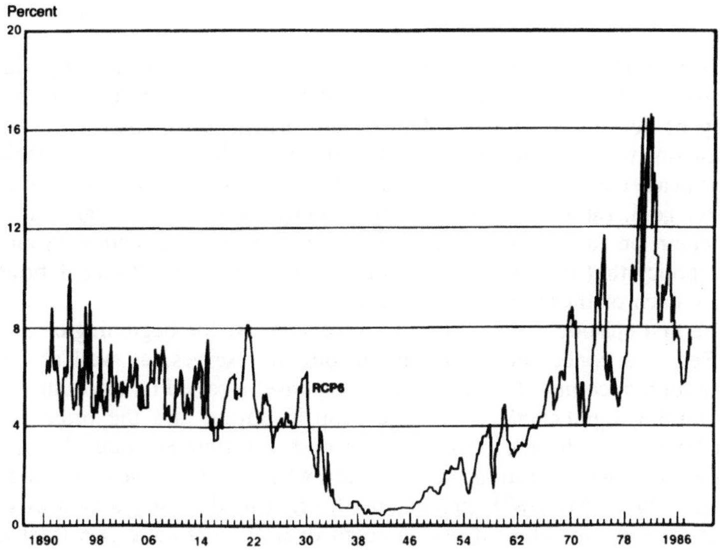

Figure 3. Commercial paper rate, level

Table 3. Summary Statistics, Commercial Paper Rate Monthly Data, Levels

Sample Period	*Standard Deviation*	*Autocorrelations*											
1890–1913	1.04	.84	.62	.46	.32	.21	.16	.14	.11	.07	.04	.02	−.01
1919–1940	2.16	.99	.98	.96	.94	.92	.90	.88	.86	.84	.83	.81	.79
1919–1928	1.23	.98	.95	.91	.87	.81	.75	.69	.63	.56	.50	.44	.38
1922–1928	.56	.91	.78	.65	.50	.37	.24	.13	.05	−.02	−.07	−.14	−.20
1929–1940	1.61	.97	.93	.89	.84	.80	.75	.71	.66	.62	.58	.54	.51
1929–1933	1.55	.94	.87	.79	.70	.61	.53	.45	.37	.31	.26	.19	.14
1934–1940	.19	.86	.73	.61	.55	.48	.44	.39	.34	.29	.23	.17	.10
1947–1987	3.43	.99	.96	.94	.92	.91	.89	.88	.87	.86	.85	.83	.82
1947–1971	1.86	.99	.97	.95	.93	.91	.88	.86	.84	.82	.81	.79	.77
1947–1973	2.02	.98	.95	.92	.88	.85	.81	.78	.76	.73	.71	.69	.67
1972–1987	3.02	.96	.89	.83	.78	.74	.69	.66	.65	.63	.59	.56	.52
1974–1987	3.01	.96	.89	.83	.78	.75	.71	.68	.67	.65	.62	.59	.56

The second point to make about Fed actions during the interwar period, however, is that on a few notable occasions the Fed departed from its policy of accommodation by deliberately driving up interest rates and contracting the economy. The idea that unifies the different episodes is that in each case the Fed's motivation was a desire to accomplish some financial market goal, rather than a desire to produce smooth output growth. In particular, on each occasion the Fed created a highly contractionary monetary policy that led to a major downturn in economic activity. I briefly review each of these episodes in turn.

The first episode is the 1920–1921 recession. By the beginning of 1920, the Fed was concerned with running out of reserves, as well as with speculation in commodity markets. In response, it raised its discount rate, contributing significantly to a large drop in output and the price level (Friedman and Schwartz, 1963). The second important episode of monetary contraction occurred in the late 1920s when the Fed restricted money growth (Hamilton, 1987), presumably leading to the early stages of the Great Depression. Here it was concern over the dramatic rise in stock prices during the mid-late 1920s, not a concern for output growth, that drove Fed actions. The third episode occurred in October 1931. After Britain left gold, the Fed raised its discount rate in order to stem gold outflows, despite the fact that the United States was in the midst of a severe downturn (Friedman and Schwartz, 1963). Finally, in 1936 the Fed was again concerned with stock market speculation, so it doubled reserve requirements, leading to the sharp but brief downturn in 1937–1938 (Friedman and Schwartz, 1963).

It is important to note that these four episodes correspond to the major disturbances in output growth during the 1919–1940 period. There are, of course, reasons to be skeptical about the Fed's role in destabilizing output in each of the episodes discussed above (see, e.g., Romer and Romer, 1989; Brown, 1956; and Temin, 1976), but the events of the interwar period strongly suggest that the Fed played a major role in the increased variability of output. The reason, again, is that the Fed was not concerned with output stability. It was concerned with maintaining what it considered stable asset market conditions.

4.3 Postwar Period

As we have seen, the postwar period has been significantly more stable than the interwar period. Does this mean that the Fed began worrying about the stability of output after WWII? The correct answer, to some extent, is probably yes. The Full Employment Act of 1946 made output stability a proper goal of monetary policy, and both textbook and academic discussions of monetary policy, as well as the Fed's *Annual Reports* and *Bulletins*, specifically address the question of maintaining full employment. Further, the Fed's experiences in the 1920s and 1930s undoubtedly taught it something about the dangers of long and variable lags.

Nevertheless, there is reason to believe that the Fed has made output more variable during the post-WWII period than it otherwise would have been. As discussed above, a number of factors all mitigate in the direction of showing that output would have become less variable even in the absence of the Fed, especially as compared to the pre-1914 period. Thus, one might have expected on a priori grounds to have witnessed a much greater stabilization relative to the pre-1914 period than actually occurred.

There is also direct evidence of the Fed's role in producing economic instability during the post-WWII period in a recent paper by Romer and Romer (1989). By reading the contemporaneous record of the Fed's policy decisions, they identify six episodes during the post-WWII period when the Fed became worried that inflation was increasing or about to increase. They then regress two measures of activity, unemployment and industrial production, on dummy variables for each of these episodes. Their results show that in each case output turns down significantly relative to its usual behavior (as represented by an autoregressive process).

A measure of the quantitative importance of the monetary shocks isolated in the Romer and Romer paper is obtained by asking what fraction of the variation in output is accounted for by the monetary shocks they identify. To this end, they examine the reduction in R^2 that results from including their monetary shock variables in simple output regressions. In the case of unemployment, this number is 23%; in the case of industrial production, the number is 15%. Obviously, these estimates are lower bounds on the amount of variation in output attributable to monetary disturbances during the post-WWII period.

The Romers' results suggest that there was a major shift in the focus of Fed policy from the interwar period to the post-WWII period. During the interwar period, the Fed appears to have placed primary emphasis on the behavior of financial markets, whereas during the post-WWII period it has worried more about the behavior of the inflation rate. One reason for this change of focus may be that the Fed learned from its mistakes. More important, the introduction of the Federal Deposit Insurance Corporation (FDIC) in 1934 probably provided more stability for financial markets than anything that the Fed could accomplish. Thus, the Fed may have felt free to pursue other goals, and indeed the Full Employment Act of 1946 made the Fed responsible for a number of other variables, including inflation. The important fact for the discussion here, however, is that the Fed contributed significantly to increased output variability during the post-WWII period.

5. Interpretation

In evaluating the evidence offered above, it is important to keep several factors in mind. First, it is possible that the Fed prevented many recessions that would otherwise have occurred, even if it introduced some that would not otherwise have occurred. Without a full structural model, it is not possible to say definitively that the Fed, on net, increased economic instability. The evidence summarized above is strongly suggestive, but it is not by itself conclusive.

Second, in both the interwar and post-WWII periods, the Fed's contribution to economic instability arose, not so much from an *inability* to guide the economy along a stable path, but from a lack of desire to do so. During the interwar period the Fed focused on financial market stability rather than output stability, while during the post-WWII period it has sacrificed output stability in favor of stabilizing inflation. There is nothing in the discussion here to suggest that the Fed is incapable of keeping output on a relatively smooth path, should it choose to do so. Thus, although this article does not provide a particularly favorable evaluation of Fed policy-making in the past, it does suggest the possibility of much better Fed policy in the future.

Notes

1. There is an extensive earlier literature on the changes in economic volatility. See in particular Burns (1960), Modigliani (1977), Bordo (1981), Romer (1986a, 1986b, 1987, 1989), Sheffrin (1988), Balke and Gordon (1989), De Long and Summers (1986a, 1988), and Miron (1989).

2. Miron and Romer (1989) show that this conclusion applies to industrial production as well as to overall GNP. In particular, they show that their index of industrial production, which is constructed in a consistent way over the entire 1884–1940 period, shows much greater intra-annual as well as annual volatility after 1914.

3. Bordo (1981) is an important exception. He examines the behavior of output over roughly the same sample periods considered here and reaches similar conclusions.

4. The standard deviation of the growth rate of Balke and Gordon's real GNP series is 4.06% for the pre-1914 period, 5.11% for the interwar period, and 2.78% for the 1947–1989 period.

5. See, for example, Hall and Taylor (1988, p. 486). De Long and Summers (1988) suggest that Fed policies might affect the average rate of growth of output. I am sympathetic to many of their arguments, but I constrain my analysis here to the more conventional view.

6. While the proponents of the system promised a host of benefits from its creation, the primary goal of monetary policy, as stated in the Fed's charter, was "to furnish an elastic currency." According to H. Parker Willis (1915, p. 75), an expert consultant to the House Banking and Currency Committee in 1912–1913 and a future secretary of the Federal Reserve Board, the potential benefits of the system were that "there will be no such wide fluctuations of interest rates...from season to season as now exist...and no necessity of emergency measures to safeguard the country from the possible results of financial panic or stringency."

7. Miron (1989) presents a more detailed analysis of the Fed's interest rate smoothing policies. Mankiw, Miron, and Weil (1987) show that the Fed began stabilizing rates almost immediately after its founding.

References

Balke, Nathan S., and Gordon, Robert J. 1989. "The Estimation of Prewar Gross National Product: Methodology and New Evidence." *Journal of Political Economy* 97 (February):38–92.

Baxter, Marianne, and Stockman, Alan C. 1989. "Business Cycles and the Exchange Rate Regime: Some International Evidence." *Journal of Monetary Economics* 23 (May):377–400.

Bordo, Michael D. 1981. "The Classical Gold Standard: Some Lessons for Today." *Review*, Federal Reserve Bank of St. Louis 63 (May):2–17.

Brown, E. Cary. 1956. "Fiscal Policy in the 'Thirties: A Reappraisal." *American Economic Review* 46 (December):857–879.

Burns, Arthur F. 1960. "Progress Towards Economic Stability." *American Economic Review* 50 (March):1–19.

De Long, Bradford J., and Summers, Lawrence H. 1986a. "The Changing Cyclical Variability of Economic Activity in the United States." In Robert J. Gordon (Ed.), *The American Business Cycle: Continuity and Change*. Chicago: University of Chicago Press.

De Long, Bradford J., and Summers, Lawrence H. 1986b. "Is Increased Price Flexibility Stabilizing?" *American Economic Review* 76 (December):1031–1044.

De Long, Bradford J., and Summers, Lawrence H. 1988. "How Does Macroeconomic Policy Affect Output?" *Brookings Papers on Economic Activity* 2:433–494.

Eckstein, Otto, and Sinai, Allen. 1986. "The Mechanics of the Business Cycle in the Postwar Era." In Robert, J. Gordon (Ed.), *The American Business Cycle: Continuity and Change*. Chicago: University of Chicago Press.

Eichengreen, Barry J. 1985. "Editor's Introduction." In Barry J. Eichengreen (Ed.), *The Gold Standard in Theory and History*. New York: Methuen.

Friedman, Milton, and Schwartz, Anna J. 1963. *A Monetary History of the United States*, 1867–1960. Princeton, N.J.: Princeton University Press.

Hall, Robert E., and Taylor, John B. 1988. *Macroeconomics: Theory, Performance, and Policy*. New York: Norton.

Hamilton, James D. 1987. "Monetary Factors in the Great Depression." *Journal of Monetary Economics* 19 (March):145–170.

Mankiw, N. Gregory, Miron, Jeffrey A., and Weil, David, N. 1987. "The Adjustment of Expectations to a Change in Regime: A Study of the Founding of the Federal Reserve." *American Economic Review* 77 (June):358–374.

Miron, Jeffrey A. 1986. "Financial Panics, the Seasonality of the Nominal Interest Rate, and the Founding of the Fed." *American Economic Review* 76 (March): 125–140.

Miron, Jeffrey A. 1989. "The Founding of the Fed and the Destabilization of the Post-1914 U.S. Economy." In Marcello de Cecco and Alberto Giovannini (Eds.), *A European Central Bank? Perspectives on Monetary Unification after Ten Years of the E.M.S.* Cambridge: Cambridge University Press.

Miron, Jeffrey A., and Romer, Christina. 1989. "A New Monthly Index of Industrial Production, 1884–1940." Manuscript, University of California, Berkeley.

Modigliani, Franco. 1977. "The Monetarist Controversy." *American Economic Review* 67:1–19.

Romer, Christina. 1986a. "Spurious Volatility in Historical Unemployment Data." *Journal of Political Economy* 94 (February):1–37.

Romer, Christina. 1986b. "Is the Stabilization of the Postwar Economy a Figment of the Data?" *American Economic Review* 76 (June):314–334.

Romer, Christina. 1987. "The Prewar Business Cycle Reconsidered: New Estimates of Gross National Product, 1869–1908." Manuscript, University of California, Berkeley.

Romer, Christina. 1989. "The Prewar Business Cycle Reconsidered: New Estimates of Gross National Product, 1869–1908." *Journal of Political Economy* 97 (February):1–37.

Romer, Christina, and Romer, David. 1989. "Does Monetary Policy Matter? A New Test in the Spirit of Friedman and Schwartz." *NBER Macroeconomics Annual*, forthcoming.

Sheffrin, Steven M. 1988. "Have Economic Fluctuations Been Dampened? A Look at Evidence Outside the United States." *Journal of Monetary Economics* 21 (January):73–84.

Temin, Peter. 1976. *Did Monetary Forces Cause the Great Depression?* New York: Norton.

Willis, H. Parker. 1915. *The Federal Reserve: A Study of the Banking System of the United States*. New York: Doubleday, Page and Co.

Zeldes, Stephen P. 1989. "Consumption and Liquidity Constraints: An Empirical Investigation." *Journal of Political Economy* 97 (June):305–346.

DATA APPENDIX

Real GNP: GNP in billions of 1982 dollars, annually 1869–1987.

Source: 1869–1928, Romer (1989), Table 2, p. 22; 1929–1982, *The National Income and Product Accounts, 1929–82*, Table 1.2, p. 6; 1983–1987, *Economic Report of the President, 1989*, Table B2, p. 310.

Implicit Deflator: implicit price deflator for GNP, 1982 = 100, annually 1869–1987.

Source: 1869–1928, Romer (1989), Table 2, p. 22; 1929–1982, *The National Income and Product Accounts, 1929–82*, Table 7.4, p. 327; 1983–1987, *Economic Report of the President, 1989*, Table B3, p. 312.

Nominal Interest Rate: open market rate of interest, New York City, prime six-month commercial paper, monthly averages of daily figures, 1890:1–1987:12, missing 1907:9, 1907:10, 1908:3, 1908:10, 1908:11, and 1909:10.

Source: 1890–1940, *Banking and Monetary Statistics, 1914–1941*, Table 120, pp. 448–51; 1941–1960, *Banking and Monetary Statistics, 1941–1970*, Table 12.5A, pp. 674–76; 1961–1987, DRI. The DRI data accord with figures published in *Banking and Monetary Statistics* (1961–1970), *Annual Statistical Digest* (1970–1986), and the *Survey of Current Business* (1987–1987). *Business Statistics 1984* cites the New York Fed as the source.

Commentary: The Behavior of Foreign Central Banks: Comparisons and Contrasts with Fed Performance

by K. Alec Chrystal

It is a great honor to be able to contribute to the celebration of the 75th anniversary of what is, perhaps, the world's most important financial institution. The global economy has changed a great deal since the 50th anniversary in 1964, and it seems quite likely that a similar gathering then would have felt it unnecessary to consider the experiences of the rest of the world. We may have been invited to the party but we would certainly not have been expected to win any of the games. However, the pace of change is such that by 2014 we may even get to blow out the candles.

My task is to see what extra insights can be added from the events in other major economies to the interpretation of the experience of the conduct of monetary policy by the Fed. This task would be daunting enough on its own. It is made even more so by the fact that my comments must necessarily be shadowed by the outstanding study presented to this conference by Professor Allan Meltzer. His article will, no doubt, become one of the standard reference points in the literature on the monetary history of the United States.

First, I should make clear what will soon become evident: I am a great deal more knowledgeable about monetary policy in the United Kingdom than in other major countries. Hence, while I shall draw partly on the experiences of other countries, I do so with some trepidation. There is a greater chance of erroneous judgments in these cases. Nonetheless, it is beneficial to take on board as wide a range of evidence about the efficacy of monetary policy as possible. Some countries have clearly learned to do it right. We can all learn from their experience.

A Potted Monetary History

It would be widely accepted that the role of monetary policy is to stabilize the value of the currency and to minimize shocks to the real economy emanating from the monetary sector. Professor Meltzer's assessment of the Fed amounts to two cheers (or perhaps one and a half) which in academic terms is about a B+.[1] The end-of-term report says, "Tried hard but could have done better." As a leading "monetarist" Professor Meltzer recommends a greater reliance on "rules" to govern the conduct of monetary policy—albeit with the possibility for contingency clauses built into the rules. Excessive discretion is what has led policymakers into error. It is essential to take a longer term view of policy rather than overreacting to the latest statistics.

It is extremely difficult to prove the counterfactual case that Fed policy under a different regime would have been "better." However, it is straightforward to look around the world at the comparative performance of central banks. The hypothesis would be that the central banks with the least political interference and the most clearly defined commitment to controlling inflation would deliver the best results. Also those which took a long-term perspective are more likely to get it right than those preoccupied with short-term priorities.

Confirmation is easily supplied by a superficial glance at some of the obvious examples. Switzerland probably conforms most closely to the monetarist ideal, while West Germany and Japan come close behind. In contrast to these, the United Kingdom has a relatively poor record, and the Bank of England is more subject to political control than any other major central bank.

It is as well to remember at the outset that, outside the United States, the problems of determining a free-standing monetary policy are of relatively recent origin. Under the Bretton Woods regime there was a monetary rule which was extremely rigorous in its effect. This rule was that the monetary authorities must maintain the exchange value of their currency against the dollar. Failure to meet an explicit exchange rate target is immediately obvious for all the world to see, and the authorities can judge very accurately how well they are doing by the inflows and outflows of foreign exchange reserves.

Under the Bretton Woods regime the n-1 countries could maintain the relative value of their currencies, but the global inflation rate was primarily the responsibility of the United States. In the 1969–1973 period, the United States clearly abdicated that responsibility. Subsequent events can be seen as the rest of the world's learning to live with the new situation. That learning process is far from over. Monetary institutions have not yet settled down. If anything, the pace of change is accelerating. It is quite possible that the monetary map will be quite different in 25 years' time (or even 10) from what it is today.

Following the adoption of floating exchange rates in 1973 (1972 in the United Kingdom), it soon became clear that some indicator of monetary conditions had to be identified. The circumstances of the collapse of

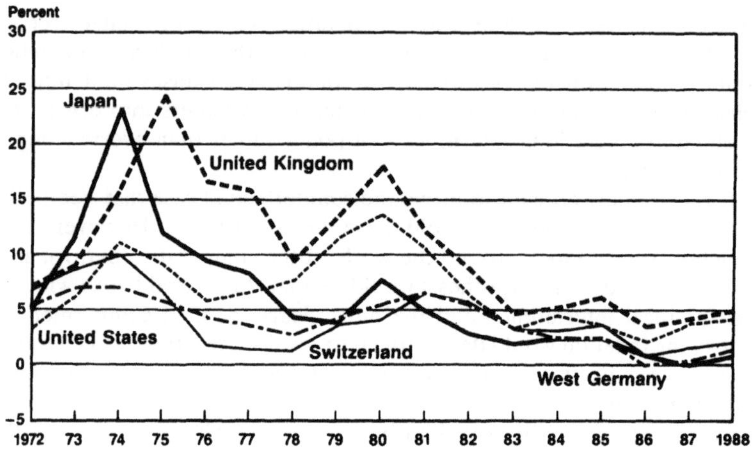

Figure 1. Consumer price inflation. *Source*: IMF Int. Fin. Stats. Yearbook '89

Bretton Woods made the inflationary experience of the early 1970s almost universally bad. International reserve holdings of dollars roughly doubled between the beginning of 1971 and the end of 1973. The counterpart to this was a substantial increase in monetary growth. The average growth rate of broad money in 1972 and 1973 was 24% for the United Kingdom, 23% for Japan, and 12% for West Germany. Not surprisingly, inflation rates in excess of 20% followed in Japan and the United Kingdom (see figure 1), while the German rate peaked at around 7%.

Following this experience of worldwide inflation virtually all central banks adopted some form of monetary targeting. Switzerland adopted an M1 target in 1975, West Germany targeted "Central Bank Money" (a weighted average of the components of M3) from 1975, and the United Kingdom targeted M3 from 1976. The Japanese never went wholly for targeting but they did go for money stock control. In 1978 they started to announce a "forecast" for M2 + CDs, the forecast incorporating the intended reactions of the central bank itself.

While Switzerland and West Germany are generally held up to be examples of "good" monetary policy, neither was consistent in meeting its targets and neither stuck to the original targeted aggregate. Swiss M1 growth of 16.2% in 1978 exceeded the target of 5%. Targeting was temporarily dropped in 1979, and a monetary base target was introduced in 1980. This target has been adhered to fairly closely in subsequent years.

West German monetary growth exceeded its target as often as not, though not by a substantial amount. After 1987, however, the Central Bank Money target was dropped in favor of an M3 target, but it is too early to say whether this will lead to a consistent improvement in the success of the authorities in meeting the targets, although there is no doubt that West Germany has continued to have great success in controlling inflation.

By way of contrast, monetary policy in the United Kingdom was an almost total disaster—notwithstanding the fall in inflation in the mid-1980s and a decade of allegedly monetarist policies. The experience with monetary targeting was unhappy, to say the least. There were nearly as many changes in targeted aggregate as there were years of targeting. The initial M3 target was replaced or supplemented from time to time by targets for M1, M2, and M0. None of these was consistently met, especially in the 1980s. The broad monetary aggregates typically grew at rates well in excess of the targets, and these targets were abandoned in 1986. Only an M0 target was retained, although it was never envisaged as being the prime guide to policy. There was an explicit return to a policy of pegging short-term interest rates, hardly the policy that any self-respecting monetarist would recommend.

The outcome of these comparative episodes of monetary targeting will surprise no one in St. Louis. The Swiss, Germans, and Japanese experienced declining inflation throughout the 1980s such that inflation over the last few years has been effectively zero. U.K. inflation declined to a low point of 3.4% in 1986 (the year in which monetary targeting was abandoned) but has since risen to a current figure of 9.8% (June 1990).

It is interesting to inquire why the U.K. government, which regards the conquest of inflation as its main priority, has abandoned monetary targets and, as a result, permitted inflation to creep back into the economy. What explains the contrast in this experience with the experience in Switzerland, West Germany, and Japan?

Part of the answer has already been offered above and that relates to the differences in constitution of the central banks. This cannot be the whole explanation, however, because the U.K. government was highly sympathetic to tight monetary control. Events made the authorities adopt a different strategy.

Velocity Precocity

The key reason why the U.K. authorities gave up on monetary targeting was that they convinced themselves that the monetary aggregates had

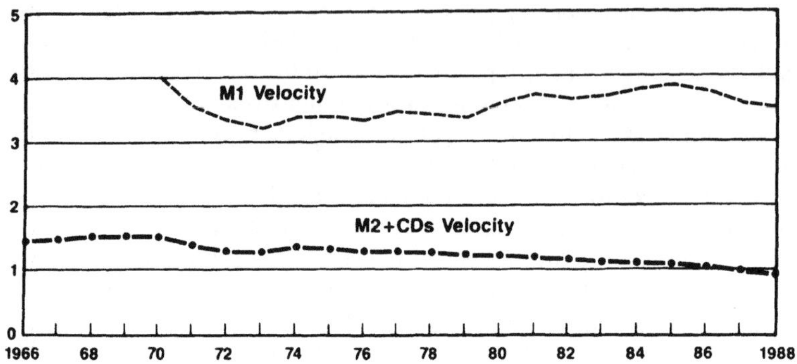

Figure 2. Japan: velocity of circulation

ceased to have any significant informational content. In contrast, the authorities in the other countries under discussion, while changing horses when one began to flag, were able to back at least one of the runners. Indeed, there is good evidence to suggest that the U.K. authorities did face a much more difficult task than some of their overseas colleagues.

That this is so can be seen clearly from the behavior of velocity in the countries concerned (see figures 1–4). Velocity has been considerably more unstable in the United Kingdom than in the other countries. The velocity of M1 was on a strong upward trend throughout the postwar period. After 1980 this turned down, and strongly so after 1983. M3 velocity also adopted a downward trend after 1980. Thus while the rapid growth of M3 in the early 1970s was a good predictor of the inflation of 1974–1975, its rapid growth in the early 1980s was followed by declining inflation and a massive recession—at least for a time.

There are two connected reasons for the instability of velocity in the United Kingdom. The most important is probably the behavior of the authorities themselves (Chrystal, 1989). In the years of pegged exchange rates the authorities used quantitative ceilings on bank lending as a tool to control the money stock. They were abolished in 1971. The resulting rapid growth of broad money was curtailed in 1973 by an alternative quantitative restriction known as the "corset." This prevented the banks from expanding their interest bearing deposits by more than a certain percentage per year. The corset was abolished in 1980, and broad money growth had a rapid spurt as the distortions unwound. This episode led the authorities to believe that M3 had ceased to be a meaningful indicator. So when its

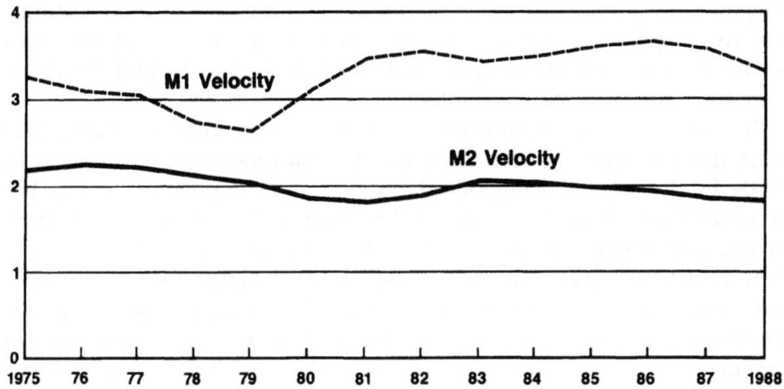

Figure 3. Switzerland: velocity of circulation

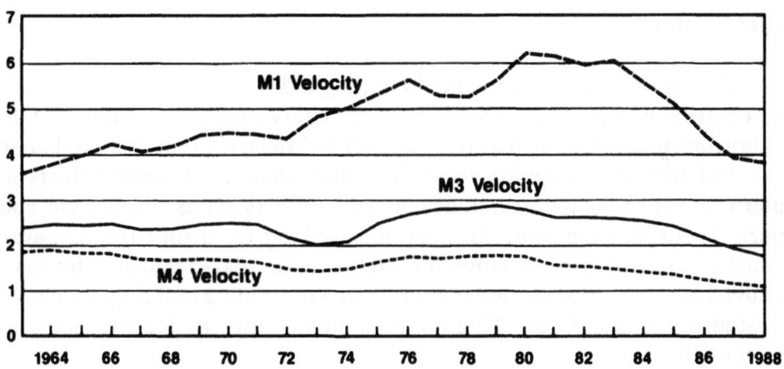

Figure 4. United Kingdom: velocity of circulation

growth again became rapid after 1985, they ignored it for far too long. Only the strong upturn of inflation, long predicted by monetarists, has convinced the authorities that this could not be allowed to go on forever.

To add to the confusion as to what was the guiding principle of U.K. monetary policy, it became clear in 1987 that the U.K. monetary authorities had replaced the money stock targets with an exchange rate target (of DM3 per pound). This was never stated in public, but the combination of this and the higher interest rates (relative to West Germany) in the United

Kingdom produced strong upward pressure on the pound. Intervention to stop its rising too fast and a lowering of interest rates fuelled a major credit boom. This first led to asset price inflation (stocks and property) followed later by a rise in retail price inflation.

In addition to the distortions created by the authorities themselves, there has undoubtedly been a period of rapid financial innovation in the 1980s in the United Kingdom. However, it is impossible to say how important that would have been in the absence of the changes introduced by the authorities. However, it does raise important questions of more than parochial interest. To what extent should the authorities resist microeconomic efficiency gains (resulting from, for example, the removal of credit rationing) in the monetary system if they make it more difficult to conduct aggregate monetary policy? Was the stability of velocity in the three successful countries just good luck? Could they, perhaps, still have to face the same problems in the future?

Goal Conflicts

The United Kingdom is not alone in finding a destructive tension between the external and internal objectives of monetary policy. All the monetary authorities make it clear that they are not indifferent to the real exchange rate and will use discretion to avoid major changes. Indeed, efforts at international exchange rate policy coordination (such as the Louvre and Plaza Accords) have done as much as anything to disrupt the domestic monetary control process. However, big swings in real exchange rates have occured in the last decade and there is a growing feeling that they should be resisted if possible. Controlling domestic money growth does not seem to be enough.

Within the European Economic Community there is a strong momentum toward the creation of a monetary union involving, as a first stage, a regime of mutually pegged exchange rates with ever-narrowing margins of fluctuation. Ultimately, the goal is to have a common currency. Added to this possible source of structural change is the 1992 program. The Second Coordinating Banking Directive, which was agreed on by heads of state at the Madrid Summit in June, provides that any bank once authorized to conduct business in its home state has a "passport" to conduct business in any other state, so long as it conforms to host country conduct of business rules. The control of member states over their domestic financial markets is bound to be diminished to some degree by these innovations.

The full implications of all these changes are hard to predict. It is possible that the pace of financial innovation will destabilize velocity in West Germany. On the other hand, it is possible that the West German authorities will resist any changes that threaten their power to control inflation. However, at the very least, the West German authorities themselves are increasingly coming to play the role of the central bank of Europe and, in this role, they will no doubt find themselves under pressure to moderate their policy from time to time in order to relieve the constraint on their more inflationary partners.

A word in defense of U.K. policy toward the EMS is due at this point. There is a general impression abroad that the current British government is holding back on moves toward economic and monetary union (EMU). Nothing could be further from the truth. All publicity has been given to Mrs. Thatcher's doubts about the later stages of the Delors Report. Anyone who has read it would also have doubts. In reality, the United Kingdom is the strongest supporter of the microeconomic single market program, which involves removal of all non-tariff barriers to trade in goods and services by the end of 1992. (Tariff barriers were phased out under the Treaty of Rome.)

The message from Europe is that some central banks have clearly learned to conduct monetary policy in a sensible way so as to achieve consistently low inflation without destabilizing the real economy. West Germany and Switzerland (plus Japan) have done it for sufficiently long now that many people would conclude that they have cracked the problem. The United Kingdom has failed, largely because it abandoned monetary targeting too soon after temporary setbacks. The stability of the underlying velocity relationships in the former countries may have been fortuitous, but it must to some degree have been due to the very stability of the policy regime. Whether this good fortune can last remains to be seen. But the prospects for substantial financial innovation in the European Community (EC) should make us urge caution.

Implications for the United States

I now return to the central theme of this conference: what all this implies for the analysis of the behavior of the Fed as interpreted by Professor Meltzer.

The Monetarist Strategy

Criticisms of the Fed for getting it wrong can probably be justified during the 1960s and 1970s when the underlying velocity relationships appear to have been stable. However, the least convincing part of Meltzer's article concerns what should have been done once it became clear that the relationships had broken down post-1981. A rule following authority would surely have tightened policy considerably in 1982 and made the recession a great deal worse. St. Louis-style equations were consistently forecasting inflation that never came. The hunt for stable relationships is still on, but, in the meantime, policymakers have to use judgment to decide what to do. My guess is that the historians of the 1980s will give the Fed at least an A– for a solid effort on a difficult question. In this respect, the problems of the Fed were much closer to those experienced by the United Kingdom than the others. However, the Fed did a better job than the Bank of England in that it managed to achieve consistently lower inflation than the United Kingdom and it did not give up entirely on monetary aggregates, realizing that the effects of financial innovation would be temporary.

Internal and External Goal Conflict

Under the Bretton Woods system it was sensible for the U.S. authorities to concentrate almost entirely upon stabilizing the dollar price level while all other countries concentrated on maintaining the relative value of their currencies. However, the U.S. authorities have clearly come to be concerned about the exchange value of the dollar, without being quite sure what instruments to use to influence it. At the present time we have the worst of both worlds so far as floating exchange rates are concerned. The authorities have periodic bouts of very active intervention followed by periods during which they show studied indifference. The bursts of activity almost certainly do more harm than good, although, under the guise of "international policy coordination," they are the flavor of the month.

The United States needs to reduce the ambiguity of its position in this area. If the intention is to have target zones for exchange rates, let them be explicit. Otherwise, monetary authorities should be prepared to state explicitly what their policy guidelines are and show that they can make them stick. Exchange rate volatility cannot be cured on an ad hoc basis. Indeed, uncertainty about the authorities' intentions is a major contributor to the problem.

Micro Efficiency and Macro Policy

One obvious area for comment from a European perspective concerns the micro-economic efficiency of the banking system. The 1992 program may well lead Europe to be served by a small number of large banks conducting the bulk of the retail business while a number of niche players survive in specialized markets, such as investment banking. Most industrial countries at present are well served by a small group of large banks. The rationalization process in Europe is only just beginning.

The United States stands in stark contrast to this situation. It is hard to believe that the U.S. financial system would not be more stable if the geographical restrictions on banking business were removed. This may not strictly be an area of Fed responsibility, but it is hard to divorce the behavior of the authorities entirely from the structure of the system with which they are working. I am aware that there is a large but inconclusive literature on the question of economies of scale in banking, but few can doubt that removal of the restrictions would lead to substantial changes in structure. Of course, such changes might induce further instability in the behavior of monetary aggregates. The question then arises again: To what extent should micro-efficiency gains be resisted in order to preserve the stability of a macro relationship?

Choice of Instruments

Alex Cukierman's article in this book is concerned with the question of why it might be sensible for monetary authorities to use interest rates as their sole short-term instrument. Monetarists generally recommend that the authorities control the monetary base and let market forces determine interest rates. Tom Melzer, in his introductory remarks, highlighted this as a key issue that monetary policymakers would like to see clarified. Nobody should be surprised to find that there are conflicting views on this subject among central bankers in Europe.

The governor of the Bank of England, for example, has put on record the view that:

> To impose quantitative restrictions on the supply of liquidity to the banks would . . . inevitably risk unacceptable volatility in the short-term interest rate. Thus when you come right down to it, the only effective instrument of monetary policy is the short-term interest rate itself (Leigh-Pemberton, 1987).

In contrast, the experience of Switzerland suggests that the position is far from clearcut. As a director of the Swiss National Bank puts it:

> In stressing the disruptive effects of monetary-base control, critics of that approach tend to overlook the fact that the extent to which the banks hold excess reserves itself depends upon the control procedures employed by the central bank. Swiss experience suggests that commercial banks are induced to hold substantial excess reserves if the central bank controls tightly the monetary base.... Interest sensitive bank reserves act as a shock absorber designed to smooth short-run fluctuations in interest rates.... On the whole, I must admit that the short-run variability of interest rates has been more pronounced in Switzerland than in countries where market rates tend to serve as operational variables for central banks. Nevertheless, the variability of interest rates engendered by our system of monetary base control has not been large enough to inconvenience the Swiss economy very much (Rich, 1987, p. 12).

The Federal Reserve Bank of Europe

Finally, I would like to present a sneak preview of the history of the first 25 years of the Federal Reserve Bank of Europe. This was formed in 1994—ironically on the 300th anniversary of the founding of the Bank of England. All EC members joined the system except for the United Kingdom. Mrs. Thatcher, who was reelected for a fourth term in 1992 with a substantially reduced majority, said that Britain would join the system "when the time was ripe," but not yet. One interesting coincidence turned out to be that the eighth district was Poland!

The Bank's head office was established in Frankfurt in order to give the new institution credibility. However, the chairmanship of the monetary policy committee was to revolve around the member nations. Under the reign of the first (German) chairman, monetary growth was established on a slow growth path. However, in subsequent years political interference from the European Commission and from the European Parliament grew, and monetary growth was allowed to accelerate. Corrective action caused a major recession.

In 2001 a computer malfunction led to a debate as to whether Europe should return to a paper-based monetary system. Representatives noted that the United States was the only monetary system still wedded to the old technology—apparently the small banks in the Midwest still liked it. The St. Louis Fed defended paper currency on the grounds that their famous equation predicted that, with no money, nominal income would have to be zero and that couldn't be a good thing.

In 2010, a summit conference between the G4—United States, Japan, the EC, and Russia—was called to deal with the large payments imbalances between the United States and the rest of the world. The U.S. trade deficit was so large that it was threatening to cause instability to the world's currency markets. Japan, the EC, and Russia reluctantly agreed to defend the dollar in the event of a major collapse. This came in the spring of 2011. However, it led to a major expansion of the world monetary base and created an inflationary cycle in the world economy.

At a conference to discuss the first 25 years of the European Fed's existence, it was argued that a base control technique should be introduced as an alternative to the current reliance on short-term interest rates. In the words of one French delegate who summarized the discussion, "*Plus ça change*!"

Note

1. The opinion at the conference seemed to be that B+ was on the high side. However, the grade seems justified by the intelligent responses to the velocity shift after 1981 and the crash of 1987.

References

Chrystal, K. Alec. 1989. "In Defense of Monetarism." In D. Llewellyn (Ed.), *Reflections on Money*. London: Macmillan.

Leigh-Pemberton, The Rt. Hon. Robin. 1987. "The Instruments of Monetary Policy." The Seventh Mais Lecture, City University Business School, May. (Later published in *Bank of England Quarterly Bulletin* 27 (August 1987): 365–370).

Rich, George. 1987. "Swiss and United States Monetary Policy: Has Monetarism Failed?" *Economic Review*, Federal Reserve Bank of Richmond (May/June): 3–16.

Commentary: The Federal Reserve Policy Process

by Donald L. Kohn

Professor Meltzer has again given us an interesting and comprehensive, if somewhat acerbic, overview of Federal Reserve performance. He has concluded that adding on the years between the 50th and 75th anniversaries does not change his overall assessment that the actions of the Federal Reserve have imposed a net cost on society. That cost is measured relative to a hypothetical path for the economy and prices based on an unspecified rule for policy using the monetary base. In the future, he would tie the tenure of the Federal Reserve Board in part to achieving an annual objective for money supply growth.

As is detailed in his article, a good deal of the ebb and flow of Federal Reserve research, debates, and changes in policy emphasis over the last 25 years has revolved around the place of the monetary aggregates in guiding policy. In sum, the Federal Reserve walked up to a monetary rule, looked over the brink for a few years, and subsequently backed away. To be sure, we never specified a rule in quite the way Meltzer would have us, or put in place the institutional framework that he would see as a needed concomitant. Still, in the 1979 to 1982 period, we came very close. I thought I might provide a useful supplement to Meltzer's review of this period by giving my views on the reasons for the shifting emphasis on the monetary aggregates, and in particular their current place in policy.

As he notes, the deemphasis of the aggregates in short-run policy implementation since 1982 has left the Federal Reserve with a somewhat eclectic, discretionary policy. The second part of my comments will describe this current situation, discussing both its strengths and its potential problems.

The Changing Role of the Monetary Aggregates

From the late 1960s to the late 1970s the monetary aggregates received increasing attention in the conduct of monetary policy. This shift owed to the confluence of two developments. First, monetary policy based on

---

I would like to thank David Small for helpful comments and discussions. The views expressed are my own and do not necessarily reflect those of the Federal Reserve Board or its staff.

adjusting nominal interest rates to recent and projected performance of the economy was not doing well. Problems of political pressures, differentiating nominal from real rates, and consistently underestimating the extent of inflation pressures meant that nominal interest rates were adjusted sluggishly and, as a consequence, real rates were kept too low and the central bank was acquiescing in, and probably contributing to, an accelerating rate of inflation.

At the same time, the monetarists had an alternative that promised improved performance. Accumulating evidence, not the least out of the Federal Reserve Bank of St. Louis, suggested an empirically robust relationship between increases in spending and prices, on the one hand, and growth of one or another of the monetary aggregates, on the other. Moreover, this relationship was sufficiently strong to suggest that the central bank ought to confine its concerns to achieving objectives for the aggregates; attention to interest rates or to the real economy would only be counterproductive.

It is important to emphasize the empirical nature of the monetarist argument. Monetarist economists made important contributions to macroeconomic theory, but at its foundation, the presciption to follow a monetary rule does not depend on a structural theory of how monetary policy affects the economy. Undoubtedly, no one from the St. Louis Fed ever thought they had anything but a reduced-form equation relating money growth to GNP.

In the last half of the 1970s, the empirical argument in favor of the aggregates was seen as so strong, and the problems with the previous policy procedures as so profound, that Congress mandated monetary aggregates objectives, and in October of 1979 the Federal Reserve adopted a reserves-oriented operating system to achieve its monetary targets. As I already noted, the new system did not meet all the criteria of those advocating tight adherence to a monetary rule. Money supply targets were adjusted from year to year; and, as a result of institutional arrangements as well as policy preference, the focus was on non-borrowed rather than total reserves, loosening the degree of control over money in short periods. However, the Federal Reserve did tolerate substantial swings in short-term interest rates in direct and automatic response to deviations of money from target.

As the new procedures interacted with strong inflation forces in the economy, interest rates soared to record levels. The consequence was a deep recession, but also a distinct break in inflation and inflation expectations that set the stage for the current expansion. In this fundamental sense, the focus on money and the procedures to control it was a major success.

Why, then, were they abandoned? The reason lies in the breakdown of those empirical regularities in the 1980s. This was primarily a result of the deregulation of rates on bank and thrift deposits, although other trends and innovations in deposit markets played a role. Deregulation was an ongoing process over several years, which changed the character of many monetary aggregates and their relationship to spending and interest rates. There is ample empirical evidence of this change. St. Louis-style reduced-form equations fit through the 1970s have essentially no predictive power in the 1980s. Some empirical studies have identified a shift in trend growth of velocity at the end of 1981. Other studies have not found a shift in trend, but have found that explaining the relationship of money to income now requires modeling the behavior of deposit offering rates, as well as taking account of one-time shifts of funds in response to certain major deregulatory episodes.

As a consequence of deregulation and innovation, distinctions among financial assets have faded, and definitions of particular bundles of those assets seem more arbitrary, especially for capturing important short-run portfolio decisions. Empirically, this has been manifest in greater interest elasticities, and hence variations in velocity. M1 has been especially affected. NOW accounts have become repositories for savings that readily shift in response to changing yield spreads, including those on time deposits. As a consequence, the velocity of this aggregate now varies over an extraordinarily wide range, and its value as a policy target essentially has been eliminated. Although much of the portfolio reallocation that affects M1 is subsumed in M2, the broader aggregate also seems to be a little more sensitive to market interest rate changes over periods of up to a year or so. Partly, this results from the lower level of opportunity costs on M2 following deregulation, so that even small changes in market rates imply large proportional changes in opportunity costs for a time, given sluggish adjustment of many deposit rates. That deposit rates can adjust has, itself, added an element of uncertainty in relating M2 to income. Depository institutions seem still to be adapting their marketing strategies in the deregulated environment, affecting the movement of opportunity costs as market interest rates change.

Owing in part to these problems with M1 and M2, most of those still proposing monetary rules have come to focus on the monetary base. Because of the large proportion of this aggregate accounted for by its currency component, the base is substantially less interest sensitive than those aggregates with higher weightings of deposits. However, this characteristic also implies that substantial variations in interest rates would be associated with efforts to keep this aggregate on a predetermined track should demand for it change. If a change in base demand reflected underlying shifts in demands for goods and serivces, the interest rate changes likely would be stabilizing for the economy, although long lags in the response of spending to interest or exchange rates could produce cycles and overshooting.

But, if changes in demand for the base reflected shifts in demand for the aggregate relative to income and interest rates, the rate movements would be destabilizing. In this regard, there seem to be more serious questions about the parameters and stability of the underlying demand functions for the base than for, say, M2. The reserves portion of the base reflects primarily transactions deposits, and, as noted above, these have become so loosely connected to income that we no longer target M1. The problem lies not only in the interest elasticity of NOW accounts, but also in the shifting role of demand deposits. Increasingly, these have become dominated by compensating balance requirements, which themselves are evolving relative to the volume of bank services as banks and customers have moved to using fees to pay for such services. The currency-income relationship also is suspect. It is difficult not to be a little careful about an aggregate, a large portion of which can not be accounted for. Questions about ownership would not be a matter for great concern if growth rates in currency were reliably related to growth rates in income or spending, but even in this regard we have experienced substantial unexplained variations in currency velocity just in the last two years.

If the base were held to a predetermined path, and if demand for it were shifting relative to income, large swings in nominal rates would be translated into unnecessary variations in real interest and exchange rates and economic activity. Policy rules have been proposed that adjust for changes in base velocity. However, these rules implement such adjustments over a period of years, implying substantial, prolonged deviations in nominal income from expectations, and in real income as well as prices and wages adjust slowly. Our experience in testing adaptive base rules within the structure of the MPS model support these conclusions. We find that unless we impose outside constraints on interest rate movements, the combined effects of low interest elasticity of the base and lags in the response of real spending and inflation expectations formation produce explosive oscillations in interest rates and income.

Evidence on past variations in base velocity, such as those cited by Meltzer, do not provide much comfort when contemplating possible movements in velocity under a base targeting rule. Such measurements were made over periods when the Federal Reserve was smoothing interest rates, which would tend to damp short-run variations in velocity. If the base itself were targeted and interest rates allowed to fluctuate over a much wider range, so would base velocity, at least within the business cycle. Such a change would be in addition to any alteration in the behavior of money holders or depository institutions from the change in policy regime.

In fact, base velocity has been quite variable in the 1980s, even after allowing for a change in trend in 1981, increasing and decreasing by amounts ranging from to 3½% to 7% within periods of just a few quarters. Movements of this sort and concerns about its demand properties have deterred the FOMC from setting objectives for the base on the several occasions when such a role has been considered.

The Current Policy Process

With the monetary aggregates no longer guiding short-run changes in reserves and money market conditions, the Federal Reserve has been reacting to information from a wide variety of sources. Longer-run trends in the aggregates contiue to play a role in judgments about the stance of policy, but interest and exchange rates—both real and nominal—get considerable attention as key variables transmitting policy and other influences to the economy. In addition, members of the FOMC look directly at data on the economy and prices in assessing whether the stance of policy is consistent with furthering the Committee's objectives. Various members of the Committee have their favorite indicatior, and some of them have been widely publicized in speeches and publications. The variety of preferences in this regard, however, masks broad underlying agreement on the objectives of policy.

The Committee has spelled out its long-run objectives in a general way—that is, to promote economic expansion through price stability. It has not specified a timetable for achieving these objectives, or a sense of the kinds of short-run tradeoffs it might be willing to tolerate in the process. Even so, in part by weighing prospects for progress toward its ultimate objectives, the Committee has been able to reach effective concensus on its intermediate-term objectives and consequently shares a yardstick against which to assess the performance of the economy and the stance of policy. There are, to be sure, disagreements on the weight to be placed on various elements in the short-run, such as inflation or employment, and the assessment of risks—that's what produces lively discussions and occasional dissents at FOMC meetings. And, while the lack of specific numerical targets may frustrate some judges of the Federal Reserve's performance, it has not seemed an unbreachable barrier to such assessments by the public or its elected representatives.

In response to the signals from a wide array of information, frequent small changes are made in the Federal Reserve's stance in reserves markets to keep the economy on track toward achieving the Committee's objectives. This operating procedure has the advantage of making use of all available information about the complex relationships in the economy—which can be especially important when these relationships are evolving in ways that may be easy to predict. Frequent adjustments of reserve positions need not signal an excessively activist policy or an attempt to fine tune the economy, in the sense of trying to achieve an outcome with more precision than is possible. Rather they can be seen as entirely rational responses to indications of changing conditions in the economy, which necessitate some change in instrument variables to raise the odds on achieving desired results.

This type of operating system has a number of problems, however. Chief among these is the well-known tendency to adjust nominal rates too slowly in the initial stages of a cycle, and then to overstay a policy stance. This tendency has the effect, as Meltzer points out, of producing a policy that is less stabilizing than it otherwise could be, and may actually be adding to business cycle amplitude. The use of a large number of indicators can contribute to this result, since some will always be giving contrary signals that could justify inaction. Moreover, in the past, the problems with a discretionary policy have not been symmetrical. The tendency, when making discretionary changes in nominal rates partly in response to economic data, has been to try and "cheat" on the side of a little more output, lending an inflationary bias to policy.

And yet, most would concede that policy has been somewhat better in the 1980s than might have been anticipated from the results of previous decades and the similarities of the current procedures to those followed then. So far, policy seems to have been reasonably successful in leaning sufficiently hard against emerging trends to keep the economy expanding and inflation confined to a fairly narrow range. The counter-cyclical pattern of policy is reflected in a different pattern of money growth and interest rate movements than previously. In previous decades, when the Federal Reserve was reacting too little too late, interest rates and money growth tended to move together, as both were dominated by cycles in income growth. Since 1982, money growth rates and interest rates have often moved in opposite directions. Policy actions to adjust interest rates in order to stabilize expansion of spending have resulted in damped money growth and rising interest rates when demands for goods and services were strong, and faster money growth and declining interest rates when demands were weak. This may be one reason for the wider variations in velocity this decade, in addition to the effects of deregulation. The swings in money growth of the last few years may connote a steadiness of purpose in the implementation of monetary policy, not the vacillation suggested by looking at money growth rates alone. In effect policy has been more stabilizing than if it had waited for signals from money growth.

The question is whether there is something in the policy process itself that helps to account for this result. I believe that there is some reason for cautious optimism on this account.

Policymakers have learned from past mistakes. There is a recognition of the adverse consequences of inflation and the ephemeral nature of tradeoffs between inflation and production and hence probably a better sense of the costs and benefits from leaning on the side of a little stronger real growth under many circumstances. And, in the implementation of policy, considerable attention is paid to differentiating real from nominal interest and exchange rates.

Moreover, there are elements of the current system that provide some longer-term discipline and can curb short-term expansionary impulses. One is reputation. In particular, the Federal Reserve has stated very clearly its intention to seek price stability and the importance it places on this objective. It is, and ought to be, quite defensive about obvious deviations from this objective, both in actual data and in projections.

Another is greater attention to expectation-driven variables, such as yield curves, exchange rates, and commodity prices. There are a host of problems interpreting these indicators: they reflect expectations of Federal Reserve actions as well as other factors affecting the economy and prices; auction markets do seem to be subject to quite a bit of volatility from time to time that is difficult to attribute to underlying economic forces that ought to concern the central bank; and, more generally, the relationship of these variables to real interest rates and the thrust of policy is complex. Still, interpreted with care, they may help policymakers judge when market participants consider conditions conducive to significant changes in inflation rates. In this regard they can be forward-looking indicators of market perceptions of the Federal Reserve's reputation.

Finally, there is continued attention to the monetary aggregates. Although they may no longer be as useful as a short-run guides to policy, there is strong evidence of a continuing relationship between trends in money and trends in prices. Thus, sustained very rapid or very slow growth in money has continued to play a role in keying policy adjustments.

Taken together, these elements have helped to provide some long-term discipline for discretionary policy drawing on a multitude of information sources. They seem to have at least limited the scope for policy mistakes, at a time when no single indicator or small set of indicators is considered a trustworthy guide to policy. Nonetheless, inflation remains unacceptably high. Whether the current policy regime will lead to the restoration of price stability, with minimum losses in production and output, remains to be seen.

Reply to Donald Kohn

by Allan H. Meltzer

During much of my professional life, academics have engaged in discussions with Federal Reserve officials and spokesmen about policies, policy procedures, and implementation. When Federal Reserve spokesmen have responded to some of the comments, proposals, criticisms, and analysis of past policies, their responses have too often been: "We know better. We have considered something of that kind, and it doesn't work. Trust us; we know what we are doing."

Regrettably, Donald Kohn's written comments are in this defensive mode. Claims are made based on evidence that is not open to scrutiny. Alternatives are dismissed without any evidence that a superior alternative is available. Instead of responding to my main criticisms of the record of the past 25 or 75 years, Kohn distorts the recent record, neglects the past, and ignores much recent work on the issues he discusses. Here are some samples.

> [T]he Federal Reserve walked up to a monetary rule, looked over the brink for a few years, and subsequently backed away.... [W]e came very close [to a monetary rule].

This is a misstatement of the facts. There is abundant evidence on that point, some of which the article cites. It does not cite the statements made by knowledgeable insiders such as Peter Sternlight and Steven Axilrod in "Money, Credit and Banking Debate" (Axilrod et al., 1982) based on a discussion of April 20, 1981, while the experiment was in process. Nor does it cite the many criticisms of the experiment made at the time, including criticisms by Robert Rasche and me, in the same debate.

The topic of the debate was: Resolved that the Federal Reserve's current operating procedures for controlling money should be replaced. This suggests that, in the opinion of many at the time, the Federal Reserve had not adopted a monetary rule or, in the view of the affirmative, adopted procedures capable of controlling money. Axilrod and Sternlight made no claim to have "come close" to a monetary rule. They claimed, instead, that a monetary rule would make interest rates too variable *under prevailing control arrangements*. Axilrod acknowledged that "if one changed the institutional environment, one would have a better shot at attaining a money objective through control of total reserves" (1982, p. 133). Kohn says:

> Why, then, were they [monetary aggregates] abandoned? The reason lies in the breakdown of those empirical regularities in the 1980s.

Kohn discusses some of the matters that are typically raised such as shifts in the aggregates, variability of velocity, and so on. He does not mention that McCallum (1987, 1989) and Meltzer (1984, 1987) proposed adaptive rules to reduce the variability arising from changes in the growth rate of velocity and fluctuations in real GNP. McCallum (1989) shows that in a variety of models—monetarist, Keynesian, and others—his rule keeps nominal GNP closer to a 3% target path than actual GNP has been to a fitted trend. The error made by the rule, on average, is about equal to the forecast error in real or nominal GNP (Meltzer, 1987) and lower than the deviations from steady growth that the Federal Reserve has achieved in practice. If followed, the adaptive rule would have avoided the two most costly mistakes—the great deflation of the 1930s and the great inflation of the 1960s and 1970s. According to Kohn,

> [B]ase velocity has been quite variable in the 1980s even after allowing for a change in trend in 1981, increasing and decreasing by amounts ranging from 3½% to 7% within periods of just a few quarters.

At best this statement is disingenuous. First, it ignores the evidence just cited on the performance of adaptive rules. Second, with minimum effort, Kohn could have run the simplest possible model,

$$V_t = a + bV_{t-1} + U_t, \quad \bar{r}^2 = .81$$

where V_t is base velocity. For the period first-quarter 1980 to first-quarter 1989, V_{t-1} "explains" 81% of the variance of V_t. The standard error of the estimate is approximately 1.2% of the mean value, and the largest error is about 2% (in second-quarter 1986), well below the errors he discusses. There is reason to believe that the error could be reduced further.

Kohn also fails to discuss a broader issue, one that is neglected by most of those who claim that control of monetary aggregates failed. "Failure" is not well defined in this context. Variability of many aggregates, interest rates, and relative prices increased. Most models predicted less accurately in the disinflation of the early 1980s than in earlier periods. This problem was not confined to monetarist models or to models in which money growth is important. As far as I know, all models, regardless of orientation, did worse than in earlier, more stable periods. Anyone who approached the problem of explaining the early 1980s in a scientific way would understand that the problem is more general than Kohn recognizes. Perhaps one of the lessons to be learned is that adaptive rules are better under these circumstances (and others) than discretionary policies based on judgment and econometric models. Kohn says:

> Our experience in testing adaptive base rules within the structure of the MPS model support these conclusions [substantial, prolonged deviations of nominal income from expectations, and in real income as well].

I cannot comment fully on results that are not made available, but I am curious what Kohn thinks these results add to the discussion. They are counter to McCallum's (1989) published results, so they may only reflect on the inadequacy of the Federal Reserve's MPS model with its minuscule interest elasticity, Phillips curve, incorrect term structure of interest rates (as described in my text), and other peculiarities.

Referring to the base, Kohn writes: "It is difficult not to be a little careful about an aggregate, a large portion of which cannot be accounted for." This comment is irrelevant. The proposed rules call for control of the *growth rate of the base*. The problem of a large currency stock, possibly held abroad, affects the level, not the growth rate. Has Kohn looked at data to learn whether the accuracy problem is worse for the growth rate of the base than for other aggregates such as GNP, inventories, or the budget deficit where measurement and conceptual problems have not been resolved? According to Kohn,

> [M]embers of the FOMC look directly at data on the economy and prices in assessing whether the stance of policy is consistent with furthering the Committee's objectives. Various members of the Committee have their favorite indicators ... The operating procedure has the advantage of making use of all available information about the complex relationships in the economy.

Almost the same statements about the FOMC have been made, or were made at the time, in the 1920s and about the period since the Accord. The data do not speak. Looking at them did not prevent deflation or inflation and other costly mistakes. Have economists or policymakers learned enough about separating permanent and transitory changes or real and nominal changes to be confident that they can reduce variability by discretionary adjustments based on available data? It is regrettable that Kohn does not address this issue. Didn't the staff use "all available information" in the 1970s when, as shown in the article, it consistently underestimated inflation for years? How has its ability to interpret the information changed? A candid discussion would not repeat the empty and meaningless phrases that the Fed staff trots out when it does not choose to respond substantively.

Yes, monetary policy has improved in the 1980s, as I recognized in my article. Society paid for the increased credibility of the Fed in the 1981–1982 recession and the lower rate of inflation that followed. The Federal Reserve learned that inflation and disinflation have greater costs and fewer benefits than they believed in the 1960s and 1970s. But inflation remains above the long-term average, and we are far from price stability. Kohn might usefully recall that the Fed took credit for the stability of the 1920s that was followed by the debacle of the 1930s. The Fed took credit for 1954–1964, but that was followed by rising inflation in the 1960s and 1970s and costly, rapid disinflation in the 1980s.

My article notes that past mistakes were "not malicious or willful acts. Many were the result of mistaken beliefs about the way policy works, or the reliance on forecasts and judgments that were faulty." What is needed now is an institutional change to increase accountability and reduce uncertainty about policy. Kohn's response tells us to trust them. We did in the past, and it often worked badly. Without a change in procedures, there is little basis for trust. Without increased accountability, the best forecast is that we will pay for more "learning from experience" in the future. Kohn's comments fail to make a case for discretion, do not respond to the criticisms, and contribute little to the dialogue.

References

Axilrod, S., Meltzer, A., Rasche, R., and Sternlight, P. 1982. "Money, Credit and Banking Debate: Is the Federal Reserve's Policy Misdirected?" *Journal of Money, Credit and Banking* 14 (February):119–147.

McCallum, B. T. 1987. "The Case for Rules in the Conduct of Monetary Policy: A Concrete Example." *Economic Review*, Federal Reserve Bank of Richmond (September/October):10–18.

McCallum, B. T. 1989. "Robustness Properties of a Rule for Monetary Policy." *Carnegie Rochester Conference Series on Public Policy* 29 (Autumn):173–204.

Meltzer, A. H. 1984. "Overview." *Price Stability and Public Policy*, Federal Reserve Bank of Kansas City.

Meltzer, A. H. 1987. "Limits of Short-Run Stabilization Policy." *Economic Inquiry* 25 (January):1–14.

SESSION II

2 WHY DOES THE FED SMOOTH INTEREST RATES?

Alex Cukierman

1. Introduction

Except for relatively short episodes, the most notable of which is the 1979–1982 period, the Fed has geared monetary policy to reduce fluctuations in short-term interest rates. Even Volcker's successful monetary experiment did not produce a permanent shift to a nominal money stock rule as advocated by monetarists. This is puzzling for several reasons, not the least of which is the fact that monetarists' prescriptions have proven to be effective in delivering price stability. The tendency to revert to a policy of interest rate smoothing seems to be rather tenacious and as old as the Fed. Thus Miron (1986) and Mankiw, Miron, and Weil (1987) report that there

---

I would like to thank Michelle Garfinkel, Nissan Liviatan, Allan Meltzer, Jeffrey Miron, and Akiva Offenbacher whose questions and reactions stimulated my thinking on the issues of this article. I also benefitted from informal discussions with Ted Balbach, Bill Brown, Glen Donaldson, Stuart Hoffman, Gary Santoni, Cliff Stone, and other participants at the conference. A previous version was written while the author was a Bundesbank Visiting Professor at Free University—Berlin.

has been a substantial change in the behavior of interest rates after the establishment of the Federal Reserve in 1914. After 1914 interest rates became substantially more persistent than prior to the founding of the Fed. Moreover, the Fed was widely expected to dampen fluctuations in interest rates. Goodfriend and King (1988) note that, prior to the Fed's creation, fluctuations in the monthly average call money rate on short-term broker loans exhibited much wider irregular and seasonal fluctuations than after 1914. Donaldson (1989a) finds that, after the foundation of the Fed, violent spikes in interest rates during financial panics virtually disappeared.

This article proposes a positive explanation for the Fed's tendency to smooth interest rates. This explanation relies on two presumptions. One is that the Fed is concerned about the stability of the financial system as well as about price stability. The other is that banks commit to loan contracts that normally stretch over longer periods than the term for which deposits are committed to them. There is little doubt that the Fed is concerned about the stability of the financial system in general and that of the banking system in particular.[1] The Fed was founded to a large extent in order to avoid financial crises (Mankiw, Miron, and Weil 1987). Its charter makes it responsible for averting such crises, and it is widely expected to do so by Congress and the public. As a bureaucracy the Fed may reasonably be expected to be more sensitive to the risks of banking failures than to adverse general economic conditions like unemployment. After all, the responsibility for the banking system is in the Fed's "own courtyard" while the responsibility for high unemployment is naturally shared by other policymaking institutions like the fiscal authority. Brimmer (1989) makes a persuasive case that on various occasions the Fed's policy was geared to safeguard the stability of the financial system.

The second presumption relies on the traditional function of banks which is to transform short-term liabilities into longer-term loan assets. Although some variable rate loans have recently developed, a large fraction of loans in the United States specifies a fixed loan rate and volume in advance for the period of the loan.[2] Many deposits, on the other hand (like demand deposits, short-term money market accounts, and large certificates of deposits—CDs) have more flexible terms both with respect to maturity and return.[3] This asymmetry is probably due to the fact that the fundamental service provided by banks on both sides of their balance sheet is liquidity. On the side of assets (loans) liquidity is provided by giving the borrower an advance unconditional assurance for the loan terms. On the side of liabilities (deposits) liquidity is provided by letting customers use their funds on demand. Another possible reason is that loan markets are more influenced by customer specific considerations than deposit markets.[4]

Be that as it may, this article takes the asymmetry in the contract provisions of loans and of deposits as given, and explores the implications of its existence for the behavior of the central bank.

The advance commitment of banks to loan terms makes them vulnerable to changes in the conditions of financial markets after they have committed their funds. For example, if after loan contracts have been made, there is an unexpected decrease in the aggregate supply of deposits, banks lose reserves and incur higher marginal costs of illiquidity.[5] In order to correct this situation, each individual bank tries to regain deposits by raising its deposit rate. Since all banks do that, there is a general increase in the total cost of funds to banks and a decrease in the profits of the banking industry. The squeeze in profits is amplified by the fact that rates rise on the entire stock of deposits after loan rates and quantities have been preset. This increases, in turn, the likelihood that some relatively weak banks will fail. Since the Fed is concerned about the stability of the banking system, it has interest in counteracting the increase in the likelihood of banking failures. Provided the price level is temporarily fixed, the Fed can temporarily offset the decrease in banks' profits by stepping up the rate of increase in reserves. This action decreases banks' demand for deposits and dampens some of the increase in the rate of interest paid on deposits, thus offsetting at least some of the increase in the risk of banking failures. However, the higher rate of reserve expansion is also costly from the point of view of the Fed, since after a while it leads to a larger rate of inflation. Hence when the cost of funds to banks unexpectedly goes down, increasing banks' profits and decreasing the likelihood of failures, the Fed puts more emphasis on the stability of the general price level and decreases the rate of growth of base money. This action dampens, in the short run, the initial decrease in the cost of funds to the banking industry.

Thus interest rate smoothing by the central bank arises as a byproduct of the bank's attempt to minimize some combination of the risks of financial instability and of the costs of inflation. The central bank directs policy mostly to increase the soundness of the banking system when the risks of financial instability are relatively high. It focuses mostly on maintainance of price stability when profits in the banking industry are high and the risks of failure are, therefore, relatively low. Since, because of the asymmetry in the structure of their contracts, banks' profits are negatively related to the level of interest rates in the short run, the central bank's actions result in interest rate smoothing. The theory implies that the Fed is concerned with the predictability of interest rates rather than with their level.[6] This article develops this intuitive mechanism more precisely and characterizes the conditions under which it operates in the presence of various shocks. In particular, shocks to the deposit market, the short-term bond market, and the loan market are considered. It shows that smoothing by the central bank arises also in the case in which, due to the existence of credit lines, the volume of loans adjusts passively to shocks to loan demand. As a matter of fact, the existence of credit lines provides another reason for the Fed to engage in interest rate smoothing.[7]

Additional implications of the article's framework are:

1. The rate of high-powered money growth behaves procyclically. More precisely, when unanticipated increases in economic activity raise the supply of bonds and the bond rate, the Fed responds by stepping up the rate of increase in base money. Rasche (1988) presents evidence suggesting that base money growth is procyclical. Similar evidence concerning M1 growth appears in Meltzer (1990).

2. The time series pattern of nominal interest rates that emerges in the presence of central bank intervention is nearer to being a random walk than their pattern in the absence of intervention. This is consistent with the findings of Miron (1986) and of Mankiw, Miron, and Weil (1987) who report that, after the foundation of the Fed, short-term rates were much closer to a random walk than prior to that.

3. The concern of the central bank for the stability of the banking system creates an inflationary bias even in the absence of employment considerations of the type discussed by Kydland and Prescott (1977), Barro and Gordon (1983), and many others. This bias makes expected rates on deposits, federal funds, and short-term bonds lower than in the absence of intervention, inducing the banking system to take higher risks by lending more.

4. Arrival of new information indicating a substantial cumulation of losses within the financial system induces the central bank to step up the rate of reserves created in the short run. This result may have some power for explaining monetary accelerations prior to the thrift industry bailout.

In order to analyze the interaction between the central bank and the banking industry precisely, it is necessary to specify the structure and type of equilibrium that characterize the banking industry. Banks are modeled as having some degree of local monopoly power (not necessarily the same) in both the loan and deposit markets.[8] Each bank picks its loan rate, the volume of loans, and its deposit rate so as to maximize profits, taking the loan and deposit rates of other banks as given. We focus on the resulting Cournot-Nash symmetric equilibrium of the banking industry. The structure of the ex post equilibrium in which the deposit rate and the demand for short-term bonds by banks is determined (for predetermined loan contracts) is discussed in section 2. Section 3 characterizes the short-term bond market equilibrium and demonstrates that, with sufficient competition in the banking sector, there is a short-run negative relationship between profits in this sector and the bond rate. The ex ante (prior to realizations of shocks) determination of loan contracts is presented in section 4. Ex ante each bank picks the loan rate and the volume of loans so as to maximize expected profits over the loans' period. In doing so, each bank takes the loan rates of other banks and the policy rule of the Fed as given. Again we focus on the Cournot-Nash symmetric ex ante equilibrium of the banking system. Section 4 also characterizes the ex ante determination of the price level which, once set, remains fixed for one period. The price level is determined at the level that clears the market for bank reserves in an ex ante sense. This way of modeling general price level determination is meant to capture the fact that prices of goods normally do not adjust instantaneously to changes in nominal shocks.[9] This temporary stickiness makes it possible for the Fed to influence interest rates in the short run.

The objectives of the central bank and the characterization of its policy appear in section 5. This section also demonstrates the existence of an inflationary bias that is induced by the central bank's concern for financial stability. The basic result of the article concerning smoothing of interest rates in the face of shocks to the deposit and the short-term bond markets is developed and discussed in section 6. For a given ex post equilibrium of the banking industry, the central bank picks the rate of expansion of the monetary base so as to minimize the combined risks of financial instability and inflation. This behavior is shown to result in interest rate smoothing. The procyclical behavior of base money growth and the tendency of short-term rates to behave more nearly as random walks in the presence of intervention is developed in section 7. The discussion is extended, and the basic smoothing result shown to carry over, to the case of credit lines in section 8. This is followed by concluding remarks.

2. Structure of the Banking Industry and the Ex Post Equilibrium

The central element of banking activity is the transformation of relatively short-term liabilities like demand deposits, certificates of deposit, and other short-term money market instruments into longer-term loans to bank customers. An important consequence of this activity is that banks have to commit to loan terms before they know with certainty the quantity and cost of their sources of funds.[10] In order to capture this fundamental asymmetry in a simple way, we postulate that each bank determines the quantity of one-period loans and their price at the beginning of each period for the period. In particular this commitment is made before various shocks that affect the economy and the banking system during the period are realized. But the volume and cost of deposits are determined within the period after the realization of those shocks. The banking industry is composed of N banks that compete for sources of funds as well as for borrowers.[11] The demand function for (real) loans facing bank i is

$$\ell(r_{\ell i}, \mathbf{r}_{\ell i}, \varepsilon_\ell) = \frac{1}{N}(A_\ell + \varepsilon_\ell - \ell_0 r_{\ell i}) - \ell \sum_{\substack{j=1 \\ j \neq i}}^{N} (r_{\ell i} - r_{\ell j}) \qquad (1)$$

where $r_{\ell i}$ is the (real) loan rate charged by bank i, $\mathbf{r}_{\ell i}$ is the vector of loan rates charged by all other banks, ε_ℓ is a stochastic shock (with zero expected value) to aggregate demand for credit, and A_ℓ, ℓ_0, and ℓ are positive parameters. Note that when all loan rates are equal this demand function reduces to $(1/N)(A_\ell + \varepsilon_\ell - \ell_0 r_\ell)$ and correspondingly the aggregate demand for loans facing the industry is $A_\ell + \varepsilon_\ell - \ell_0 r_\ell$. Hence ℓ_0 is a measure of the sensitivity of *total* demand for credit to an increase in the loan rate. The parameter ℓ measures the degree of local monopoly power of each bank. The higher it is, the more customers are lost by the individual bank when it raises its rate and all other banks maintain their rates at fixed levels. Hence, given N, a higher ℓ implies a smaller degree of local monopoly power. Equation (1) represents the demand for loans facing a bank after the realization of intra-period shocks. The demand facing it at the beginning of the period is the same expression with $\varepsilon_\ell = 0$. If during the period ε_ℓ is (say) positive, there is an incrememtal demand of ε_ℓ/N which is not satisfied by the bank since all loan contracts have been concluded at the beginning of the period.[12]

The (real) supply of deposits function facing bank i is

$$d(r_{di}, \mathbf{r}_{di}, \varepsilon_d) = \frac{1}{N}(A_d + \varepsilon_d + d_0 r_{di}) + d \sum_{\substack{j=1 \\ j \neq i}}^{N} (r_{di} - r_{dj}) \qquad (2)$$

where r_{di} is the (real) rate paid on deposits by bank i, $\mathbf{r}_{di}$ is the vector of rates paid on deposits by all other banks, ε_d is a stochastic shock (with zero expected value) to aggregate deposit supply, and A_d, d_0, and d are positive parameters. The parameter d_0 measures the sensitivity of aggregate deposit supply to a change in the average deposit rate. The parameter d measures the degree of local monopoly power in the deposit market for a given number of banks. The lower d, the less competitive is the banking industry in the deposit market.

The required reserve ratio against deposits is τ. Hence the (real) required reserves of bank i are

$$r\rho_i = \tau d(r_{di}, r_{di}, \varepsilon_d). \tag{3}$$

There is an economywide short-term bond market. The (real) bond rate, r_b, is determined on the stock exchange. It is, therefore, influenced by the within-period realizations of the various shocks that affect the economy. The non-bank real demand for bonds is

$$\varepsilon_b^d + s_0 r_b \tag{4}$$

where ε_b^d is a stochastic shock to the real demand for bonds with zero mean, and s_0 is a positive parameter. Banks choose their bond portfolios after the realization of stochastic shocks within the period. In order to maintain the complexity of the model at a manageable level, it is assumed that bonds are traded only once within a period after the realization of shocks. Furthermore, only one-period bonds that mature just prior to trade-in bonds in the next period are considered. This specification abstracts from the function of bonds as secondary liquidity. But it does account for the tendency of banks to reduce their bond portfolios when they lose reserves, thus bringing out part of the function of bonds as secondary reserves as well as the effect of reserve losses on bond market equilibrium.[13]

In addition to the interest it pays on deposits, the individual bank incurs various costs that are associated with illiquidity. Those costs increase at an increasing rate with the degree of the bank's illiquidity which is measured, in turn, as the difference between the required reserves of the bank and its actual (real) level of reserves. More precisely, the costs of illiquidity are:

$$c(\rho_i - r\rho_i) = \begin{Bmatrix} \frac{c}{2}[\alpha - (\rho_i - r\rho_i)]^2 & \text{for } \alpha - (\rho_i - r\rho_i) \geq 0 \\ 0 & \text{otherwise} \end{Bmatrix}. \tag{5}$$

Here ρ_i are the actual (real) reserves of the bank, α is a non-negative parameter, and c is a positive parameter. The costs of illiquidity are zero whenever actual reserves exceed required reserves by more than the threshold α. But once the difference between actual and required reserves drops below the threshold, the costs of illiquidity become positive and increase at an increasing rate with further increases in illiquidity. Two presumptions underlie this specification. One is that as the difference between actual and required reserves decreases, the individual bank dips more heavily into the discount window and incurs higher implicit penalties from the Fed. The other is that the lower this difference, the higher the amount of managerial and other resources devoted by the bank to execute trades in the federal funds market. Obviously each of those presumptions alone is sufficient to generate increasing marginal costs of illiquidity as specified in equation (5).

Abstracting from inessential items, the balance sheet of an individual bank implies that total assets, which are composed of reserves, bonds, and loans, are equal to total deposits. Letting R_i,B_i,L_i, and D_i denote, respectively, the nominal quantities of reserves, bonds, loans, and deposits of bank i, its balance sheet identity can be written

$$R_i + B_i + L_i = D_i. \tag{6}$$

Dividing by the price level and rearranging

$$\rho_i = d(r_{di}, r_{di}, \varepsilon_d) - \ell(r_{\ell i}, r_{\ell i}, \varepsilon_\ell) - b_i \tag{6a}$$

where b_i is the real stock of bonds held by the bank. The general price level, P, for each period is determined at the beginning of the period so as to clear the market for the monetary base in an ex ante sense.

It is useful to summarize the timing of events. Loan contracts covering both the price and the quantity of loans and the general price level are determined at the beginning of each period. Within the period the timing of events is as follows. First, the short-term bonds carried over from the previous period mature, then the intra-period shocks realize, and finally decisions about new bond portfolios and the interest rate on deposits are made.

The ex ante determination of the price level, the loan rate, and the volume of loans are discussed in section 4. Here we focus on the ex post, within period, equilibrium of the financial system for previously predetermined values of the price level, the loan rate, and the amount of outstanding loans.

Taking those variables, the bond rate, and the deposit rates of all other banks as given, the individual bank chooses its own deposit rate and the amount of bonds so as to maximize real profits. Those profits are equal to revenues from loans minus interest paid on deposits and the costs of illiquidity. Using equations (3) and (6a) in (5), and noting that revenues from loans as well as their quantity are predetermined, the maximization problem of bank i can be written:

$$\begin{aligned} \max_{\{r_{di}, b_i\}} \; & r^p_{\ell i}\, \ell^p_i + r_b b_i - r_{di} d(r_{di}, r_{di}, \varepsilon_d) \\ & - \tfrac{c}{2}[\alpha + \ell^p_i + b_i - (1 - \tau) d(r_{di}, r_{di}, \varepsilon_d)]^2 + u_i \end{aligned} \tag{7}$$

where u_i is an idiosyncratic stochastic shock to bank i's profits that realizes concurrently with ε_d and ε_b. The sum of the u shocks over banks satisfies $\Sigma_{i=1}^{N} u_i = 0$. The superscript "p" designates variables that have been predetermined at the beginning of the period. For simplicity, and without much loss of generality, we set $\alpha = 0$. The formulation in equation (7) is based on the presumption that the single bank operates in the range for which the costs of illiquidity are positive. As explained in note 14, this always is the case when the real return on bonds is positive. Substituting the particular form of the deposit demand function from equation (2) into (7) and differentiating with respect to r_{di} and b_i, the first order conditions for bank i's optimization are:[14]

$$-\frac{1}{N}(A_d + \varepsilon_d) - \left(\frac{2d_0}{N} + (N-1)d\right)r_{di} - d\sum_{\substack{j=1\\ j\neq i}}^{N}(r_{di} - r_{dj})$$
$$+c(1-\tau)\left(\frac{d_0}{N} + (N-1)d\right)\Bigg(\ell_i^p + b_i - (1-\tau)$$
$$\cdot\left\{\frac{A_d + \varepsilon_d + d_0 r_{di}}{N} + d\sum_{\substack{j=1\\ j\neq i}}^{N}(r_{di} - r_{dj})\right\}\Bigg) = 0 \tag{8a}$$

$$r_b - c\left(\ell_i^p + b_i - (1-\tau)\left\{\frac{A_d + \varepsilon_d + d_0 r_{di}}{N} + d\sum_{\substack{j=1\\ j\neq i}}^{N}(r_{di} - r_{dj})\right\}\right) = 0. \tag{8b}$$

As in any oligopolistic market, the decisions of bank i depend on the decisions of other banks in the industry. In particular, as can be seen from the first order conditions in (8), the choice of r_{di} and of b_i by bank i depends on the deposit rate of all other banks in the industry. In a Nash equilibrium the choice made by each bank has to be such that, given the optimal choices of all other banks, the individual bank is also at an optimum. We focus here on a symmetric Nash equilibrium of the banking industry in which

$$r_{di} = r_d, \quad b_i = b \text{ for all } i. \tag{9}$$

Substituting equation (9) into (8) and solving for r_d and b, the equilibrium values of the deposit rate and of the individual bank demand for bonds are[15]

$$r_d = -\frac{1}{D}(A_d + \varepsilon_d) + (1-\tau)\left(1 - \frac{d_0}{D}\right)r_b \tag{10a}$$

$$b = -\ell^P + (1 - \tau)\left(1 - \frac{d_0}{D}\right)\frac{\varepsilon_d}{N} + \left(\frac{1}{c} + (1 - \tau)^2 \frac{d_0}{N}\left(1 - \frac{d_0}{N}\right)\right) r_b \qquad (10b)$$

where

$$D \equiv 2d_0 + N(N - 1)d. \qquad (11)$$

The features of those solutions are plausible. The deposit rate offered by banks is higher the higher the return on bonds and is lower the higher the ex post demand for deposits. In a wider model with an explicit federal funds market r_d and the federal funds rate will normally move in tandem. Hence, within the present model, r_d can also be thought of as a proxy for the federal funds rate. The demand for bonds by the individual bank is an increasing function of the bond rate and is smaller, ceteris paribus, the larger the amount of loan commitments that have been made at the beginning of the period.

Substituting equations (10) into the profit function of the individual bank in (7) and rearranging, the profits of an individual bank are:[16]

$$\pi_i = (r_\ell^p - r_b)\ell^p + \frac{1}{DN}\left(1 - \frac{d_0}{D}\right) \cdot \left((1 - \tau)d_0 r_b + A_d + \varepsilon_d\right)^2 + \frac{r_b^2}{2c} + u_i. \qquad (12)$$

Depending on whether the ex post value of the bond rate is smaller or larger than the precommited loan rate, a larger volume of loans is beneficial or detrimental to profits ex post. Since $\Sigma_{i=1}^N u_i = 0$ the (ex post) profits of the entire banking industry are:

$$\pi = N\pi_i = (r_\ell^p - r_b)N\ell^p + \frac{1}{D}\left(1 - \frac{d_0}{D}\right) \cdot [(1 - \tau)d_0 r_b + A_d + \varepsilon_d]^2 + \frac{N}{2c} r_b^2. \qquad (13)$$

3. The Short-Run Negative Relationship Between the Bond Rate and the Profits of the Banking Industry

The effect of an increase in the real rate on bonds on the profits of the banking system after the conclusion of loan contracts can be obtained by differentiating equation (13) with respect to r_b. The resulting expression is

$$\frac{\partial \pi}{\partial r_b} = N\left(\frac{r_b}{c} + 2(1-\tau)\frac{d_0}{D}\left\{1 - \frac{d_0}{D}\right\}\frac{(1-\tau)d_0 r_b + A_d + \varepsilon_d}{N} - \ell^p\right). \quad (14)$$

The term $(1/N)[(1-\tau)d_0 r_b + A_d + \varepsilon_d]$ is somewhat smaller than the ex post equilibrium volume of deposits at a representative bank. ℓ^p is the volume of loans at a representative bank. The expression $2(1-\tau)(d_0/D)$ $(1 - d_0/D)$ which multiplies the deposit-related term is substantially smaller than 1 already for a moderately large N since $(1-\tau)(1 - d_0/D) < 1$ and d_0/D tends to zero as N gets larger.[17] Since r_b is a fraction r_b/c is also smaller than 1 if $c > r_b$ which seems a relatively mild restriction. The upshot is that if the marginal cost of illiquidity is not too small and the number of banks moderately large, the last negative term in equation (14) dominates the sign of $\partial\pi/\partial r_b$ and an increase in the bond rate decreases the profits of the banking industry. Either condition alone may be sufficient to induce this negative effect. The remainder of the discussion is based on the presumption that a within-period increase in the bond rate squeezes the profits of the banking system.

The intuition underlying this total negative effect is as follows: An increase in the bond rate induces two opposing effects on the profits of the banking industry. On one hand, there is an increase in the return on the bond portfolio and a related upward adjustment in the quantity of bonds held by each bank (see equation (10b)), both of which tend to increase the profits of banks. On the other hand, the more lucrative bond rate causes an intensification of the banks' competition for funds and results in an increase in the deposit rate (see equation (10a)) on the *entire* stock of deposits. This market effect reduces the profits of the banking industry. If banks had not previously committed a large part of their funds to loans, they would have increased their investment in the bond market also by decreasing the amount of loans offered to customers as well as by increasing the loan rate. However, the previously made commitment to a certain level of loans limits the banks' ability to take advantage of the better bond market opportunities. The larger this commitment, the more limited is the ability of banks to increase their bond portfolio because of increasing costs of illiquidity. This limitation is reflected in equation (10b) which implies that the total amount of earning assets of a bank (loans + bonds) is limited by a constant which depends on r_b and on the shock to the demand for deposits. Thus the ability of banks to take advantage of the more lucrative bond rate is limited by past commitments of funds. However, the increase in the deposit rate increases the cost of all funds, including those that are needed to fulfill the obligation to previously contracted loans. As a consequence the negative market-induced effect of an increase in r_b on profits dominates the direct positive effect.

We turn next to a characterization of the (ex post) bond market equilibrium. Let ε_b^s be a (zero mean) shock to the real supply of bonds during the period. Let EB be the nominal supply of bonds as anticipated at the beginning of period t.[18] All unindexed variables refer to period t. Since ε_b^s is that part of the nominal supply of bonds which was not anticipated (as of the beginning of the period), the actual real supply of bonds during the period is:

$$\frac{EB}{P^p} + \varepsilon_b^s.$$

The superscript "p" attached to the price level, P, denotes the fact that the price level has been predetermined by the ex ante equilibrium at the beginning of the period. Details concerning price level determination appear in section 4 below. The real rate on bonds during the period is determined by clearing of the bond market. The public's demand for bonds is given by equation (4) and the demand of the banking system is given by (10b) multiplied by the number of banks. Summing up these two components of demand for bonds, equating to the supply of bonds, and solving for r_b, we obtain:

$$r_b = K\left(\frac{EB}{P^p} + N\ell^p - \varepsilon_b - (1 - \tau)\left(1 - \frac{d_0}{D}\right)\varepsilon_d\right) + R(\varepsilon_b, \varepsilon_d) \quad (15)$$

where

$$\varepsilon_b \equiv \varepsilon_b^d - \varepsilon_b^s \quad (16a)$$

$$K \equiv \frac{1}{\frac{N}{c} + (1 - \tau)^2 d_0\left(1 - \frac{d_0}{D}\right) + s_0} \quad (16b)$$

and the term $R(\cdot)$ represents the reaction function of the Fed. The determination of this function is discussed toward the end of section 6. Equation (15) states that, in the absence of intervention, the equilibrium real rate on bonds is lower the higher are the intra-period shocks to the excess demand for bonds (ε_b) and to the demand for deposits (ε_d). It is higher when the volume of loans to which the banking system precommited at the beginning of the period is higher and the higher is the expected supply of bonds at that time. The intuition underlying the effects of EB and of ε_b is obvious. The positive relationship between ℓ^p and r_b is due to the fact, mentioned earlier, that the larger the volume of loan precommitments, the smaller the increase in the demand of the banking system for bonds when r_b goes up. As a result, its attenuating effect on the rise in r_b is weaker the larger ℓ^p. Finally, the depressing effect of ε_d on the bond rate is due to the fact that a positive shock to the demand for deposits induces a decrease in the equilibrium deposit rate (see equation (10a)) and increases the demand of banks for bonds. This increased demand decreases the real rate on bonds. The discussion of the term $R(\cdot)$ is left to section 6.

We turn next to the intra-period effects of the shocks ε_b and ε_d on the profits of the banking industry. Since, from equation (13), ε_b affects π only through r_b and since $\partial\pi/\partial r_b < 0$ it follows that

$$\frac{\partial\pi}{\partial\varepsilon_b} = \frac{\partial\pi}{\partial r_b}\frac{\partial r_b}{\partial\varepsilon_b} > 0. \tag{17}$$

An increase in the excess demand for bonds increases the profits of the banking system in the short run. A change in ε_d affects profits directly, as well as through the change it induces in the bond rate. Hence

$$\frac{d\pi}{d\varepsilon_d} = \frac{\partial\pi}{\partial\varepsilon_d} + \frac{\partial\pi}{\partial r_b}\frac{\partial r_b}{\partial\varepsilon_d}. \tag{18}$$

But from (13)

$$\frac{\partial\pi}{\partial\varepsilon_d} = \frac{2}{D}\left(1 - \frac{d_0}{D}\right)[(1 - \tau)d_0 r_b + A_d + \varepsilon_d] \tag{18a}$$

which is positive as long as the demand for deposits is positive. Since $\partial\pi/\partial r_b < 0$ and since, from (15), $\partial r_b/\partial\varepsilon_d < 0$, the total effect of an increase in ε_d on the profits of the banking industry is positive.

The upshot is that the existence of unanticipated shocks to the excess demand for bonds or to the demand for deposits *after* the conclusion of loan contracts creates a negative correlation between the bond rate and the profits of the banking industry. It is easy to establish, by using (10a), that a similar negative correlation exists between profits and the deposit rate r_d.

4. Determination of the Loan Rate, the Volume of Loans, and the Price Level

Each individual bank is aware of the fact that after the realization of shocks, during the period, the equilibrium values of b and of r_d will depend on ε_d and on r_b in a way that is given by equations (10). However, as of the beginning of the period, the bank does not know the intra-period realizations of ε_d and of r_b. It therefore picks the loan rate $r_{\ell i}$ and the volume of loans ℓ_i so as to maximize the expected value of profits taking the relations in (10) into consideration. Hence the ex ante maximation problem of the individual bank is obtained by substituting equations (10) and (1) into the profit function of the individual bank in (7) and by taking the expected value of this expression. The resulting ex ante optimization problem of the individual bank is:

$$\begin{aligned}\operatorname*{Max}_{r_{\ell i}} E &\Bigg[r_{\ell i}\Bigg(\frac{A_\ell+\varepsilon_\ell-\ell_0 r_{\ell_i}}{N}-\ell\sum_{\substack{j=1\\ j\neq i}}^{N}(r_{\ell i}-r_{\ell j})\Bigg)\\ &-\frac{1}{N}\left\{(1-\tau)\left(1-\frac{d_0}{D}\right)r_b-\frac{A_d+\varepsilon_d}{D}\right\}\left\{A_d+\varepsilon_d+d_0\left((1-\tau)\left(1-\frac{d_0}{D}\right)r_b-\frac{A_d+\varepsilon_d}{D}\right)\right\}\\ &+r_b\left\{(1-\tau)\left(1-\frac{d_0}{D}\right)\frac{\varepsilon_d}{N}-\frac{A_\ell+\varepsilon_\ell-\ell_0 r_{\ell i}}{N}-\ell\sum_{\substack{j=1\\ j\neq i}}^{N}(r_{\ell i}-r_{\ell j})\right.\\ &\left.+\left[\frac{1}{c}+(1-\tau)^2\frac{d_0}{N}\left(1-\frac{d_0}{D}\right)\right]r_b\right\}-\frac{r_b^2}{2c}\Bigg].\end{aligned} \tag{19}$$

The first order condition for an internal maximum of this problem is

$$\frac{A_\ell-\ell_0 r_{\ell i}}{N}-\ell\sum_{\substack{j=1\\ j\neq i}}^{N}(r_{\ell i}-r_{\ell j})-\left(\frac{\ell_0}{N}+(N-1)\ell\right)\left(r_{\ell i}-Er_b\right)=0. \tag{20}$$

Again we focus on a symmetric (ex ante) Nash equilibrium in which

$$r_{\ell i}=r_\ell \quad \text{for all } i. \tag{21}$$

Using equation (21) in (20) and rearranging, the loan rate is predetermined at

$$r_\ell^p=\frac{A_\ell}{D_L}+\left(1-\frac{\ell_0}{D_L}\right)Er_b \tag{22}$$

where

$$D_L\equiv 2\ell_0+N(N-1)\ell. \tag{23}$$

The corresponding volume of loans contracted by a single bank at the beginning of the period is (from equation (22) and the expected demand for loans in a symmetric equilibrium):

$$\ell^P=\left(1-\frac{\ell_0}{D_L}\right)\frac{A_\ell-\ell_0 Er_b}{N}. \tag{24}$$

In order to find Er_b we substitute equation (24) into (15), take expected values of the resulting expressions, and solve for Er_b. The resulting expression is:

$$Er_b = \frac{K\left[\frac{EB}{P^p} + \left(1 - \frac{\ell_0}{D_L}\right)\right]A_\ell}{1 + K\ell_0\left(1 - \frac{\ell_0}{D_L}\right)}. \tag{24a}$$

In order to fully characterize Er_b it is still necessary to specify how P^p and EB are determined. The remainder of this section is devoted to the first issue. The expected value, EB, of the supply of bonds depends, inter alia, on what banks know about the open market policy of the central bank. Since this policy is specified only in the next section, the precise characterization of EB is presented there.

We turn next to the price level which is determined by the condition that the market for nominal bank reserves clears in an ex ante sense. The advance determination of the price level for the period is meant to capture the well-accepted fact that prices of many goods and services on real markets do not respond to shocks immediately.

From equations (6) and (6a) the demand of an individual bank for reserves after the realization of shocks is

$$R_i^D(\cdot) = P[d(\cdot) - \ell^p - b] \tag{25}$$

where ℓ^p and b are given in equations (24) and (10b), respectively, and the explicit form of $d(\cdot)$ can be obtained by substituting equations (9) and (10a) into equation (2). Since in equilibrium $d(\cdot)$, ℓ^p and b are identical across all banks, the intra-period total demand for reserves is N times the single bank demand in (25):

$$R^D(\cdot) \equiv \sum_{i=1}^{N} R_i^D(\cdot) = PN[d(\cdot) - \ell^p - b] \equiv Px. \tag{25a}$$

Since $R^D(\cdot)$ depends on the intra-period realization of shocks and of the bond rate, it is not known with certainty at the beginning of the period when the price level is determined. Let R be the total nominal quantity of reserves made available to the banking system during the period. Since reserves respond, through the policy of the central bank, to intra-period shocks, their supply is also not known with certainty at the beginning of the period. We postulate that the price level is determined so as to equate the expected value of the natural logarithm of the demand for reserves with the expected value of the natural logarithm of reserves' supply.[19]

$$ElnR^D(\cdot) = ElnR \tag{26}$$

Using equation (25a) in (26) and rearranging

$$lnP = ElnR - Elnx \equiv lnR_{-1} + E\mu - Elnx \tag{26a}$$

where

$$\mu \equiv ln\frac{R}{R_{-1}} \text{ or } R = R_{-1}e^{\mu}. \tag{27}$$

Here use has been made of the fact that the nominal reserves, R_{-1}, of the previous period are known with certainty at the beginning of the current period. Note that *ln P* is directly proportional to the *ln* of the last period's reserves plus the expected rate of growth of reserves and is inversely related to *Elnx*. The analogy to the traditional money market clearing condition used to determine the price level is evident: the price level is higher the higher the expected supply of nominal reserves for the period and the lower the expected real demand for reserves as measured by *E ln x*.

5. Central Bank Objectives and Behavior

A main, self-acknowledged goal of the Federal Reserve both by law and custom is the preservation of the stability of the financial system in general, and that of the banking system in particular (*Federal Reserve Bulletin*, July 1984, p. 548).

This objective of the Fed is more likely to be attained the higher the profits are of the banking system, particularly if the Fed does not know the realizations of the idiosyncratic shocks, u_i, across individual banks (equation (7)). This statement can be elaborated by noting that the profits of a single bank in equation (7) are composed of a common component that includes all the terms except the last one which is idiosyncratic to the individual bank. If the common component of profits is large, even banks with particularly adverse realizations of u_i will be solvent, but if the common component of profits is small even banks with moderately adverse u_i's may run into difficulties.[20] Thus the higher the profits of the banking system, the smaller the probability of a serious financial crisis. Therefore, if the Fed values financial stability, it should, ceteris paribus, prefer a state of nature with higher profits in the banking industry to a state with lower profits. However, as total profits increase further, the incremental contribution to financial stability most probably diminishes. We shall model those features by postulating that one component of the objective function of the central bank is a function, $f(\pi)$, which increases in π but at a decreasing rate. In addition, as in Barro and Gordon (1983), the central bank dislikes inflation. Thus the entire objective function of the central bank may be written[21]

$$-\tfrac{1}{2}(\ln P_{t+1} - \ln P_t)^2 + gf(\pi_t),\ f'(\cdot) > 0,\ f''(\cdot) < 0. \tag{28}$$

Here $\ln P_{t+1} - \ln P_t$ is the rate of inflation between period t and period $t+1$, π_t are the profits of the banking industry in period t and g is a positive parameter that measures the relative concern of the central bank for financial stability versus price stability. This formulation reflects a basic externality that is internalized by the Fed. Each bank cares only about its own profits, but the Fed cares about the profits of the entire industry because of the connection between this aggregate and financial stability.

The profits of the banking system after the realization of intra-period shocks are given by equation (13). The discussion in section 3 implies that an intra-period decrease in the bond rate can increase the profits of the banking system in the short run. Since the price level is fixed, the central bank can temporarily decrease the bond rate by performing open market purchases of bonds, thus injecting additional reserves into the banking industry. Provided every dollar of bonds purchased generates a full additional dollar of reserves[22]

$$dR_t = -dB_t. \tag{29}$$

Combining equations (15) and (29),

$$dr_{bt} = \frac{K}{P^p} dB_t = -\frac{K}{P^p} dR_t \text{ or } \frac{dr_{bt}}{dR_t} = -\frac{K}{P^p} < 0 \tag{30}$$

where

$$B_t \equiv E_{t-1}B_t + \varepsilon^s_{bt}. \tag{31}$$

Equation (30) confirms the ability of the central bank to decrease the interest rate on bonds for a predetermined price level. But

$$\frac{dr_{bt}}{d\mu_t} = \frac{dr_{bt}}{dR_t}\frac{\partial R_t}{\partial \mu_t} = -\frac{K}{P_t^p} R_{t-1} e^{\mu} \tag{32}$$

where the extreme right-hand equality follows from equations (27) and (30). Equation (32) may be restated as:[23]

$$\frac{dr_{bt}}{d_{\mu_t}} = -K\bar{x}e^{\mu_t - E\mu_t} < 0,\ \bar{x} \equiv E\ln x. \tag{32a}$$

The time index has been deleted from the term $E\ln x$ since this expected value is time invariant due to the fact that all shocks are transitory. For the same reason $E\mu_t$ turns out to be time invariant as well.[24] This invariance in conjunction with equation (26a) implies:

$$\ln P_{t+1} - \ln P_t = \ln R_t + E\mu - \bar{x} - (\ln R_{t-1} + E\mu - \bar{x}) = \mu_t. \quad (33)$$

Substituting equation (33) into (28) and recognizing explicitly the dependence of banks' profits on ε_{dt} and on ε_{bt} and μ_t through their effects on r_{bt}, the objective function of the central bank may be restated as

$$\underset{\mu_t}{\text{Max}} - \tfrac{1}{2}\mu_t^2 + gf[\pi_t(\varepsilon_{dt}, r_{bt}(\varepsilon_{bt}, \mu_t))]. \quad (28a)$$

This restatement emphasizes the basic intra-period tradeoff confronting the central bank. It may, if it wishes, increase the profits of the banking system by stepping up the rate of nominal reserve creation, μ_t. Such a policy increases the profits of banks by decreasing the bond rate and decreases the probability of financial instability. This is a benefit for central bank objectives. But an increase in the rate of reserve creation also increases the rate of inflation between the current and the next period, and that is a cost. The choice of μ_t involves weighing the benefits of increased financial stability against the costs of higher inflation. The first and second order conditions for an internal maximum of equation (28a) are, respectively:

$$F_\mu \equiv -\mu_t + gf'(\pi_t)\frac{\partial \pi_t}{\partial r_{bt}}\frac{dr_{bt}}{d\mu_t} = 0 \quad (34a)$$

$$F_{\mu\mu} \equiv -\left[1 - g(K\bar{x})^2\left\{f''(\pi_t)\left(\frac{\partial \pi_t}{\partial r_{bt}}\right)^2 + f'(\pi_t)\left[\frac{N}{c} + 2(1-\tau)^2\frac{d_0}{D}\left(1 - \frac{d_0}{D}\right)\right]\right\} + gK\bar{x}f'(\pi_t)\frac{\partial \pi_t}{\partial r_{bt}}\right] < 0. \quad (34b)$$

Since (from the discussion in section 3) $\partial\pi_t/\partial r_{bt}$ is negative and (from equation (32a)) $dr_{bt}/d\mu_t$ is also negative, the first order condition in equation (34a) implies that the rate of reserve creation by the central bank is positive for *every* possible realization of the intra-period shocks. Thus central bank concern for the stability of the banking system creates an inflationary bias similar to the one produced by the Kydland-Prescott (1977) and Barro-Gordon (1983) employment motive. But there is an important difference. In the case of the employment motive perfect foresight with respect to central bank policies by the public neutralizes any potential effect of nominal policies on real variables. As explained in the remainder of this section, this is not the case here. The realization by banks of the central bank's policy induces them to charge lower real loan rates and to supply a larger real quantity of credit.

In order to determine the effect of the central bank's policy on the loan market it is necessary to complete the characterization of EB. This is needed to obtain a fully specified solution for Er_b in equation (24a). Banks are aware of the inflationary bias of the Fed and take that into consideration when forecasting the bond rate at the beginning of the period. In particular, they know from equation (29) that

$$B = B_{-1} + dB_F = B_{-1} - dR$$

where dB_F is the amount of bonds purchased by the Fed through open market operations during the period. Using equation (27) and the approximation $e^{\mu} \cong \mu$, we obtain

$$dR = R_{-1}\mu.$$

Substituting this equation into the previous one and taking expected values,

$$EB = B_{-1} - R_{-1}E\mu = B_{-1} - R_{-1}gEf'(\pi)\frac{\partial \pi}{\partial r_b}\frac{\partial r_b}{\partial \mu} < B_{-1}. \quad (24b)$$

The last equality follows by rearranging the first order condition in equation (34a) and by taking expected values.[25] The inequality follows from the inflationary bias of the central bank. Equation (24b) implies that in the absence of expected changes in the supply of bonds from non-central bank sources, private banks expect the Fed to purchase some of the existing debt because of the Fed's concern for the stability of the banking system. Note that the *higher* this concern relative to the concern for price stability, the larger g and the lower EB. But a lower expected stock of bonds leads (through equation (24a)) to a lower expected real bond rate and (through equation (22)) to a lower loan rate and to a higher volume of commercial loans. The upshot is that the inflationary bias of the central bank produces a permanent downward effect on loan rates and that this effect is stronger the higher g. This effect is permanent in spite of the fact that the Fed's ability to affect real rates is limited only to the time interval over which the price level is fixed. The reason is that the central bank has this bias in every period and is known by banks to have it when they set their loan rates at the beginning of each period.

Thus, in contrast to the employment motive that only gives rise to an inflation bias but does not affect real variables, the financial stability motive induces *both* an inflationary bias and an expansion in the real quantity of loans.

6. An Explanation for the Fed's Tendency To Smooth Interest Rates

We saw in section 2 that an unexpected intra-period decrease in the demand for deposits or an increase in the bond rate due to an upward shock to the supply of bonds or a downward shock to the demand for bonds decreases the profits of the banking industry. When profits are lower the likelihood of bank failures is larger and the marginal value to the Fed of an incremental increase in the profits of the banking industry is larger. The Fed is, therefore, more willing to tolerate larger increases in bank reserves, even if they increase the rate of inflation provided the decrease in profits is thereby attenuated.

But, as explained in section 4, the Fed can dampen the short-run decrease in banks' profits by stepping up the rate of reserve creation, thereby decreasing the bond rate and the deposit rate (see equations (32a) and (10a)). The Fed's tendency to follow such a policy is stronger when unanticipated shocks to financial markets raise the bond rate and the deposit rate and concurrently decrease profits. On this view the Fed has no long-term concern about the level of interest rates per se. However, due to the short-run negative correlation between the bond rate and the profits of the banking industry, the Fed at least partially offsets unanticipated increases in interest rates in order to dampen the adverse effect that such increases have on the profits and the stability of the banking system. This is consistent with the minutes from the February 1963 report of the Federal Advisory Council (FAC) to the Board. The FAC advised the board that "the principal thesis of the Council's thinking was that bankers would accommodate to almost any policy of restraint when it was applied gradually, but that sudden twists caused serious dislocations" (Woolley, 1984, p. 118, footnote 9).

Conversely, when unanticipated shocks decrease interest rates and increase the profits of banks, the value to the Fed of further increases in profits is diminished. It therefore puts more emphasis on reducing the rate of inflation by reducing the rate of reserve creation below its mean value. As a result, the decrease in interest rates is not as large as it would have been without an active policy on the part of the Fed.

The upshot is that the central bank smoothes short-run fluctuations in real rates. When shocks push rates unexpectedly above their mean level, the bank steps up the rate of reserve creation and dampens the increase in rates. When shocks decrease rates below their mean level, the bank slows down the rate of reserve creation and dampens the decrease in rates.

We turn now to a more precise demonstration of those intuitive results. In order to gain a better understanding of the processes involved, it is convenient to examine first the response of the Fed to each shock in isolation. Consider the Fed's response to an unanticipated shock to the excess demand for bonds, ε_b. Performing a comparative statics experiment with respect to ε_b on the central bank's first order condition in equation (34a) and evaluating the resulting change in the rate of growth of reserves at the no-shocks equilibrium, we obtain[26]

$$\frac{d\mu}{d\varepsilon_b} = \frac{NgK^2\bar{x}}{-F_{\mu\mu}}\Bigg[f''(\pi)N\Bigg\{\frac{r_b}{c} + 2(1-\tau) \cdot \left(1 - \frac{d_0}{D}\right)\frac{d_0}{DN}\Big((1-\tau)d_0 r_b + A_d\Big) - \ell^p\Bigg\} + f'(\pi)\left\{\frac{1}{c} + \frac{2}{N}(1-\tau)^2\frac{d_0^2}{DN}\left(1 - \frac{d_0}{D}\right)\right\}\Bigg]. \tag{35}$$

Since $-F_{\mu\mu}$ is positive by the second order condition in equation (34b), the sign of this expression depends on the sign of the bracketed expression which is negative if and only if

$$\theta \equiv \left|\frac{f''(\pi)}{f'(\pi)}\right| > \frac{\frac{1}{c} + \frac{2}{N}(1-\tau)^2\frac{d_0}{D}\left(1 - \frac{d_0}{D}\right)}{N\left[\frac{r_b}{c} + 2(1-\tau)\left(1 - \frac{d_0}{D}\right)\frac{d_0}{D}\frac{(1-\tau)d_0 r_b + A_d}{N} - \ell^p\right]^2}. \tag{36}$$

The right-hand side of equation (36) tends to zero as N becomes large and is likely to be small already for a moderately large number of banks. The left-hand side is formally analogous to a coefficient of absolute risk aversion. In the present context it measures how quickly the marginal contribution of additional profits to banks' stability diminishes with the level of profits of the banking industry. It may also be interpreted as reflecting how quickly the marginal "utility" of the Fed from further increases in banks' stability decreases with additional increases in stability. It obviously may reflect a mixture of both elements. The first element is determined by the structure of the economy while the second depends on the preferences of the central bank. We refer to θ as the index of aversion to instability remembering that, in general, it is affected by both the structure of the economy and the preferences of the central bank. The higher θ the quicker the decrease in the marginal utility of profits because of the combined effects of further profits on stability and of more stability on the objectives of the central bank. The condition in equation (36) is satisfied if the index of aversion to instability is sufficiently large. The following proposition summarizes the main qualitative result.

Proposition 1: For a sufficiently large number of banks and/or a sufficiently large index of aversion to instability, the central bank decreases the rate of growth of reserves when the intra-period excess demand for bonds increases. The precise condition appears in equation (36).

Since the condition in (36) is likely to be satisfied even for moderately large values of N and of θ, the rest of the discussion is based on the presumption that it is satisfied and that, therefore,

$$\frac{d\mu}{d\varepsilon_b} < 0. \tag{35a}$$

An immediate consequence of equation (35a) is that the central bank smoothes fluctuations in the bond rate. This can be seen by noting, from equation (15), that a decrease in ε_b raises the bond rate. Equation (35a) implies that the central bank reacts to this increase by stepping up the rate of reserves creation, which from (32a), pushes the bond rate in the opposite direction.

We turn now to the response of the central bank to an unanticipated shock to the demand for deposits. Performing a comparative statics experiment with respect to a change in ε_d on the first order condition in equation (34a), it can be shown that the central bank responds to an increase in ε_d by decreasing μ provided conditions similar to those in proposition 1 are satisifed. The derivation and the precise condition are in part 1 of the Appendix. The main qualitative result is summarized in the following proposition.

Proposition 2: For a sufficiently large number of banks and/or a sufficiently large index of aversion to instability, the central bank responds to an unanticipated increase in the demand for deposits by slowing down the rate of reserves expansion.

Proposition 2 implies that the central bank attenuates fluctuations in the bond rate which are due to unanticipated shocks to the demand for deposits. The argument is similar to that used when the origin of shocks is in the bond market. A decrease in the demand for deposits raises interest rates. The central bank responds, according to proposition 2, by stepping up the rate of reserve creation thus at least partially offsetting the short-run increase in rates.

In summary, if either of the following holds: (1) The number of banks is large, (2) The index of aversion to instability is sufficiently large,[27]

$$\frac{d\mu}{d\varepsilon_b} < 0, \quad \frac{d\mu}{d\varepsilon_d} < 0 \tag{37}$$

and the central bank smoothes interest rates in the face of short-run shocks to both the bond and deposit markets.

In general, shocks to both the bond and the deposit market may occur simultaneously and not always in the same direction. It is, therefore, not possible to rule out *particular* configurations of shocks for which one of r_b or r_d increases and profits still increase because the other rate decreases by a sufficient amount. However, such cases will not be typical if the correlation between profits and interest rates is negative in the short run. Provided the shocks ε_d and ε_b have symmetric distributions and are independent, the covariance between the profits of the banking industry and the bond rate is[28]

$$\text{cov}(\pi, r_b) = -N\left[\ell^p + \frac{r_b^*}{c}\right]\text{Var}\ (r_b) \tag{38}$$

where Var (r_b) is the intra-period variance of the bond rate around its no-shocks value, r_b^*. Since the real bond rate is usually positive, the expression in equation (38) is negative, confirming that, in the absence of intervention, the profits of the banking industry are negatively correlated with the bond rate.[29]

In general, the Fed responds to a combination of the shocks ε_b and ε_d. If the realization of shocks changes profits in a given direction, the Fed responds by altering the rate of change of reserves so as to move the bond rate in the same direction. Since, in the absence of intervention, profits and the bond rate are negatively correlated, this implies that, on average, the Fed acts so as to dampen fluctuations in r_b. Equations (37) and (32a) imply that the Fed responds to an increase in either of ε_b or ε_d by moving the short-term bond rate in a direction that is opposite to the effect of these shocks on the bond rate in the absence of intervention. This is formalized by the Fed's response function,

$$R(\varepsilon_b, \varepsilon_d),$$

that appears as one of the determinants of the equilibrium short-term bond rate in equation (15). Since, in the absence of intervention, the effect of increases in ε_b and in ε_d on r_b is negative, the partial derivative of $R(\cdot)$ with respect to either argument is positive. Hence the main result of the article, stated in terms of equation (15), is that the effects of ε_b and ε_d on r_b through the Fed's response function are opposite in sign to the direct effects of those shocks on r_b.

Note that the existence of a non-zero correlation between ε_b and ε_d does not alter the fact that the central bank needs to intervene. But the sign and magnitude of the correlation affects the extent of intervention. A positive contemporaneous correlation between ε_b and ε_d is likely to increase the necessity for the Fed's intervention while a negative one is likely to reduce it. However, except for the extreme case in which movements in ε_b and in ε_d, in the absence of intervention, exactly offset each other, leaving the profits of the banking system unaltered, some intervention is necessary. A sufficiently high degree of negative correlation between the shocks may alter the sign of the partial derivatives of $R(\cdot)$. On the other hand, positive serial correlation between ε_b and ε_d reinforces the likelihood that the partial derivatives of $R(\cdot)$ are positive. Provided the shocks ε_d and ε_b are mostly affected by common disturbances to the supply of funds, the second case seems more likely.

As noted above, the hypothesis about the Fed's behavior embedded in equation (28) reflects a basic externality. Each financial institution cares only about its own profits, but the Fed is concerned about the profitability of the entire system. Hence when there is an unexpected cumulation of losses across a number of financial institutions, the Fed's reaction can be expected to be more vigorous. In order to see this effect in isolation, suppose that the profits of the entire banking system in equation (13) are unexpectedly reduced by an exogenous amount L. To determine the central bank's reaction to this event, we perform a comparative statics experiment with respect to L on the first order condition in equation (34a). The resulting expression is:

$$\frac{d\mu}{dL} = \frac{g}{F_{\mu\mu}} f''(\pi) \frac{\partial \pi}{\partial r_b} \frac{dr_b}{d\mu} .$$

Since $\partial\pi/\partial r_b < 0$ and $F_{\mu\mu} < 0$ by the second order condition in equation (34b), this expression is positive. Hence an accumulation of unexpected losses across wide segments of the financial system induces the central bank to expand high-powered money at a higher rate. This result may have some power in explaining recent monetary accelerations as being partially due to the arrival of new information about the magnitude of losses in the thrift industry.

7. Implications for the Procyclical Behavior of Money Growth and the Time Series Characteristics of Nominal Rates

The shock ε_b to the excess demand for bonds may be taken as a proxy for the cyclical position of the economy. When it is negative, there is an excess supply of bonds due to high cyclical activity. Conversely, a positive value of ε_b is associated with low cyclical activity. Since, from equation (37), the central bank steps up the rate of reserve creation, μ, when ε_b is negative and reduces it when ε_b is positive, the behavior of μ is procyclical. There is evidence that base money growth in the United States behaves procyclically (Rasche, 1988). ε_b can also be interpreted as a seasonal shock to the demand for liquidity of the type that induced financial panics in the pre-Fed era (Donaldson, 1989b).

Miron (1986) and Mankiw, Miron, and Weil (1987) find that after the creation of the Fed, short-term nominal rates became nearer to random walks than prior to that time. Friedman and Schwartz (1963, p. 293) report a similar phenomenon. To examine whether this change could have been caused by the Fed's concern for the profits and the stability of the financial system, I compare the behavior of the nominal bond rate in the presence of central bank intervention with its behavior in the absence of intervention. From equation (15) the short-term nominal bond rate in the presence of intervention is[30]

$$n_b^I = r_b^I + E^I\mu = K\left[\frac{E^IB}{P^{pI}} + N\ell^{pI} - \left(\varepsilon_b + (1-\tau)\left(1 - \frac{d_0}{D}\right)\varepsilon_d\right)\right] + R(\varepsilon_b, \varepsilon_d) + E^I\mu \tag{39a}$$

where the superscript "I" designates equilibrium values in the presence of interest rate smoothing by the central bank. In the absence of intervention the reaction function $R(\cdot)$ vanishes and there is no systematic expectation of inflation—the expected value of μ is zero. Hence without a central bank the equilibrium value of the nominal bond rate is

$$n_b = r_b = K\left[\frac{EB}{P^p} + N\ell^p - \left(\varepsilon_b + (1-\tau)\left(1 - \frac{d_0}{D}\right)\varepsilon_d\right)\right] \tag{39b}$$

where, only in this section, variables that do not carry the index I denote the equilibrium values of these variables in the absence of any intervention by the central bank.

Since the shocks ε_b and ε_d are transitory, the expected values of n_b^I and of n_b conditional on the realizations of those shocks are, respectively,

$$K\left[\frac{E^I B}{P^{pI}} + N\ell^{pI}\right] + E^I \mu \tag{40a}$$

$$K\left[\frac{EB}{P^p} + N\ell^p\right]. \tag{40b}$$

In order to judge whether one time series is more nearly a random walk than another, it is necessary to specify an index of nearness to a random walk. I use as a measure of the nearness of a time series to a random walk the absolute value of the difference between the current state of the series and its predicted value given the current state. For a random walk this index is zero, and it increases monotonically as the series departs more from a random walk. From equations (39) and (40) this measure, with and without intervention, respectively, is:

$$\left|-K\left[\varepsilon_b + (1-\tau)\left(1-\frac{d_0}{D}\right)\varepsilon_d\right] + R(\varepsilon_b, \varepsilon_d)\right| \tag{41a}$$

$$\left|K\left[\varepsilon_b + (1-\tau)\left(1-\frac{d_0}{D}\right)\varepsilon_d\right]\right|. \tag{41b}$$

Since the partial derivatives of $R(\cdot)$ are both positive, the index of nearness to a random walk is always smaller in the presence of interest rate smoothing than in its absence.[31] The upshot is that the theory presented in this article is consistent with the change that occured in the time series properties of short-term interest rates after the creation of the Fed as reported in Miron (1986) and Mankiw, Miron, and Weil (1987).

Strictly speaking, this result has been demonstrated only for the case in which exogenous shocks are white noises. However, I believe that, as long as the Fed smoothes only purely transitory movements in interest rates, the same argument extends to a wide variety of specifications for the exogenous shocks. When the shocks have some predictable persistence, the forecasts in equations (40) incorporate this persistence. Since the Fed smoothes out only purely transitory shocks, its reaction function still depends only on terms like ε_b and ε_d which now have to be interpreted as the transitory parts of the exogenous shocks. Subject to this reinterpretation equations (41) remain the same and the previous argument extends to the more general specification.[32]

8. Extension to the Case of Credit Lines

To this point the analysis was based on the assumption that the entire volume of loans is predetermined before the realization of shocks during the period of the loan. In practice part of banking credit takes the form of credit lines in which borrowers are free to determine the actual amount borrowed, up to a predetermined ceiling, after the realization of shocks (Brady, 1985).

This section examines the robustness of the main result of the article to this alternative form of loan contract. Specifically it is assumed now that banks passively accommodate any intra-period changes in the demand for loans at the loan rate which was set at the beginning of the period.

The main difference between this framework and the previous one is that now shocks to the demand for loans affect the ex post profitability of the banking industry in addition to shocks to the bond and deposit markets. The loan rate is still determined by solving the problem in equation (19). Before shocks realize $E\varepsilon_\ell = 0$. Hence the ex ante maximization problem with lines of credit is formally equivalent to the same problem when loan volume is determined ex ante and the equilibrium loan rate for both problems is given by equation (22). The difference is that now the volume of intra-period loans is determined by the ex post demand for loans instead of being equal to ℓ^p from equation (24) as was previously the case. Equation (10a) still represents the ex post equilibrium level of r_d.

The ex post equilibrium demand for bonds by the individual bank is given by equation (10b) with ℓ^p replaced by

$$\ell(r_\ell^p, r_\ell^p, 2_\ell) = \frac{A_\ell + \varepsilon_\ell - \ell_0 r_\ell^p}{N}. \tag{42}$$

Similarly the expression for total profits of banks in equation (13) remains the same except that ℓ^p is replaced by the expression in (42). As a consequence, profits become dependent on the shock, ε_ℓ, to the demand for loans. Since the intra-period demand for bonds by banks depends now on ε_ℓ, the bond rate becomes a function of ε_ℓ, too. The precise relation between r_b and ε_ℓ is obtained by substituting equation (42) instead of ℓ^p in equation (15). An intra-period increase in the demand for loans increases the bond rate. The reason is that banks have to supply a larger demand for credit. This reduces their liquidity. They partially restore liquidity by reducing their bond portfolios. This pushes the bond rate up.

If the loan rate is larger than the bond rate, an unexpected increase in the demand for loans generally has an ambiguous effect on the profits of the banking system. On one hand, profits are squeezed, as in the previous case, because of the increase in the bond rate brought about by the larger demand for loans. On the other hand, since $r_\ell^p > r_b$, a substitution of loans for bonds increases profits. However, for a sufficiently large number of banks the negative effect on profits is likely to dominate. Details appear in part 3 of the Appendix. We shall therefore proceed under the presumption that

$$\frac{d\pi}{d\varepsilon_\ell} = \frac{\partial\pi}{\partial\varepsilon_\ell} + \frac{\partial\pi}{\partial r_b}\frac{\partial r_b}{\partial\varepsilon_\ell} < 0. \tag{43}$$

The maximization problem of the central bank and the corresponding first and second order conditions remain as in equations (28a) and (34) except that banks' profits now also depend on the realization of the shock ε_ℓ. Totally differentiating the first order condition of the central bank in (34a) with respect to ε_ℓ, evaluating at the no-shocks equilibrium, and rearranging

$$\frac{d\mu}{d\varepsilon_\ell} = \frac{gK\bar{x}}{F_{\mu\mu}}\left[f''(\pi)\frac{\partial\pi}{\partial r_b}\frac{d\pi}{d\varepsilon_\ell} + f'(\pi)\left(\frac{\frac{N}{c} + (1-\tau)^2 d_0\left(1-\frac{d_0}{D}\right)\frac{2d_0}{D}}{\frac{N}{c} + (1-\tau)^2 d_0\left(1-\frac{d_0}{D}\right) + s_0} - 1\right)\right]. \tag{44}$$

$F_{\mu\mu} < 0$ by the second order condition. Equation (43) implies that the first term in brackets on the right-hand side of (44) is negative. Since $2d_0/D < 1$ and $s_0 > 0$, the second term is negative, too. Hence

$$\frac{d\mu}{d\varepsilon_\ell} > 0. \tag{45}$$

The central bank responds to the increased demand for credit by increasing the rate of reserves creation. It thereby, at least partially, offsets the upward effect of this increased demand on the bond rate. The bank's attempt to preserve the profits of the banking industry within a "reasonable range" induces it to accommodate changes in credit demand.

The upshot is that the major result of the article—that the central bank smoothes fluctuations in interest rates—extends to the case in which credit is allocated to customers via credit lines. As a matter of fact, in the presence of credit lines, the bank smoothes fluctuations in interest rates that are due to shocks to the loan market as well as to shocks to the bond and deposit markets. Since shocks to the demand for credit are positively correlated with the cycle, the procyclical response of reserves growth is amplified by the existence of credit lines.

8. Concluding Remarks

The explanation for the Fed's tendency to dampen fluctuations in interest rates relies on the presumption that the interest rate on all loan contracts is determined prior to the determination of the cost of funds to banks. The assumption that this contractual arrangement applies to *all* loans is made for simplicity and is not essential. Even if the interest rate on *part* of bank loans is adjusted simultaneously with changes in the cost of funds, the Fed will have an incentive to smooth interest rates provided the fraction of loans with predetermined rates is sufficiently large. This observation implies that the incentive of the Fed to engage in interest rate smoothing depends on the degree of inflexibility in the terms of banks' loans. In particular when, other things the same, a larger fraction of credit is marketed via variable rates loans, the central bank's tendency to smooth interest rates diminishes. But since the correlation between the rate to which variable rate loans are indexed and the cost of funds to banks is not perfect, the incentive to smooth rates does not disappear.[33]

A basic implication of this article is that financial instability is more likely when interest rates rise. This is consistent with the evidence in table 1 of Donaldson (1989a) who finds that in the pre-Fed era interest rates rose to very high levels during financial panics.[34]

Some concern of the central bank for banks' profits can always be justified on the ground that sufficiently high profits are necessary for the stability of the banking system. But the intensity of this concern (measured by g in equation (28)) may also be due to "captive regulator" elements in the motives of the central bank. Such motives tend to strengthen the tendency toward interest rate smoothing. In any case this article has no implications for the extent to which the policy of interest rate smoothing followed by the Fed is due only to its concern for the public interest or also to "captive regulator" elements. Woolley (1984) attributes some weight to such elements, particularly during the early seventies.

The analysis in this article abstracted from the required reserve ratio as an instrument of short-run policy first because it is seldom used as such by the Fed. This raises an interesting question concerning the reason for such allocation of instruments. A probable answer is that the impact of open market operations on interest rates and banks profits is more immediate and clearcut than that of changes in reserve requirements that affect the financial system with a lag. In addition, reserve requirements are not as flexible as open market operations since their span is limited to the positive range ($\tau \geq 0$).

In order to maintain the analytic framework within managable proportions we have abstracted from possible dependencies between the demand for loans and deposits at the individual bank (Cukierman, 1978). We have also abstracted from the difference between borrowed and unborrowed reserves. This distinction, following the useful analysis in Goodfriend (1982), could probably be incorporated in the framework of this article.

However, it is unlikely that such extensions will alter the basic result of the article.

Note that the controversy about whether the business cycle is largely due to monetary factors (Friedman and Schwartz, 1963) or to real factors (Plosser, 1990) does not affect the arguments in this article. The reason is that interest rate smoothing and an inflationary bias of policy arise as a consequence of the interaction between the Fed and the banking system even in the absence of a short-run Phillips curve.

In closing, note the following interesting implication of the article's framework: an unexpected increase in the supply of bonds by the federal government to finance an increase in the budget deficit triggers (by raising the bond rate) increased monetization by the monetary authority in the short run. Again, this is due to the concern this authority has for the stability of the banking system.

Notes

1. See, for example, *Federal Reserve Bulletin* (July 1984, p. 548). Bernanke (1983) argues persuasively that financial crises retard capital formation, thereby inducing a real output cost.

2. The fraction of credit marketed through such contracts was even larger prior to the acceleration of inflation in the seventies.

3. The maturity of demand deposits and of money market accounts is obviously at the continuous discretion of depositors.

4. A bank normally has to invest some resources in gathering information about a borrower before granting a loan. No similar investment is necessary in order to accept a deposit.

5. The rise in costs partially reflects the increasing difficulties of borrowing successively larger amounts at the discount window.

6. This is consistent with Woolley's (1984, p. 72) observation that bankers care little about the ease or tightness of monetary policy as long as they are not caught by surprise.

7. See Brady (1985).

8. Due to locational and other idiosyncratic characteristics.

9. A similar device has been used in Brunner, Cukierman, and Meltzer (1983). A totally different view of the origin of the Fed's ability to affect interest rates is presented by Goodfriend (1987). In Goodfriend's model the price level adjusts instantaneously to always clear the money market. In his model the central bank affects the nominal interest rate by changing the expected rate of inflation. This is done by altering the current price level for a given expected future price level. By contrast here the short-run fixity of the price level enables the central bank to temporarily affect both the real and the nominal short-term rates in the short run. Shiller (1980) presents evidence that supports the view that the Fed has some temporary influence on short-term real rates.

10. This asymmetry is due to the fact that borrowers need to know the period for which funds are available with certainty in advance while depositors prefer to retain as much flexibility as possible.

11. The banking industry model is a variant of the model in Cukierman and Sokoler (1988).

12. The case in which, due to the existence of credit lines, banks passively accommodate fluctuations in the demand for credit after the realization of shocks is discussed in section 8.

13. Treasury bills and other good quality short-term paper are the most frequently used real-life counterparts of the "bonds" in the model (Tobin, 1982).

14. Equation (8b) confirms that if $r_b > 0$ the costs of illiquidity are positive in the individual bank's equilibrium.

15. The solution for b incorporates the assumption that the ex ante Nash equilibrium which determines the amount of loans given out at the beginning of the period is also symmetric. It also incorporates the assumption that this solution occurs in the non-negative range of b. Details appear in section 4.

16. Again, use has been made of the fact that the ex ante equilibrium is also symmetric. See also previous note. Note, however, that in spite of the symmetry of both the ex ante and the ex post equilibria, profits may differ across banks due to different realizations of the idiosyncratic default shocks u_i.

17. For $N = 1{,}000$ and $d_0 = 100$, d_0/D is equal to 0.0001.

18. Letting the time index t refer to within-period realizations of shocks, a more explicit form for this expectation is $E_{t-1}B_t$ since at the beginning of period t only the realization of period's $t - 1$ shocks are known. The more explicit notation is utilized in section 5.

19. This specification abstracts from the existence of cash.

20. Incomplete information by the central bank about the realizations of the $u_i - s$ and of profits across individual banks makes it difficult to apply bank specific measures and increases the reliance of the central bank on industrywide measures to preserve profits. Even if the realizations of the $u_i - s$ were known to the central bank, the latter may find it preferable and more in the spirit of free markets to use industrywide instruments rather than bank-specific interventions. Brimmer (1989) argues that except under extraordinary circumstances, the Fed prefers generalized to specific measures.

21. To focus on the consequences of the interaction between the central bank and the private banking system in isolation, we abstract from other possible motives for inflation like the employment and the revenue motives.

22. In a model with cash this will be the case if the real demand for cash is constant. A more general formulation could incorporate leakages into cash, but it is unlikely that this would alter the main qualitative result of the article.

23. The demonstration follows: from (26a) $P_t^p = \exp[ln\, R_{t-1} + E\mu_t - \bar{x}]$. By definition $R_{t-1} = \exp[ln\, R_{t-1}]$. Substituting those two terms into (32) and rearranging, we obtain (32a).

24. An elaboration of this statement appears later.

25. Note from equation (26a) and (27) that $ln\, P_{t+1} - ln\, P_t = ln \dfrac{R_t}{R_{t-1}} = \mu_t$.

Hence the expected rate of inflation is also equal to $E\mu$ and the nominal loan rate is equal to $r_\ell^p + E\mu$.

26. Since there is no danger of confusion, the time index t is omitted. Evaluation of the derivative in (35) at the no-shock equilibrium is strictly correct for small shocks. For large shocks the expression in (35) also depends on ε_d, ε_b and on the actual rate of growth of reserves, but the general qualitative results are similar.

27. Note that either condition alone may be sufficient for the result in (37) and interest rate smoothing.

28. The covariance is evaluated around the no-shocks value of π and r_b in the absence of central bank intervention. Details appear in part 2 of the Appendix.

29. When ε_b and ε_d are positively correlated, the following additional expression appears on the right-hand side of (38):

$$\frac{\frac{2d_0}{D}\left(1 - \frac{d_0}{D}\right)(1 - \tau)}{\left[\frac{N}{c} + (2 - \tau)^2 d_0\left(1 - \frac{d_0}{D}\right) + s_0\right]^2}\left[\frac{E\varepsilon_d\varepsilon_b^2}{(P^p)^2} + \frac{2(1 - \tau)}{P^p}\left(1 - \frac{d_0}{D}\right)E\varepsilon_b\varepsilon_d^2\right].$$

But for a sufficiently large number of banks it is dominated by the negative terms in (38).

30. The first order condition in (34a) implies that (omitting the time index)

$$E^I\mu = gEf'(\cdot)\frac{\partial\pi}{\partial r_b}\frac{dr_b}{d\mu}.$$

Since $f'(\cdot) > 0$, $\partial\pi/\partial r_b < 0$, and $dr_b/d\mu < 0$ this expression is positive.

31. In this context "always" means of all possible realizations of ε_b and ε_d except the case for $\varepsilon_b = \varepsilon_d = 0$ for which the indices for the two regimes trivially coincide.

32. If, for example, the typical shock is specified as a first order Markoff process, $\nu_{t+1} = \rho\nu_t + \eta_t$, the predictable persistent part as of period t is $\rho\nu_t$ and the purely transitory part is $(1 - \rho)\nu_t$.

33. Financial institutions can also partially hedge their net maturity position through the use of future markets. However, some residual risk usually remains since available standardized future contracts are not fully tailored to meet the idiosyncratic hedging needs of individual banks.

34. See also Donaldson (1989b).

References

Barro, R. J., and Gordon, D. B. 1983. "A Positive Theory of Monetary Policy in a Natural Rate Model." *Journal of Political Economy* 91 (August):589–610.

Bernanke, B. S. 1983. "Nonmonetary Effects of the Financial Crisis in the Propagation of the Great Depression." *American Economic Review* 73 (June):257–276.

Brimmer, A. F. 1989. "Distinguished Lecture on Economics in Government: Central Banking and Systemic Risks in Capital Markets." *Journal of Economic Perspectives* 3 (Spring):3–16.

Brady, T. F. 1985. "Changes in Loan Pricing and Business Lending at Commercial Banks." *Federal Reserve Bulletin* 71 (January):1–3.

Brunner, K., Cukierman, A. and Meltzer, A. H. 1983. "Money and Economic Activity, Inventories and Business Cycles." *Journal of Monetary Economics* 11 (May):281–319.

Cukierman, A. 1978. "The Horizontal Integration of the Banking Firm, Credit Rationing and Monetary Policy." *Review of Economic Studies* 65 (February): 165–178.

Cukierman, A., and Sokoler, M. 1988. "Monetary Policy in Israel—Past, Present and Future." Presented at the May 1988 Conference of the "Pinhas Sapir Economic Policy Forum." Also published in Hebrew in *Economic Quarterly* (1989), No. 139.

Donaldson, R. G. 1989a. "Sources of Panics: Evidence from the Weekly Data." Discussion Paper 149, Woodrow Wilson School, Princeton University, October.

Donaldson, R. G. 1989b. "Panic, Liquidity and the Lender of Last Resort." Discussion Paper 150, Woodrow Wilson School, Princeton University, October.

"The Federal Reserve Position on Restructuring of Financial Regulation Responsibilities." 1984. *Federal Reserve Bulletin* 70 (July):547–557.

Friedman, M., and Schwartz, A. J. 1963. *A Monetary History of the United States: 1867–1960*. Princeton, N.J.: Princeton University Press.

Goldberg, M. A. 1982. "The Sensitivity of the Prime Rate to Changes in Money Market Conditions." Research Paper in Banking and Financial Economics, Financial Studies Section, Division of Research and Statistics, Board of Governors of the Federal Reserve System.

Goodfriend, M. 1982. "A Model of Money Stock Determination with Loan Demand and a Banking System Balance Sheet Constraint." Federal Reserve Bank of Richmond *Economic Review* 68 (January):3–16.

Goodfriend, M. 1987. "Interest Rate Smooothing and Price Level Trend-Stationarity." *Journal of Monetary Economics* 19 (May):335–348.

Goodfriend, M., and King, R. G. 1988. "Financial Deregulation, Monetary Policy and Central Banking." Federal Reserve Bank of Richmond *Economic Review* 74/5 (May/June):3–22.

Kydland, F. E., and Prescott, E. C. 1977. "Rules Rather than Discretion: The Inconsistency of Optimal Plans." *Journal of Political Economy* 85 (June):473–492.

Mankiw, N. G., Miron, J. A., and Weil, D. N. 1987. "The Adjustment of Expectations to a Change in Regime: A Study of the Founding of the Federal Reserve." *American Economic Review* 77 (June):358–374.

Meltzer, A. H. 1990. "The Federal Reserve at Seventy Five." In M. Belongia (Ed.), *Monetary Policy on the 75th Anniversary of the Federal Reserve System—Proceedings of the 14th Annual Economic Policy Conference of the Federal Reserve Bank of St. Louis*. Boston: Kluwer Academic Publishers.

Miron, J. A. 1986. "Financial Panics, the Seasonality of the Nominal Interest Rate, and the Founding of the Fed." *American Economic Review* 76 (March):125–140.

Plosser, C. I. 1990. "Money and Business Cycles; A Real Business Cycle Interpretation." In M. Belongia (Ed.), *Monetary Policy on the 75th Anniversary of the Federal Reserve System—Proceedings of the 14th Annual Economic Policy Conference of the Federal Reserve Bank of St. Louis*. Boston: Kluwer Academic Publishers.

Rasche, R. 1988. "Demand Functions for U.S. Money and Credit Measures." Econometrics and Economic Theory Paper No. 8718, Department of Economics, Michigan State University, May.

Shiller, R. J. 1980. "Can the Fed Control Real Interest Rates?" In S. Fischer (Ed.), *Rational Expectations and Economic Policy*. Chicago and London: University of Chicago Press.

Simpson, T. D., and Parkinson, P. M. 1984. "Some Implications of Financial Innovations in the U.S." *Federal Reserve Bulletin* 70 (August):621–622.

Tobin, J. 1982. "The Commercial Banking Firm: A Simple Model." *Scandinavian Journal of Economics* 84, No. 4:495–530.

Woolley, J. T. 1984. *Monetary Politics—The Federal Reserve and the Politics of Monetary Policy*. Cambridge: Cambridge University Press.

APPENDIX

1. Comparative statics with respect to ε_d and precise characterization of the conditions underlying proposition 2.

Totally differentiating the first order condition in (34a) with respect to ε_d, evaluating at the no-shocks equilibrium, and rearranging

$$\frac{d\mu}{d\varepsilon_d} = \frac{gK\bar{x}}{F_{\mu\mu}}(1-\tau)\left(1-\frac{d_0}{D}\right)\left[f''(\pi)\frac{\partial\pi}{\partial r_b}Z_1 + f'(\pi)Z_2\right] \qquad \text{(A1a)}$$

$$Z_1 \equiv \frac{2}{D}\left(d_0 r_b + \frac{A_d}{1-\tau}\right) - K\frac{\partial\pi}{\partial r_b} \qquad \text{(A1b)}$$

$$Z_2 \equiv \frac{2d_0}{D} - \frac{\dfrac{N}{c} + \dfrac{2d_0^2}{D}(1-\tau)^2\left(1-\dfrac{d_0}{D}\right)}{\dfrac{N}{c} + d_0(1-\tau)^2\left(1-\dfrac{d_0}{D}\right) + s_0} r. \qquad \text{(A1c)}$$

Since $F_{\mu\mu} < 0$, $d\mu/d\varepsilon_d < 0$ if and only if the expression in brackets on the right-hand side of ($A1a$) is positive. Provided $r_b > 0$ and the demand for deposits at a zero deposit rate is positive $Z_1 > 0$ since $\partial\pi/\partial r_b < 0$. Hence a necessary and sufficient condition for $d\mu/d\varepsilon_d < 0$ is

$$\theta \equiv \left|\frac{f''(\pi)}{f'(\pi)}\right| > \frac{Z_2}{Z_1 \frac{\partial \pi}{\partial_{r_b}}}. \tag{A2}$$

The denominator of this expression is negative. By using the definition of D and rearranging, it can be shown that

$$Z_2 \gtreqless 0 \text{ as } N^2(N-1) \lesseqgtr 2\frac{d_0}{d}\frac{s_0}{c}. \tag{A3}$$

If $N^2(N-1) \leq 2\frac{d_0 s_0}{d\,c}$ the condition in (A2) is always satisfied since in this case the right-hand side of (A2) is either negative or zero. If N is large enough to make $N^2(N-1) > 2d_0s_0/dc$, the right-hand side of (A2) is positive. However, for a sufficiently large N the right-hand side of (A2) tends to zero from above so that even if θ is moderately large the condition in (A2) is satisfied. This can be seen by using equation (14) and (16b) to rewrite the right-hand side of (A2) as

$$\frac{Z_2}{Z_1 \frac{\partial \pi}{\partial r_b}} = \frac{1}{N} \cdot \frac{\dfrac{2d_0}{D} - \dfrac{\frac{1}{c} + \frac{2(1-\tau)d_0}{D}g(N)}{\frac{1}{c} + (1-\tau)g(N) + \frac{s_0}{N}}}{\left(\frac{1}{c} + \frac{2(1-\tau)d_0}{D}g(N)\right)r_b + 2\frac{A_d}{D}g(N) - \ell^p}$$
$$\cdot \frac{1}{\dfrac{2T}{D} - \dfrac{\left\{\frac{1}{c} + \frac{2(1-\tau)d_0}{D}g(N)\right\}r_b + 2\frac{A_d}{D}g(N) - \ell^p}{\frac{1}{c} + (1-\tau)g(N) + \frac{s_0}{N}}} \tag{A4}$$

where

$$g(N) \equiv \frac{d_0}{N}(1-\tau)\left(1 - \frac{d_0}{D}\right); \quad T \equiv d_0 r_b + \frac{A_d}{1-\tau}.$$

When N becomes large, $g(N)$ tends to zero and the last two terms on the right-hand side of (A4) tend to

$$\frac{1}{\left(\frac{r_b}{c} - \ell^p\right)^2}$$

while $1/N$ tends to zero. Hence for N sufficiently large (A4) tends to zero from above so that condition (A4) is satisfied even for small values of θ.

2. Derivation of the covariance in equation (38)

Let π^*, r_b^* be the values of π and r_b at the no-shocks equilibrium. From (13) and (15)

$$\pi^* = (r_\ell^p - r_b^*)\, N\ell^p + \frac{1}{D}\left(1 - \frac{d_0}{D}\right)[(1 - \tau)d_0 r_b^* + A_d]^2 + \frac{N}{2c}(r_b^*)^2. \quad \text{(A6)}$$

By definition

$$\operatorname{cov}(\pi, r_b) \equiv E(\pi - \pi^*)(r_b - r_b^*). \quad \text{(A7)}$$

Equation (38) is derived by using (13) and (A6) in (A7), rearranging and using the statistical independence of ε_b and ε_d and the fact that $E\varepsilon_b^3 = E\varepsilon_d^3 = 0$ by symmetry of the distributions of ε_d and of ε_b.

3. Demonstration that an increase in ε_ℓ reduces banks' profits if the number of banks is sufficiently large

Replacing ℓ^p in equation (13) with the expression from equation (42) and differentiating totally with respect to ε_ℓ

$$\frac{d\pi}{d\varepsilon_\ell} = \frac{\partial\pi}{\partial\varepsilon_\ell} + \frac{\partial\pi}{\partial r_b}\frac{\partial\pi_b}{\partial\varepsilon_\ell}$$

$$= r_\ell^p - r_b + \frac{\left(\frac{1}{c} + \frac{2(1-\tau)d_0}{D}g(N)\right)r_b + \frac{2}{D}g(N)(A_d + \varepsilon_d) - \ell(r_\ell^p, r_\ell^p, \varepsilon_\ell)}{\frac{1}{c} + (1-\tau)^2\frac{d_0}{N}\left(1 - \frac{d_0}{D}\right) + \frac{s_0}{N}} \quad \text{(A8)}$$

For N sufficiently large this expression tends to

$$\lim_{N\to\infty}\frac{d\pi}{d\varepsilon_\ell} = r_\ell^p - r_b - c\,\ell(r_\ell^p, r_\ell^p, \varepsilon_\ell). \quad \text{(A9)}$$

Obviously if $r_\ell^p \le r_b$ this expression is unambiguously negative. However, even when $r_\ell^p > r_b$ it is likely to be negative if the costs of illiquidity as measured by c are not negligible. For $c = 1$, for example, the expression in (A9) is negative provided:

$$\ell(r_\ell^p, r_\ell^p, \varepsilon_\ell) > r_\ell^p - r_b.$$

Commentary

by Michelle R. Garfinkel

In his article, Alex Cukierman has undertaken the difficult task of rationalizing the observation made by many that a goal or an intermediate objective of monetary policy in the United States is to smooth fluctuations in interest rates. In a setting where banks serve to transform short-term liabilities into long-term loans for their customers, he argues that if the Fed is concerned about both the stability of the banking system and price stability, then optimal monetary policy involves reducing the variance of interest rates. Although other economists have suggested that an objective of financial stability motivates a policy of smoothing interest rates—for example, Goodfriend (1987)—Cukierman formalizes this idea by studying a choice-theoretic model of monetary policy in which the banking system is specified on the basis of micro-principles.[1] In equilibrium, by trading off the costs of financial instability against those of inflation, the Fed dampens short-term movements in interest rates. The equilibrium tradeoff, however, involves what Cukierman calls an "inflationary bias." Without going into much of the technical detail of his analysis, my comments on his positive theory focus on his modeling strategy and his choice of an equilibrium.

The Usefulness of Choice-Theoretic Modeling of Policy

Although I am sympathetic to Cukierman's modeling strategy, I suspect that many people are not. With this in mind and to fulfill my role as a discussant, the usefulness of choice-theoretic modeling deserves a few comments. Critics invariably argue that, in any positive theory of policy, the assumptions are so crucial to the predictions of the model that the predictions have little content. In Cukierman's theory, the assumptions include not only the Fed's preferences but the assumed structure of the economy as well. Even if one accepts that the Fed's preferences are price stability and stability in financial markets, what ensures that smoothing interest rates generates the best possible outcome? In other words, could there be an alternative set of institutional arrangements that could make everyone, or at least the Fed, better off? The institutional arrangements assumed in Cukierman's model are meant to capture the essential characteristics of the banking system. Without any rationalization of these institutions, however, his positive theory of monetary policy might seem incomplete.

Indeed, the assumed institutional arrangements themselves create friction in the economy that forces the Fed to face the tradeoff between financial and price stability with only one instrument, the growth of reserves. On a closer inspection, however, the reader sees that there could be two instruments available to the Fed in Cukierman's article—not only the growth of reserves, but the reserve requirement ratio. But only the first instrument is considered. If the Fed were permitted to manipulate the reserve ratio, then it might be able to achieve both of its goals simultaneously without smoothing interest rates or doing so to a lesser extent.[2]

To take choice-theoretic modeling to an extreme, one must believe that our historically given institutions were established in an optimal way. Accordingly, it is conceivable that the institutions were chosen so as to maximize the benefits of having a competitive banking system while minimizing the costs of financial instability. Given this optimal tradeoff, financial instability might not be a concern in day-to-day monetary policy.

Even in the context of Cukierman's model, it is not immediately obvious what financial stability is or why it should be desired by the Fed. Since there is no possibility of default on loans, financial crises are precluded in the model. The lack of a meaningful notion of financial stability is underscored in Cukierman's formulation of the Fed's objective function. In particular, he translates financial stability of the banking system into a function of the banking industry's total profits. Even in the absence of any shocks to credit markets, the model implies that the Fed chooses to add reserves to the banking system to enhance banks' profits. That is, without any apparent need for interest rate stabilization, the Fed tolerates inflation. But the Fed is less willing to tolerate a positive inflation when profits are above than when they are below their mean value. Hence, we might interpret his analysis as suggesting that the Fed's policy of smoothing interest rates is being driven by its desire to maximize banks'profits (as suggested by Cosimano and Van Huyck (1989)) while stabilizing prices. Why maximizing banks' profits would be considered desirable, from a social welfare perspective, remains unclear.

On a more technical note, the result that the Fed smooths interest rates appears to be partly driven by the assumption that the various shocks to the credit market are independent. In a general equilibrium framework, however, one might expect there to be a negative correlation between shocks to the demand for bonds and to the demand for demand deposits since these assets are at least partial substitutes. In this case, the effect of a negative shock, say, in the excess demand for demand deposits (which will depress profits) would be partially offset by an accompanying positive shock to the excess demand for bonds without any actions by the Fed. Hence, a negative correlation of demand shocks, not considered in Cukierman's partial equilibrium analysis, would weaken the need for the Fed to smooth interest rates.

Game-Theoretic Aspects of Monetary Policy

My second set of comments on Cukierman's article relates to his particular choice of an equilibrium—a one-shot Nash equilibrium, in which the banks take the Fed's policy as given and, more important, the Fed takes the behavior of the banks as given. As a dominant and presumably rational player in this model, the Fed would realize that it could be better off if it set its policy after taking into account the policy's impact on banks' behavior. By ignoring the game-theoretic or, equivalently, the strategic aspects of monetary policy in his model, Cukierman derives a suboptimal policy for the Fed.

The suboptimality is reflected in an inflationary bias. That is, the equilibrium inflation rate that he derives generally is not equal to the equilibrium inflation that would emerge if the Fed realized the impact that its policy had on banks' behavior. That inflation is positive, however, could overstate the inefficiency. Indeed, an equilibrium inflation that is positive stems partly from the Fed's preference to maximize bank profits because, under Cukierman's assumptions, profits are increasing in reserves. Hence, from the Fed's perspective, the positive inflation is not necessarily suboptimal. But because the Fed does not recognize and exploit the indirect dependence of banks' profits on its own actions through their effect on banks' policies, the equilibrium inflation in Cukierman's solution generally will not equal the optimal rate.

In fact, and in contrast to the typical game-theoretic models of monetary policy, the inflation bias need not be positive in this model. Whether the bias is positive or negative depends on how expected reserve creation by the Fed indirectly affects banks' profits as well as actual inflation. The ambiguity of the sign of the bias arises because, in Cukierman's model, the total effect of expectations on the Fed's utility through its effects on banks' profits and actual inflation depends on parameter values. To illustrate the possible outcomes, I present in the Appendix a simple game-theoretic model that focuses on expectations' effects on bank profits. The results, which are only summarized here, are fairly intuitive. If the effect of inflation expectations on bank profits is negative, then the marginal benefit of inflation through its direct and indirect effects is lower than that of the direct effect. The optimal policy would keep inflation lower than the policy in the Nash one-shot solution; in this case, the bias can be positive. If the effect of expectations on bank profits is positive, however, then the bias will be negative. This basic idea is that an optimal policy would keep inflation higher than in the Nash one-shot solution since expectations of higher inflation consistent with the optimal policy would carry an additional marginal benefit for banks' profits. In any case, provided that the effect of expectations on the Fed's objective function is non-zero, a policy that recognizes its effects on expectations will dominate the policy derived by Cukierman.

The optimal policy, however, might not be a feasible outcome in the absence of some commitment technology.[3] If banks assume the Fed adheres to the optimal policy and banks make their decisions accordingly, the Fed would have an incentive to invalidate their given expectations. Of course, rational forward-looking banks cannot be fooled systematically and, as a result, will take the Fed's incentive into account when forming their expectations and making their decisions. In the absence of binding commitments, the optimal policy might not be feasible so that the equilibrium could be characterized by an inflationary bias. But, if the Fed recognizes the importance of its reputation, then the magnitude of the bias can be reduced.[4]

In the context of the simple model presented in the Appendix, where the information structure is complete, the game-theoretic considerations of monetary policy do not affect the Fed's desire to smooth interest rates or the feasibility of doing so. Reputational considerations can reduce the inflationary bias without sacrificing financial stability. If the Fed had some private information (for example, a forecast about future shocks to credit markets) that was never observed directly by banks, however, then the efficacy of the reputational mechanism to reduce the inflationary bias is weakened.[5] In this case, it is likely that the Fed would face an additional tradeoff—namely, one between reducing the inflationary bias and accommodating those shocks. One would expect that as the inflationary bias became very large and the variance of shocks to the credit market became very small, the Fed's desire to smooth interest rates would approach zero.

Moreover, in the context of Cukierman's model, where the behavior of banks is explicitly modeled, one would expect that the game-theoretic considerations would affect the Fed's desire to smooth interest rates. Specifically, the Fed's policy of smoothing interest rates (and maintaining a positive inflation) induces banks to devote a larger amount of resources to make loans than they would otherwise. This incentive arises because banks anticipate that subsequent positive demand shocks in the bond market, which would otherwise adversely affect their profits, will be offset by the Fed. But the greater amount of resources committed to loans hampers the banks' ability to take advantage of an unexpected increase in interest rates on bonds. The indirect effect of reducing short-term fluctuations in interest rates, then, is that any given positive shock will require a greater response by the Fed, implying higher inflation. If the Fed realized this effect, it might be less willing, than one would be led to believe by Cukierman's analysis, to tolerate a positive inflation or to smooth interest rates.

Notes

1. Barro (1989) offers an alternative motivation stemming from the optimal theory of public finance that implies smoothing distortionary taxes intertemporally.
2. As argued by Goodfriend and King (1988), however, the Fed need not rely on reserve requirements to smooth out interest rate fluctuations.
3. See Cosimano and VanHuyck (1989) for a related analysis of the feasibility of the optimal policy that attempts to target the federal funds rate and total reserves simultaneously.
4. See, for example, Barro and Gordon (1983) who illustrate how, through reputational considerations, the Fed can indirectly control expectations. The reputational equilibrium policy results in a smaller inflationary bias that approaches zero as the Fed's discount factor approaches one.
5. For example, see Canzoneri (1985), who shows that once it becomes difficult to verify that the Fed has followed the reputational policy, the reputational mechanism might not be operational to reduce the inflationary bias.

References

Barro, Robert J. 1989. "Interest-Rate Targeting." *Journal of Monetary Economics* (January):3–30.

Barro, Robert J., and Gordon, David B. 1983. "Rules, Discretion and Reputation in a Model of Monetary Policy." *Journal of Monetary Economics* (July):101–122.

Canzoneri, Matthew B. 1985. "Monetary Policy Games and the Role of Private Information." *American Economic Review* (December):1056–1069.

Cosimano, Thomas, F., and Van Huyck, John B. 1989. "Dynamic Monetary

Control and Interest Rate Stabilization." *Journal of Monetary Economics* (January):53–64.

Goodfriend, Marvin. 1987. "Interest Rate Smoothing and Price Level Trend-Stationarity." *Journal of Monetary Economics* (May):335–348.

Goodfriend, Marvin, and King, Robert G. 1988. "Financial Deregulation, Monetary Policy, and Central Banking." Federal Reserve Bank of Richmond Working Paper Series No. 88–1, April.

APPENDIX

To illustrate the game-theoretic aspects of monetary policy and the emergence of an inflationary bias in the sort of Nash equilibrium chosen by Cukierman, it is helpful to study the following simple model of monetary policy. Following Cukierman's approach, I assume that the Fed dislikes inflation, μ_t, and wants to maintain the profitability of the banking industry, π_t. In time $t = 0$, before the state of nature is realized and actions are taken, the Fed's expected lifetime utility is given by

$$F_0 = E\left\{\sum_{t=0}^{\infty} \delta^t f_t\right\}, \quad 0 < \delta < 1, \tag{1}$$

where

$$f_t = -\tfrac{1}{2}(\mu_t^2 + g(\pi_t - \pi^*)^2), \quad g > 0,$$

and $E\{x_t\}$ is the unconditional expectations operator. δ represents the Fed's discount factor and g measures the importance of financial stability relative to price stability. Here, in contrast to Cukierman, I assume that the Fed wants to minimize deviations of the banking industry's profits from some target level, π^*. Profits of the banking industry are given by the following:

$$\pi_t = p_0 + p_1\,\mu_t + p_2\,\mu_t^e - \eta_t, \quad p_1 > 0, \tag{2}$$

where η_t, an i.i.d. shock to the credit market that reduces profits of the banking industry, has an expected value of zero and a finite variance, σ_η^2. The parameters, p_1 and p_2, capture the impact of actual inflation and expectations of inflation, respectively. Although it is assumed that $p_1 > 0$, p_2 can be positive or negative.

Before the realization of η_t, banks form their expectations of the Fed's policy, μ_t^e, and upon the subsequent realization of η_t, the Fed chooses μ_t.[1] The solution to this model depends on the banks' expectation of μ_t, which ultimately depends on the Fed's strategy. Two strategies are considered below.

Nash One-Shot Equilibrium

Assuming that the Fed ignores the indirect effect of its policy on bank profits through the effect on expectations, the Fed's optimization problem reduces to a sequence of one-period problems. Maximizing equation (1), subject to (2), with respect to μ_t yields the following first order condition:

$$-\mu_t - g(\pi_t - \pi_t^*)p_1 = 0 \tag{3}$$

for $t = 0, 1, \ldots, \infty$. Substituting (2) into (3), solving for μ_t and taking expectations, yields the banks' expectations for μ_t:

$$\mu_t^e = \frac{p_1 g(\pi^* - p_0)}{1 + p_1 g(p_1 + p_2)} \tag{4}$$

for all t. Even in the absence of any shocks, banks expect a positive inflation provided that $\pi^* > p_0$ and $p_1 + p_2 > -1/p_1 g$. By combining (3) and (4), one can verify that the Nash equilibrium inflation rate is given by the following:

$$\mu_t^N = \frac{p_1 g}{1 + p_1 g(p_1 + p_2)}(\pi^* - p_0) + \frac{p_1 g}{1 + p_1^2 g}\eta_t, \tag{5}$$

for all t. Note that the banks' expectations are rational.

A more articulated specification of the economy is necessary to interpret equation (5) as a policy of interest rate smoothing. To relate (5) to Cukierman's solution, assume that the shock to credit markets decreases bank profits by increasing interest rates in the absence of a policy response.

But assume that the parameter, p_2, in the profit function (2) implicitly captures a negative effect of money creation and, hence, inflation on interest rates. Then, according to (5), by partially accommodating the shock, the Fed dampens fluctuations in interest rates as in Cukierman's analysis.

Commitment Equilibrium

Assuming that the Fed recognizes the impact of policy on expectations and it can make binding commitments, it will announce the following contingent rule:

$$\mu_t^A = c_0 + c_1\eta_t, \tag{6}$$

where the coefficients, c_0 and c_1, are determined below. Given this announcement, expectations are formed by

$$\mu_t^e = c_0. \tag{7}$$

The coefficients, c_0 and c_1, are chosen to maximize the expectation of the Fed's objective function (1), subject to (2), (6), and (7). The first order conditions to this problem are given by

$$-E\left\{\sum_{t=0}^{\infty}\delta^t[c_0+c_1\eta_t-g(p_1+p_2)(p_0+p_1(c_0+c_1\eta_t)+p_2c_0-\eta_t-\pi^*)]\right\} = 0 \tag{8a}$$

$$-E\left\{\sum_{t=0}^{\infty}\delta^t[(c_0+c_1\eta_t)\eta_t-gp_1\eta_t(p_0p_1(c_0+c_1\eta_t)+p_2c_0-\eta_t-\pi^*)]\right\} = 0 \tag{8b}$$

By solving for the coefficients, one can verify that the equilibrium inflation rate is given by the following expression:

$$\mu_t^c = \frac{(p_1 + p_2)g}{1 + g(p_1 + p_2)^2}(\pi^* - p_0) + \frac{p_1 g}{1 + p_1^2 g}\eta_t. \tag{9}$$

A comparison of (5) to (9) reveals that the inflationary bias, given by

$$\frac{-gp_2(\pi^* - p_0)}{(1 + p_1 g(p_1 + p_2))(1 + g(p_1 + p_2)^2)}, \tag{10}$$

is non-zero provided that p_2 does not equal zero and p_0 does not equal the target rate for banks' profits, π^*. Maintaining the assumption that $p_0 < \pi^*$ and $p_1 + p_2 > -1/p_1 g$, the inflation bias is positive if $p_2 < 0$ and is negative if $p_2 > 0$.[2] However, the coefficient on the shock is the same for both solutions. Hence, the game-theoretic aspects of policy considered here do not affect the Fed's response to shocks to credit markets.

By comparing the Fed's expected utility under the Nash equilibrium,

$$F^N = -\frac{g}{2(1-\delta)}\left[\frac{(1+p_1^2g)(\pi^*-p_0)^2}{(1+p_1g(p_1+p_2))^2}+\frac{\sigma_\eta^2}{(1+p_1^2g)}\right], \tag{11a}$$

to that under the commitment equilibrium,

$$F^c = -\frac{g}{2(1-\delta)}\left[\frac{(\pi^*-p_0)^2}{(1+g(p_1+p_2)^2)}+\frac{\sigma_\eta^2}{(1+p_1^2g)}\right], \tag{11b}$$

one can verify that the Nash equilibrium is inefficient:

$$F^c - F^N = \frac{g^2p_2^2[\pi^*-p_0]^2}{2(1-\delta)\,[1+g(p_1+p_2)^2][1+p_1g(p_1+p_2)]^2}. \tag{12}$$

The difference in the Fed's expected utility under the two solutions indicates the inefficiency of the inflationary bias. Provided that bank profits depend on expected policy—i.e., $p_2 \neq 0$—and $\pi^* \neq p_0$, the Nash equilibrium will be suboptimal.[3]

Notes to Appendix

1. For simplicity, it is assumed that the Fed directly controls inflation through its monetary policy actions. In a more sophisticated analysis, as in Cukierman's, one would expect that inflation is partly determined by expectations of policy actions in equilibrium. While this complication does not affect the Nash outcome, it would affect the commitment outcome. Nevertheless, the qualitative results on the relation between the inflationary bias and the effect of expectations on banks are unchanged, except where noted below.

2. If inflation were positively related to expectations of inflation indirectly through banks' decisions, the inflation bias could be positive even if $p_2 > 0$. But the inflation bias is more likely to be negative when $p_2 > 0$ as the effect of expectations of inflation on the equilibrium inflation rate approach zero.

3. The notion that the optimal policy necessarily is not a subgame equilibrium strategy when commitments are not possible can be verified by substituting the expectation of μ_t^c and (2) into (1) and solving the Fed's optimization problem. Given that banks expect the Fed to adhere to (9), the Fed's best cheating policy, given by

$$\mu_t^{ch} = \frac{gp_1(1+p_1^2g)(\pi^*-p_0)}{1+p_1g(2p_1+p_2)} + \frac{gp_1}{1+p_1g(2p_1+p_2)}\eta_t,$$

does not equal the optimal policy (9) and, hence, violates expectations. If banks were rational, they would never form expectations under the assumptions of (6) and (9). Therefore, without considering reputational effects of monetary policy, as in Barro and Gordon (1983), or a commitment technology, the commitment solution is not feasible.

3 PRECOMMITMENT TO RULES IN MONETARY POLICY

Edmund S. Phelps

This article is about the issue of what role might usefully be played by the commitment of the monetary authorities to a rule or book of rules in their monetary policy.

The first section takes up the question of whether in fact there are any rules that promise to be both operational and attractive. Here I have rounded up the "usual suspects" though without any compunction to give them all equal attention. One restriction is that candidacy has been restricted to "nominal" rules if for no other reason than the fact that requiring the central bank to stabilize a "real" variable, such as the real interest rate or the real exchange rate or the unemployment rate, would certainly be a non-starter in today's thinking. In this section I try to see what are the merits and demerits of the idea of expressing the target in terms of a band, hence an upper and lower bound.

The second section steps back from the particular rules and norms considered earlier to discuss some underlying questions of a more general nature. One of these questions concerns the meaning of the distinction between rule and discretion. Is there some latent function, to use Merton's term, lurking behind the manifest function of the proposed rules? Certainly a more precise vocabulary for analyzing the issues involved is desirable.

Another question here is the sort of "price stability" that is best for the rule to aim for. With trivial adjustments and adapters, most of the rules can accommodate a wide range of underlying monetary objectives. There is, for example, a wide family of nominal GNP rules, ranging from rules in "levels" to rules in "rates of change" and from rapidly rising trend paths or high average rates to the opposite; and although some members of this family are undoubtedly regarded as black sheep that are best forgotten, a conscientious appraisal would have to give explicit reasons for rejecting some in the family and embracing others. Is zero inflation (in terms of the Consumer Price Index, say) better than "moderate" inflation? Is stability of the price-level path around a steadily rising target path better than a constant inflation rate target (with last period's error therefore having no effect on today's target)?

A further question concerns "start-up" considerations. Is there to be a provisional rule during some early (and trial!) period to be followed by a normal rule if and when the economy has adapted to the provisional rule and the expectation of the normal regime to follow? More generally, what provisions are to be made for changes in the rule when circumstances change? Will the adopted monetary rule, if there is one, be the first experiment to escape the law of unintended consequences?!

1. Some Rules and Rule Modifications Under Current Discussion

When one thinks of monetary rules one thinks first of the classic examples, and so I will begin with the monetary standard that is oldest but not least of those covered here.

1.1 Pegging the Price of Gold

This is the system of gold convertibility without backing, not the system of gold backing without convertibility. Under this monetary standard, the stock of money, which is paper money, determines (jointly with other factors) the nominal price of gold (and of every other good), and is continuously varied as required to stabilize that nominal (or money) price; the real price of gold—the price relative to the Consumer Price Index—would be determined entirely by real factors, such as the industrial demand for gold, if all nominal prices and wages were instantaneously flexible, though under nominal stickiness of the general price or wage level, which is posited here, nominal disturbances in the demand or supply of money will in general have some indirect (transient) effect on the real price. (A stickiness-augmented version of, say, the model in Barro (1979) as extended by Barsky and Summers (1987) gives the picture.)

Why gold? In the previous century there was no available index of the general price level, only indexes of the money prices of certain individual goods and assets. (The official U.S. Consumer Price Index was born in 1919, five years after the British one.) So as a practical matter price stability was apt to be translated as stability of the publicized index of an individual commodity, such as gold. Price stabilization of gold was fully operational since there was an open market in it and a fairly broad one at that. Perhaps the history of earlier times when the stock of gold was the stock of money also gave gold an edge over alternative commodities.

But this monetary standard had the defect of its virtues. Since gold was special, not a general basket of goods, there could be changes in the equilibrium level or path of gold's relative price. If there occurred a decline in the marginal efficiency of capital and hence a fall in the expected real rate of interest, the opportunity cost of holding gold for industrial and ornamental use would be decreased, so the real price of gold would rise. If nominal prices were not sticky, they would drop by just enough to leave the money price of gold unchanged; with nominal prices or wages sticky, however, the nominal price of gold will temporarily rise in concert with the real price. The rule of stabilizing the nominal gold price will then require a contraction of the money supply—by an open market sale of gold—with the result that real cash balances are constricted and employment is consequently depressed until the de-sticking of nominal wages and prices has returned activity to the "natural rate" of unemployment and corresponding level of employment. The reverse problem arises, of course, in the event of an increase in the marginal efficiency.[1]

The presence of a liability of an enterprise does not tell us much about the bottom line, however. It is an *asset* of this sort of monetary standard, its advocates say, that when real interest rates are low and hence the real price of gold is high, open-market sales would be needed to stabilize the nominal price; for typically, their argument goes, low real rates are the result of financial or monetary disturbances (such as a decline of liquidity preference or easier banking regulations) at home or abroad which tend to stimulate boom conditions; likewise, the real price of gold is typically depressed when business activity is strangling on high real interest rates. This defense of the gold convertibility standard interprets periods of strong gold prices in the opposite way from the more Keynesian perspective of the previous paragraph.

I am disinclined to cast any doubts whatsoever on the second premise—that high real interest rates rather typically (though I would not suppose always) go hand in hand with weakness in the capital-goods industries and indeed the whole economy; that is a feature of the sort of non-monetary theory of slumps that I have been developing since the prototype models in the Fitoussi-Phelps monograph (1988). But, rather surprisingly, recent empirical analysis has turned up a weakness in the other premise—the assumption that the real gold price is high when the real interest rate is low. One examination, the Barksy-Summers contribution, seems to confirm the importance of the real interest rate as an element of the opportunity cost of holding gold, so that when the real rate goes up the real price goes down. However, a statistical analysis by Vincent Reinhart (1989) finds that there is little or no negative correlation between those two variables in U.S. historical times series. At the very least this finding serves as a caution against implicitly basing aggressive changes in the supply of money on changes in the real price of gold.

A full and balanced assessment of gold convertibility as a monetary standard is not what I want to supply, nor is there much demand for it. But I would close by agreeing with Cooper (1982) that the arbitrariness of whatever money price of gold is settled upon would be a strike—if not two strikes—against the credibility of that system as a bulwark against an eventual expansion of the money supply in inflationary proportions.

1.2 Stabilizing the Consumer Price Level

This standard was, I believe, the norm favored by most monetary experts in the early decades of this century. It may be complained that this norm of monetary policy is not a genuine rule since the central bank could not keep the price level errorlessly on the desired trend path. However, there are good reasons for discussing it anyway. Moreover, borrowing a device conceived by Robert Hall for use in nominal GNP stabilization, we could imagine that the central bank does a tolerable job of stabilizing the price level *predicted* next period in some average of private forecasts.

Whether the actual price level is the target or whether the expected price level serves as the intermediate target, dedicating monetary policy exclusively to price stability has encountered many objections. There is, for example, the objection that a supply shock, more precisely one that drives up the supply price of output more than the demand price, would occasion a contraction of the money supply under this standard;[2] as prices rose with the upward push of costs and the monetary authorities sought to drive the price and cost levels back down, the result would be a lengthening of the distance that nominal wages would have to drop (relative to trend) before they restored employment to the normal level, and a widening of the initial decline in employment. More generally, the goal of single-mindedly minimizing the variability of the price level around the specified trend path suffers from a property pointed to by John Taylor's notion of a trade-off between price variability and unemployment variability: that goal accepts a huge increase in unemployment variability at the margin for the last little bit of reduction in price variability (Taylor, 1981).

There is the radical objection, parallel to the early objection to employment stabilization voiced by Friedman (1953), that, even with the best will in the world, a central bank that is encouraged to adopt an activist approach to price-level stabilization is apt to destabilize the price level compared to the result that would follow from adoption instead of a rule expressed in terms of a comparatively attainable intermediate target such as a fixed money-supply growth rate rule. Too often the activist will jump the wrong way when it is better not to respond at all, owing to the complicated structure of the disturbances. If the actual price level is the target, not the consensus prediction, it is plausible (at least to me) that the price level could suffer a run of mistakes, driving it some 10% off the target before the monetary authorities took steps that would send it back to target with high probability; even if the central bank instead adopts the predicted price level as an intermediate target, it is imaginable that errors could cumulate for quite a while. Nevertheless, the condition Friedman himself derives such that an activist money-supply policy would be variance-reducing does not look blatantly unrealistic. (See Chand, 1986, for an empirical analysis of output stabilization.) Moreover, as the late Henry Wallich used to complain, if the velocity of money follows a non-stationary process, say a random walk, and in fact the velocity of money drifts away, the fixed money-supply path would *never* cause the price level to return to the target path—and to those devoted to stability of the price level around a precommited path, that is a big strike against. I suspect that Friedman's position commands a great deal of sympathy not so much because we fear the central bank will for long periods miscalculate the direction in which to move but because we suppose the central bank would frequently shy away from price-level stabilization, implicitly admitting other desiderata.

On a different plane, and a point that applies to the next two standards as well as the present one, is the objection that this "stabilization" of the price level, either the actual or the predicted, is not very operational. It is not operational since no outsider would be able to tell whether the monetary authorities were truly conducting their monetary management so as to "stabilize." The very notion of stabilizing is ambiguous: does it mean minimizing the variance or the range or some other moment of the distribution, and what of possible trade-offs between variance tomorrow and variance in subsequent periods? Would the central bank be permitted to use what they claimed was the best practice model, perhaps one of their own construction, or have to use some off-the-shelf model with which the macroeconomic fraternity was widely familiar? Such considerations have led many economists, including notably some of the leading monetarists, to oppose such monetary targets as excessively vague and thus far too open to abuse by the authorities to be desirable.

There are some other rather general objections to the class of stabilization targets of which price-level stabilization is a member, but I set these aside until later in the article.

In closing, perhaps note should be taken, for the sake of completeness, of the proposal for a "tabular" standard made by Irving Fisher (1920). Under this scheme, fiat money would be mandated to be exchangeable for a daily specified amount of gold, say. If the consumer price level rose in terms of the fiat money, the authorities would increase the gold worth of the fiat money. In this way the gold value of contracts would be protected from inflation and deflation. Generalizing the idea, Hall (1982) suggested that a basket of four commodities, the price of which closely followed the Consumer Price Index, could be used in place of gold, so that, to a close approximation, the real value of contracts (the value in terms of consumer goods) would be protected. No one among present-day economists seems to have been persuaded (including Hall) that this standard is preferable to price-level stabilization by the ordinary methods of fiat-money management.

1.3 Stabilizing the Average Money Wage

In his 1936 book Keynes envisioned that monetary policy would be dedicated to stabilizing the average level of nominal wage rates about some prespecified target path. It is an advantage (at least a possible advantage) of this objective that if a supply shock occurred that drove up the price level there would, in general, be no call under the rule for a sharp contraction of the money supply, as there would under price-level stabilization; so there would not be a planned slump, the central bank would not have to sell more debt to the public, increasing the burden of the debt, and wealthowners would share more in the real-income adjustment. More generally, if one thinks of labor-market dynamics as a wage-wage process in which the path of the general wage level rises or falls in relation to the expected trend path as employment is above or below the natural employment level, a policy that somehow forestalled deviations of the wage path from the desired trend path would also forestall deviations of unemployment from the natural rate. By the time of Bretton Woods, 1946, Keynes had seemingly moved on to the exchange rate as the thing to stabilize. But if the U.S. dollar is the key currency, the American central bank must pick a monetary policy other than fixing an exchange rate already fixed by other countries.

Although in a wage-wage world the general wage level does not bear any direct impact of a supply shock, such as an oil shock or a shock to the capital stock, Taylor's point carries over to the present norm: wage-level stabilization does not as a byproduct achieve the greatest possible stability of employment. The reason is that animal spirits can overtake wage setters, driving up the wage level without any change of the environment inducing them to do so, and since such a disturbance forces the monetary authority to tighten money, employment is thereby destabilized.

The other two objections to price level stabilization also carry over here: the objection that the general wage level is hard to control, and the objection that there might be incentives within the bureaucracy of the central bank militating against strict adherence to the wage stabilization goal in many situations.

One might infer from all this that stabilizing of the general wage level is at least as good as stabilizing the general consumer price level—indeed better. However, most economists have favored the latter system. Perhaps they have assumed that the public can better cope with the information-processing costs and mistakes caused by a wandering (typically upward drifting) wage level accompanied by a well-anchored price level than with a wandering price level accompanied by a well-anchored wage level. (Is that tied up with the fact that a household buys many goods and sells few kinds of labor services?) Another consideration is the prevalence of indexing wages to the Consumer Price Index. If you cannot stabilize the wage level when the price level rises, you have to stabilize the price level to stabilize the wage level. (Happily, indexation seems to have receded in the 1980s in the United States, but it is still quite important in many countries.)

1.4 Stabilizing the Nominal GNP

The fathers of this proposed norm include James Tobin, Robert Hall, Allan Meltzer, and Bennett McCallum. (I would appreciate learning of others.) Every successful idea, John Kennedy remarked after the Bay of Pigs, has many fathers, while every failure is an orphan. It is evident that this proposed norm is an idea with which many economists are happy to be associated.

The proposal to stabilize the nominal GNP around a prespecified target path has two attractions. One of these is that such a policy will tend to counter a disturbance to the velocity of money with a change of the money supply in the opposite direction; a positive velocity shock—in Keynesian terms, a positive IS shock or a negative LM (or liquidity preference) shock—will drive up output and inflation (thus gradually push up the price level), and these observations will signal the central bank to tighten up. This seems to be an advantage over the monetarist rule of inflexibility in the supply of money, though stabilization of the price level has the same advantage (alongside some disadvantages noted above). The second attraction of nominal GNP stabilization is that it will not tend to drive down the money supply in the event of a supply shock: the shock will drive down output, and though it will tend also to drive up the price level, the nominal GNP is likely to be driven down as well; the observation of a reduced nominal GNP will then signal the central bank to increase the money supply. This seems to be an advantage over the price-level stabilization norm, though (absent indexation) the wage-level stabilization norm shares this advantage.

Does this nominal GNP stabilization proposal, in whatever concrete form it may be given, contain some ghastly error? There seems to be little problem with the long-run properties of this norm, assuming that mechanisms exist that can be counted on to create a tendency for the economy to gravitate toward a natural rate of unemployment (whether or not that natural rate is permanently disturbed by permanent real shocks). It could be remarked here that a large change in the trend rate of growth of the supply of output (at the natural rate) would translate into a change in the trend rate of inflation. That problem could be met, of course, by a mid-course change in the growth rate of the nominal GNP target path. Allowing such amendments opens the policy to abuse, however. A central bank faced with having to drive down the actual nominal GNP might be tempted to adjust upward the target growth rate of nominal GNP as the path of expediency.

The short-run operating characteristics of such a stabilization policy are only beginning to be subjected to critical scrutiny. A recent paper by the Fed economist Vincent Reinhart[3] points out that were nominal GNP stabilization to be perfectly realized, a supply shock, if it jerks output down while it pushes up the sticky price level smoothly, would imply an upward jump of the money supply to drive the nominal GNP back to the target path. Households would be driven to work overtime and to step up their consumption despite the possibly temporary setback to real wage rates. The transition time to the new steady state is prolonged by the stabilization of nominal income, and there is a consequent welfare loss in Reinhart's general-equilibrium model with utility-maximizing consumers. The lesson Reinhart would have us draw is:

• Real income responds faster than real cash balances to a supply shock. If output variability traces typically to aggregate supply shocks rather than to financial shocks, a nominal money-supply rule will better govern the path of real income and employment than will a nominal GNP rule.

• Real cash balances respond faster than real income to a financial shock. If output variability is typically due to financial shocks more than supply shocks, a nominal GNP rule will better manage the path of real income and employment than will a nominal money-supply rule.

A glance at the behavior of real wage rates and of nominal GNP in the years of the first oil shock does not convince me, however, that this particular shock had the assumed property of driving down output faster than it drove up the price level. If anything, that experience reinforces my normal predilection for models in which the nominal stickiness is in wages rather than prices. (I also feel there is more to the prosperity-depression story than nominal stickiness, but that is another matter.)

A small point I would add apropos short-run properties is that some kinds of supply shocks are contractions of the natural employment level brought about by certain kinds of fiscal shocks, foreign or domestic, acting through the real interest rate. (See Fitoussi-Phelps, 1988, for the beginnings of this line of models.) In the event of such a shock there will be a tendency for nominal GNP to rise provided that some part of the rise in real interest rates is expressed in higher nominal rates as well; the velocity of money, V, will be stimulated, and hence MV too at the initial M. Under the stabilization rule being considered, therefore, the money supply will be contracted (relative to trend). Under Reinhart's criterion, the speediness of our adjustment to our straitened circumstances, this downward kick may be a good thing. However, I imagine it would be possible to build a model in which a certain amount of overshooting in the downward trajectory takes place, owing perhaps to some accelerator principle, in which case a tightening of money might be undesirable.

To the objection that the central bank is hardly capable of stabilizing the nominal GNP—that the standard is not operational—there have been two interesting responses thus far.

Bennett McCallum has done a great deal of work studying simulations of an economy operating on the basis of a concrete error-correcting rule for monetary policy aimed at stabilizing nominal GNP about a linear-logarithmic path. This rule specifies that the proportionate rate of change of the monetary base be increased each quarter by a fixed trend amount *plus* a term indicating the extent to which the ratio of base to nominal GNP was growing over the past four years *plus* a term proportional to the "error"—the logarithmic excess of the target level over the actual level of the nominal GNP (McCallum, 1988, p. 5 of typescript, ca. eq. (1)). McCallum finds that these simulations, carried out with three quite different kinds of macroeconomic models of nominal GNP, all represent his rule as performing very well in stabilizing the nominal GNP.

One misses, though, a demonstration of how well that rule does with regard to the stability of the employment path and the Consumer Price Index, to take two leading desiderata. One would also like to see a comparative study of this rule pitted against rival rules, such as the ones discussed above. In short, the research done by McCallum so far is necessary but not sufficient.

Hall's response to the problem of finding an operational rule is the suggestion of stabilizing as a sort of intermediate target the predicted nominal GNP of some average of private commercial forecasting models. Such a procedure would undoubtedly remove a great deal of discretion from the central bank. The bank would have difficulty explaining why it could not take actions that would move forecasts of the nominal GNP into a close neighborhood of the target path. But the authorities could always claim that they were not making any systematic policy mistake and were only the victims of a chance run of errors, which would be clear to all in a short time.

A criticism that Hall himself has made of the nominal GNP stabilization principle is that when unemployment is above its long-run tendency, the natural rate, while at the same time the nominal GNP is on target, the operation of the rule does nothing to hasten the recovery of the economy; similarly, when unemployment is too low, the rule does not rush employment back to base. He would modify the rule in the following way. Instead of having the central bank implicitly aim for a price level that is inversely proportional to output, or expected output, so that PY—familiar notation for GNP price deflator times real GNP, hence an expression giving nominal GNP—tends to be a constant, Hall would have policy aim for a price level target that is an increasing function of the unemployment rate. For example, the price-level target expressed in index form, with a normal level of 100, would be 8 points above normal for every point by which the observed unemployment rate exceeded its "normal" level (Hall, 1987, p. 140). It is clear that this rule could be expressed equivalently in terms of a relation between the deviation of the nominal national income target from some trend-path normal target and the observed unemployment rate. In fact, if the Hall coefficient above is equal to the coefficient in Okun's Law, about 2.5, his price level target would give a nominal GNP target that is invariant to the current unemployment rate. I believe it is the case that this idea is already present in an implicit way in the series of papers by Taylor, already referred to, in which what looks like an aggregate demand schedule, $Y = -cP$, is interpreted by Taylor as, in effect, a sort of monetary-policy function, the coefficient c being subject to policy choice; the difference is only that Hall, quite reasonably, makes the demand price a function of unemployment rather than output (although Taylor must have considered alternative formulations as well).

There seems to be some dissonance here. When a supply shock strikes, the Reinhart criterion of avoiding "prolonged" transitions would have the central bank pop the economy onto the new Ramsey-Solow-Prescott optimal path; that may mean a contraction of the money supply, which would dampen or prevent or reverse a rise of the price level. The Taylor-Hall criterion provides that, "[as] unemployment rises, the allowable price level rises as well .... When the economy [recovers] and unemployment falls toward its normal level, ... the Fed ultimately has to achieve the [normal] price target. But the linkage to unemployment *cushions* the economy in the desirable way in the short run" (Hall, 1987, p. 140). I believe the latter approach makes sense if the shock is a temporary one or is a permanent one that causes only a transient rise of the unemployment rate above an unaffected natural rate; the Taylor-Hall approach meets the problem that the mean money wage, being sticky, cannot decline as fast as (one may presume) an ideal social planner would have it do. The former approach if, to take the less controversial case, a supply shock of a permanent nature has occurred that, perhaps by depressing real interest rates and thus also the velocity of money, has reduced national income; the Reinhart criterion responds by virtuously refusing to accept the opportunity to keep employment above its newly reduced natural level in order to smooth the money GNP. There does seem to be room for coexistence of these two points. But these dissonant themes raise a problem. How do we decide whether the supply shock is permanent and the change in the unemployment rate so far observed reflects a change in the natural rate of unemployment or whether instead the whole thing is a passing disturbance? Will Ben McCallum's labors ever be done?

1.5 Modified Monetarism: Bands Around the Normal Monetary Base

Ever since the classic case for monetarism built by Friedman, monetarist proposals for stabilizing the monetary base or some other monetary aggregate around a regularly rising target path have always had the attractions that they are at least operational—no one really doubts that the central bank can control the base and, indeed, most money-like aggregates—and their inflexibility, while earning them criticisms from a short-term perspective, has the advantage that, theoretically at least, they limit the damage that can occur over the long term—as no one doubts that hyperinflation is virtually impossible if the monetary base is held almost constant. The recent proposal by Thomas Melzer (1988) envisions upper and lower bands around some normal, or mid-range, path of the monetary base.

The merit of this proposal, it strikes me, is that it translates to the management of the monetary base the advantages that have been noted in the scheme of bands around the exchange rate within which the rate might fluctuate freely. Short-term disturbances are left free to have effects in the desired direction usually, since only rarely if at all will the exchange rate press up against either band, while the mere existence of the bands imparts a dampening effect on the volatility of the exchange rate, since it is known that the possible future developments growing out of current or foreseen disturbances cannot in the future drive the exchange rate beyond the bands. Analogously, the use of bands permits the central bank in its managements of the monetary base to respond sensitively and energetically to short-term considerations when disturbances arise while preserving the public's confidence that the bank will not and cannot generate rapid inflation in perpetuity.

That said, it has to be conceded that there remains the monetarist problem that a marked change in the trend growth of the velocity of the monetary base or in the trend growth of potential output would necessitate either the acquiesence in a long-term inflation rate much higher or lower than that originally envisioned or else a sort of constitutional reconvening to retune the parameters of the bands. I have the feeling that when push comes to shove the bands would be retuned every decade or so, and after long experience with that they would come to be seen as paper tigers, though perhaps useful symbols of official resolve never to countenance permanent high inflation.

2. Some Basic Considerations in the Choice of a Rule

I have tried in the previous section to limit the comments made for or against each rule discussed above to criticisms that are specific to the rule under discussion or to some subset of the various rules taken up. Here I will venture some comments of a more general nature.

2.1 The Uneasy Case for Having Any Coercive and Fixed Rule

The terms currently in use to discuss this subject do not seem altogether revealing of what is at issue. Robert Barro and Donald Gordon (1983) begin one of their papers by explaining that "[i]n a discretionary regime the monetary authority can print more money and create more inflation than people expect.... [C]ommitments on monetary behavior, as embodied in... rules, eliminate the potential for ex post surprises."

It strikes me that this way of putting things, which goes back to the classic discussion of "rules versus authorities" by Simons (1936) which, although not wrong as far as it goes, is a little misleading. It seems to overlook the point that the behavior of authorities left to their discretion can be presumed to be describable by a rule. "When I am permitted to do what I feel like doing, I make it a rule to...." In fact, some economists of a neoclassical bent, such as Thomas Sargent and, I believe, Robert Lucas, sometimes propose that we forget the utility function that was traditionally imputed to the household and think instead of the household's decision rules. Of course, monetary policymaking is not like choice in the vegetable section of the grocery store, as the government is playing a sort of game with the public, and that gives policy choice some special features, as we all know. We might want to regard the government in our formal theories as a Machiavelli out to extract from us what is possible by hook or crook, including surprise tactics. But is it really well established and persuasive that a self-interested bureaucracy, without any exogenous disturbances triggering such behavior, would "play" a mixed strategy against us, swooping down helicopter drops of dollar bills on us under cover of night when we least expect it? Where is the historical example of such behavior? True, one can see that there have been and will always be situations in which great uncertainty attaches to policy, so any move and even a non-move taken at the discretion of the central bank would come as a surprise; but in such situations a rule-loving regime would also generate uncertainty that it would change the rule or tinker with the prevailing one. It is analogous to the choice between a dirty float and an adjustable peg with regard to the foreign-exchange rate.

The radical proposal that is the substance of the "Chicago view," ever since Simons, is that the central bank be required to obey a rule that is not the one it would follow if it were not constrained. A better way of terming the dichotomy is "contingent contract versus discretion." The agent contracts with the principal—the public—to respond in certain ways to specified eventualities (in return for salary and the emoluments of office). Some deep observations about the possibility of an incentive-compatable contract are made in Matthew Canzoneri (1985).

The role of reputation in contractual behavior and discretionary behavior also seems to me to be viewed rather oddly these days. In an early essay of mine on inflation policy (Phelps, 1967), the government maximizes an intertemporal objective function, using a discount rate that expresses its own time preference, subject to a side condition on the adaptive behavior of the expected rate of inflation. In the steady state the inflation rate is just high enough that the government would not gain on balance from a surprise move to push up the inflation rate to a still higher level. The government enjoys a reputation for being unwilling to tolerate a greater inflation rate than the one currently expected, and driving up inflation higher (at least temporarily)—even if the government subsequently backed down after a while—would cost because it would give the government a reputation (at least temporarily) for being willing to tolerate a higher inflation rate than previously estimated. So reputation is the key consideration in shaping the discretionary equilibrium. From that viewpoint Barro and Gordon had it upside down when they wrote: "When . . . rules are in place, the policymaker has the temptation each period to 'cheat' . . . . However, this tendency to cheat threatens the viability of the rules equilibrium and tends to move the economy toward the inferior equilibrium under discretion. [But] because of the repeated interactions between the policymaker and the private agents, it is possible that reputational forces can support the rule." (Barro and Gordon, 1983, p. 101). The numerous proposals for a rule to impose on the central bank—from the gold standard on down to today's nominal national income target—are calls for an enforced contingency plan; it is the behavior of the bank when left to its own discretion that is self-regulated by its own regard for its reputation with respect to tolerance for inflation. Thus, as I see it, the present article is *not* about the behavior rule observed in a reputation equilibrium of a monetary policy game (though central bank incentives are a factor in considering the enforceability of any imposed rule).[4]

What these rules *are* about is coercive, possibly even once-for-all constraints on the "agents" carrying out their "contract" at the central bank. I presume that shifting to such a procedure would require some sort of legislative assent by the U.S. Congress. If the experience of recent decades has taught us anything, it is that the legislature sometimes does the unexpected, that the consequences of the legislation are sometimes quite different from what the legislature intended, and it sometimes takes a long time if it is feasible at all to develop a consensus over how to overhaul the legislation. Perhaps it would be better not to go down that road lest it prove full of disappointing turns with no way by which to get back.

2.2 Price-Level Stabilization Versus Inflation Stabilization

Another issue is what the target variable should be, the desired inflation rate or the desired price level (at the current moment). In the older way of looking at what the government ought to do, and perhaps even what it did do, the actual inflation rate chosen by the government was shown to be a function of the state in which it found itself, and the state variable—a single variable that sufficed to describe fully the situation—was the expected inflation rate that had been "learned" by the public from its recent and more distant experience. In recent years Mankiw (1987) and Grilli (1989) are among the authors who, extending an earlier effort of mine (Phelps, 1973, 1989), have sought to explain inflation behavior in terms of the collection of seignorage over time. Of course, if there are no disturbances, this solution gives the path of the price level as well as the path of the inflation rate, since the initial price level is a known datum. But in general there will be unforeseen shocks, which raise the question of whether it is *optimal* to go on following the desired "inflation-rate policy," treating as a bygone the jump of the price level that may have occurred, or whether a truly optimal policy will aim always to get back onto some desired path of the price level.

For decades the conventional wisdom on this question, I note, was that, insofar as efficiency of money as a unit of account and medium of exchange is concerned, little would be served by following inflation by deflation and deflation with inflation. Axel Leijonhufvud (1968), commenting on Keynes' veiw on this question, says that Keynes did not think that if the economic ship strayed near Scylla it ought to be condemned to spend equal time near Charybdis. (Yet Keynes does speak of a "wage path" as the objective of monetary policy, not a wage-inflation rate, in chapter 19 of the 1936 book.) In fact, the contrary position—that inflations and deflations should be reversed, rolled back—deserved some satire. Often the preference for stability of the price level around a path (rather than for stability of the inflation rate around zero) was defended with the claim that an unreversed upward drift of the price level cheats previous contractors of their expected and presumptively just deserts. But under no criterion of justice with which we were familiar then or now would it be invariably optimal to impair the careers of some young people in order to save some retired people from a loss of real wealth and real pensions. If anything, the presumption is that an aggregate windfall loss to the economy should be shared in some way.

Now I sense that the pendulum of sophisticated opinion has swung away from inflation stabilization toward (precommitment to) a target path of the level of some variable, whether the price level or nominal GNP level or something else. It has come to be argued that monetary efficiency requires first and foremost the stability of the consumer price level. Thus Hall writes,

> [T]he purchasing power of the dollar is a basic unit of measurement to the public. Many important economic decisions, especially those made by the general public, are stated in terms of the dollar. A drifting price level interferes with good economic planning .... [The problems of pension decisions and mortgage decisions are cited.] Although a policy of inflation stabilization would solve some of those problems, price level stabilization would be even better. It is well within the power of monetary policy to promise a 30-year-old worker today that the purchasing power of the dollar at the time of his retirement 35 years later will be within 10 percent of what it is today (Hall, 1987, p. 142).

However, this argument in no way shows or suggests that price-level stabilization dominates inflation stabilization. Certainly there is no chance that price-level stabilization would give as smooth a behavior of the inflation rate as inflation-rate stabilization; the economy in the former case might shuttle between Scylla and Charybdis so violently that those workers would lose their jobs before they could think about pensions and mortgages. The argument only persuades that price-level stability is a consideration alongside inflation stabilization. It is a reasonable conjecture that, under any optimality criterion from the familiar set, an optimal policy will settle for aiming the price level part way back to the previous target path when driven off it by shocks. When negative real shocks occur, some group or groups in the economy must suffer an unplanned real windfall loss and it does not seem like a safe policy to guarantee so many groups protection against a real loss to them from a higher price level that there is no one or almost no one left on whom the adjustment can fall.

2.3 How High a Steady Inflation Rate Is Reasonable?

It is frequently (though not always) easier to talk about the above rules on the assumption that they are calibrated so as to deliver, in the expected-value sense, a steady price level, say, a steady Consumer Price Index, or, under the alternative formulation, a zero inflation rate on average from the current moment forward. But in reality the calibration is a decision to be faced up to in the event that any of the rules reached the stage of being considered for implementation.

One question, which is the subject of this section, is what steady inflation rate over the lengthy past would be optimal if the central bank were constrained by its rule to go on generating that steady rate (whatever the ups and downs around it) over the indefinite future? In other words, what is the best steady state to inherit and preserve? I recently summarized and updated my own position on this matter (Phelps, 1989) so it is not essential for me to state it here in any detail, and besides there is not the space to do so. Suffice it to say that stability considerations, relating to the nonexistence of equilibrium with a negative nominal interest rate and the volatility of a low nominal-interest-rate equilibrium, and public-finance considerations, relating to the optimality of having some revenue from an inflation tax, argue against zero as the best steady-state inflation rate (and *a fortiori* against negative rates). I assume we would not want to count on a continuation of the extraordinary *real* interest rates of the Nippo-Italo-Reagan era, with its *après moi* mentality, to continue with little or no abatement into the next century.

A reply sometimes heard is that, although a cost-benefit analysis does not give the answer of zero, zero enjoys an advantage with respect to credibility that is not shared by higher inflation rate targets such as 3 or 1.5 and so on. But in the present context of monetary rules that reply is not very persuasive. If the procedures of the central bank are going to be dictated by a fixed rule, the public will sensibly expect the rule to be followed, and they will work out the inflation implications accordingly.

I am somewhat afraid that if a public discussion of the calibration of the rule were to take place, piety would win out over optimality, leaving us with a rule designed to work well for an economy—if only a mythical economy—*capable* of working well with a zero average rate of inflation. But this capability is far from assured.

2.4 The Startup Problem

A question that the introduction of any rule, particularly a rule that has no break-in-period features, is how it would perform in the early months and years of its operation, a period over which the economy will not have had the opportunity to adjust fully to it. Robert Gordon (1985) is one of those who have worried about the "startup" properties of the rules being discussed these days.

A simple example is the problem raised when the economy is fully adjusted to steady inflation at 1% per quarter, say, and the rule calls for zero change per quarter. If the log of the CPI has been going up like the series . . . 97, 98, 99, and stands this quarter at 100 when the rule is to be introduced, we do not want the implied target over the future to be 100, 100, 100 and so forth. A better possibility is 110, 110, 110, with the understanding that undoubtedly the policy will "underfulfill" its "quota" in the first few periods, since no firm will want to jump its price immediately to 110, on an index basis, when it expects most other firms to be following their usual schedule with regard to prices and wages and hence not likely to jump the gun in the same way. This provision for "catch-up" and adjustment to the rule could accompany a nominal GNP rule or a monetary base rule as well as (more obviously) a price-level rule.

The real problem is not a conceptual one of failing to address the near term but, rather, the difficulty of figuring how best as a practical matter to do it—particularly, to avoid overdoing it and underdoing it.

3. Conclusion

As I worked my way through this article I wondered whether its tone would be precisely the on-the-one-hand-on-the-other that would be expected from a liberal like me. I also worried that it would appear to be an endorsement, cheerful or grudging, of the idea of a rule when, in fact, my visceral reaction to them is negative (though I do not suppose inalterably so). But in reviewing the article I see that its predominant message is one of skepticism and caution about the wisdom of proceeding with any of the rules that the profession has proposed so far. If, in fact, we are now moving inexorably toward the adoption of a rule, let us do what we can to avert the worst risks that such a rule, whatever its benefits, is apt to bring.

Notes

1. I found what seems to be the same objection to this monetary standard in Cooper (1982). "... [I]n periods of high 'animal spirits' in the business and financial community, Federal Reserve credit could rise substantially, only to be sharply reduced as buoyant spirits give way to pessimism and a period of heavy conversion sets in, leading to a drop of Federal Reserve credit below its historical trend under the regime" (p. 255 in Eichengreen edition).

2. This point rests on a Keynesian analysis of supply shocks such as that based on the wage-wage view of the labor market (rather than a wage-price or indexation-based view) in my early treatment of the problem (Phelps, 1978). Today, rather tentatively, I would say that the natural unemployment rate itself—more precisely, the natural rate path—is shifted up by an adverse supply shock, though this effect is conceivably vanishing over the far future.

3. Not a young man in a hurry (though he will get there as fast anyway), he prepared this article as the eighth chapter of his dissertation, to which he is still adding.

4. At the substantive level, there is little difference between the determination of the "discretionary" government in my article (Phelps, 1967) and the determination of what the authors cited call the "rule equilibrium" in their paper (Barro and Gordon, 1983). The main difference is that the latter article imputes to the public a more drastic souring of expectations in the event the government engages in some surprise inflation than that envisioned by the adaptive-expectations premise in my article.

Both articles show that the steady-state equilibrium inflation rate will be lower—thus nearer to the ideal rate sustaining "full liquidity"—the lower the government's discount rate is.

References

Barro, Robert J., and Gordon, David B. 1983. "Rules, Discretion, and Reputation in a Model of Monetary Policy." *Journal of Monetary Economics* 12 (July): 101–121.

Barsky, Robert L., and Summers, Lawrence H. 1988. "Gibbon's Paradox and the Gold Standard". *Journal of Political Economy* 96 (June):528–550.

Canzoneri, Matthew B. 1985. "Monetary Policy Games and the Role of Private Information." *American Economic Review* 75. (December):1056–1070.

Chand, Sheetal. 1984. "The Stabilizing Role of Fiscal Policy" *Finance and Development* vol. 21, no. 1 (March).

Cooper, Richard N. 1982. "The Gold Standard: Historical Facts and Future Prospects." *Brookings Papers on Economic Activity* 12 (Spring):1–45; abridged and reprinted in Barry Eichengreen (Ed.), *The Gold Standard in Theory and History*. New York and London: Methuen, pp. 251–271.

Fisher, Irving. 1920. *Stabilizing the Dollar*. New York: Macmillan.

Friedman, Milton. 1953. "The Effects of a Full-Employment Policy on Economic Stability." In M. Friedman (Ed.), *Essays in Positive Economics*. Chicago: University of Chicago Press.

Gordon, Robert J. 1985. "The Conduct of Domestic Monetary Policy." In A.

Ando et al. (Eds.), *Monetary Policy in our Times*. Cambridge: MIT Press.

Grilli,Vittorio. 1989. "Seigniorage in Europe." In M. deCecco and A. Giovannini (Eds.), *A European Central Bank*? Cambridge: Cambridge University Press, pp. 53–78.

Hall, Robert E. 1982. "Explorations in the Gold Standard and Related Policies for Stabilizing the Dollar." In R. E. Hall (Ed.), *Inflation: Causes and Effects*. Chicago: University of Chicago Press, pp. 111–122.

Hall, Robert E. 1987. "Monetary Strategy with an Elastic Price Standard." In *Price Stability and Public Policy*. Kansas City: Federal Reserve Bank of Kansas City, pp. 137–159.

Mankiw, N. Gregory. 1987. "The Optimal Collection of Seignoriage." *Journal of Monetary Economics* 20 (September):327–341.

McCallum, Bennett T. 1988. "Robustness Properties of a Rule for Monetary Policy." Carnegie-Rochester Conference Series on Public Policy, vol. 29. *Money, Cycles, and Exchange Rates: Essays in Honor of Allan H. Meltzer*, pp. 173–204.

Melzer, Thomas C. 1988. "A Proposal for the Adoption of Monetary Base Growth Contraints." Mimeo., St. Louis: Federal Reserve Bank of St. Louis.

Phelps, Edmund S. 1967. "Phillips Curves, Expectations of Inflation and Optimal Employment Over Time." *Economica* 34 (August):254–281.

Phelps, Edmund S. 1978. "Commodity-Supply Shock and Full-Employment Monetary Policy." *Journal of Money, Credit and Banking* 10 (May):206–221.

Phelps, Edmund S. 1973. "Inflation in the Theory of Public Finance." *Swedish Journal of Economics* 75 (January):67–82.

Simons, Henry C. 1936. "Rules versus Authorities in Monetary Policy." *Journal of Political Economy* 44 (February):1–30.

Taylor, John B. 1981. "Stabilization, Accommodation, and Monetary Rules." *American Economic Review Papers and Proceedings* 71 (May):145–149.

Tobin, James. 1983. "Monetary Policy: Rules, Targets and Shocks." *Journal of Money, Credit and Banking* 15 (November):506–518.

Commentary

Manfred J. M. Neumann

Edmund Phelps' article reviews coercive rules for monetary policy. Since Friedman's proposal of a simple *k*% money rule, economists have come up with a great variety of more sophisticated rules. A common objective of all rules is to hinder the agent central bank from producing permanent inflation, while some rules aim in addition at enforcing a certain degree of employment stabilization. There is no ideal rule, of course; each rule has its merits as well as drawbacks, as Phelps points out. Consequently, it seems we need a comparative evaluation in order to determine which of the various proposals is the most promising in terms of a lasting welfare gain to the central bank's principal, the private sector.

However, this is not what this article is about. Instead Phelps informs us about his apparently deep-rooted skepticism about the wisdom of constraining monetary policy by any rule. To cite him: "I worried that it [the article] would appear to be an endorsement . . . of the idea of a rule when, in fact, my visceral reaction to them is negative." But why bother to discuss pros and cons and even startup problems of rules, if one fundamentally believes that any coercive rule is likely to produce more damage than good? What strikes me about the article is the unconstructive, if not negative, attitude. Doesn't it imply that the status quo is the better world, if not—as the French philosopher Voltaire's Candide used to believe—the best of all worlds? Clearly, the message underlying this article is the traditional one that unconstrained discretion—possibly supported by some kind of reputation—is the superior solution. This may be true. However, I would have preferred the case for discretion to be made explicit and, if possible, to be backed up by some evidence.

In what follows I will discuss alternative concepts of price stability and examine whether coercive rules are capable of providing commitment to this goal. Finally, I will put forward an alternative solution.

Price Stability and Its Attainability by Coercive Rules

It is commonplace that monetary policy should aim at price stability. While policymakers for good or bad reasons prefer to shy away from committing themselves to a precise concept of price stability, economists employ several stability concepts or norms with markedly different economic implications. In the rules debate, at least three different concepts are employed.

Consider the following decomposition of the realized rate of change of the general price level,

$$\Delta p_t = \Delta \bar{p}_t + \varepsilon_t + s_t \tag{1}$$

where $\Delta \bar{p}_t$ is the rationally expected permanent rate of inflation based on period $t - 1$ information (excluding information on s_t), ε_t is a normally distributed one-time price level change with zero mean that is supposed to summarize the price level impact of normally distributed real and nominal shocks, and s_t is a shift-term intended to represent unfrequent and unusual one-time changes of the price level, caused, for example, by changes in the rates of turnover or excise taxes or by an oil-price shock.

A first concept of price stability requires monetary policy to hold constant the actual price level over the long run.

$$\text{Average } p = p^* \tag{2}$$

This norm underlies Hall's "monetary strategy with an elastic price standard" (Hall, 1984). He permits short-run variation in the price level but requires that it be brought back to a fixed level in the medium to long run. This implies shielding the owners of nominal assets and nominal contracts from the real consequences of one-time price level changes, ε_t and s_t. I agree with Phelps (1990) and Meltzer (1984) that the value judgment on which this concept of price stability is based is unclear and, moreover, that its adoption is likely to impose unnecessary real costs. For example, what welfare gain is to be expected from having the central bank remove the price level effect of an increase in the value-added tax rate? Doesn't it, on the contrary, enforce an unnecessary loss of output and employment?

A second concept of price stability is zero-inflation-cum-countercyclical-stabilization. The norm requires to set expected permanent inflation at zero but to permit and create inflation surprises such that an optimal stabilization of short-run fluctuations of output around its normal path is achieved. Hence the norm implies to choose a variance of price level change that is (optimally) related to the variances of predetermined real and nominal shocks.

$$\Delta \bar{p}_t = 0 \wedge \delta^2_{\Delta p} = \text{opt.} < \delta^2_\varepsilon \tag{3}$$

This second concept of price stability is an imago that has long inspired economists to search for operational procedures that promise an approximation to the ideal state as closely as possible. The main problem with this stability norm is that it presupposes a central bank which is sufficiently well informed about current stochastic shocks and about the structure and speed of shock transmission.

The least demanding price stability norm, finally, requires the central bank to set the expected permanent rate of inflation at zero and to avoid any unanticipated changes of the money supply.

$$\Delta \bar{p}_t = 0 \wedge \delta^2_{\Delta p} = \text{subopt.} < \delta^2_\varepsilon \qquad (4)$$

This is the price stability norm underlying Friedman's $k\%$ rule of money creation. It implies to accept price level variation that one would eliminate under conditions of a perfectly informed central bank, and it does so in order to "prevent money itself from being a major source of economic disturbance" (Friedman, 1968).

The three price stability norms have in common that expected permanent inflation is to be set at zero. Is this a sensible target for a real world economy or—as Phelps suggests—only for a mythical economy? Phelps mentions two arguments in favor of a positive rate of inflation.

First, a stable equilibrium requires the nominal interest rate to be non-negative. This is certainly correct. But given that a zero permanent rate of inflation is compatible with a strictly positive permanent (real) rate of interest, I fail to see the point.

Second, public-finance considerations suggest that it is suboptimal to avoid the inflation tax, the argument being that the costs of distortions from financing a given level of government expenditure by taxation can be minimized by choosing the optimal mix of direct taxes and inflation tax (Phelps, 1973).

The logic of the argument is indisputable, though it bypasses the question of distributional justice given that the distribution of taxable personal income does not match the distribution of personal money holdings. However, the empirical relevance of the argument is in question: First, given that we are lacking sufficient empirical knowledge to compute the optimal rate of inflation reliably, we may easily end up with higher costs from distortions by picking some positive rate than with a zero rate. Second, there is revealed-preference type of evidence available which suggests that the true optimal rate of inflation is hardly larger than a measured rate of 2%. Otherwise we should have observed the population of Switzerland or of Germany demanding more inflation than they actually got in the past.

Which of the various policy rules discussed in recent years is likely to achieve price stability in the sense of an expected permanent rate of inflation of zero? Generally, this depends on whether the rule is capable of

Table 1. Monetary Policy Rules and Price Stability

Rules	*Response to* *Current Shocks*	*Trend Change in* *Velocity*	*Output Supply*	*Guarantees Expected Inflation of Zero*
Outcome based				
Pure discretion	Yes	Yes	Yes	No
Nominal GNP	Yes	Yes	No	No
Instrument based				
Friedman (1968)	No	No	No	No
Melzer (1988)	Yes[1]	No	No	No
McCallum (1987)	No	Yes	No	No
Meltzer (1984)	No	Yes	Yes	Yes[2]

[1] Provided shocks are not too large.
[2] Over the longer run.

taking automatically into account trend changes in the velocity of money and in the normal rate of output growth.

Table 1 lists various rules and provides information on their compatibility with the third price stability concept. There is no need to discuss the rules in detail. The important point relevant to our discussion is that, with the exception of one, no rule satisfies our price stability norm. Pure discretion suffers from the time-consistency problem. Non-contingent rules, whether based on outcomes or on instruments, suffer from not taking account of trend changes in the velocity of money (Friedman's rule and Melzer's Bundesbank-style rule) and/or of trend changes in output supply (nominal GNP rule and McCallum's rule).

The only rule that promises an expected zero-rate of inflation for the long run is Allan Meltzer's rule. It is completely retrospective by setting the current base money growth equal to a three-year moving average of the difference between the growth rates of real output and of monetary base velocity. The rule's unique advantage of an automatic adjustment of base money growth to trend changes has its costs: it takes three years until the adjustment is completed. Consequently, the rule does not guarantee expected zero inflation for the medium run.

Of course, one might argue that in the advent of trend changes in velocity or output growth all rules can be adjusted accordingly. But here I strongly agree with Phelps: permitting amendments opens the Pandora-box of policy abuse. It is likely that amendments will become a hot issue in the political arena, especially if, say, a fall in the trend growth of output supply is diagnosed. Hence there is the danger that amendments will be used to put the price stability goal into the asides.

On the Ultra-Conservative Central Banker

Let me finally address the question of whether we really need a coercive rule in order to achieve a solution where citizens can be fairly confident that the permanent rate of inflation will be close to zero over several years ahead.

From history we know that central bankers are used to promising price stability and creating permanent inflation nevertheless. And the application of game theory (Barro and Gordon, 1983) has sharpened our understanding of why this is so. Given that central bankers desire or are obliged by government to stabilize prices and employment, and given that they cannot make a binding commitment to expected zero inflation, the equilibrium solution is the time-consistent positive rate of inflation.

It was for this reason that more than 20 years ago monetarists, notably Milton Friedman, opened the rules debate. They believed that there was no other way than to constrain central bankers by a coercive rule in order to achieve zero inflation for the medium to long run.

However, there is an alternative to rules coercion that has barely been explored so far. I propose to write a constitution for the central bank that sets the positive incentive for central bankers to deliver zero expected inflation.

The solution is not a completely unfamiliar one:

- Free central bankers from the obligation of employment stabilization and from an explicit obligation of having to support government policies in general.
- Free them from having to lend to government and from having to purchase Treasury bills and bonds.
- Free them from having to support a specific exchange rate target.
- Ask for professional competence by applying restrictive eligibility criteria for members of the central bank's board or policy committee. Provide them with contracts of a minimum duration of four political cycles (16 years) and pay salaries that match those in private industry.
- Require a qualified majority (e.g., of two to one) in parliament for any change of the central bank law.

In summary, the alternative to coercion by a specific rule is the provision of independence. It is noteworthy that in contrast to any of the proposed coercive rules we have suggestive evidence on the likely performance of a commitment to independence; see Parkin and Bade (1985). For example, the Deutsche Bundesbank and the Schweizerische Nationalbank are the most independent central banks in the world. We know that Germany and Switzerland enjoyed a much lower rate of inflation over the past 40 years than most if not all other countries while living standards in these two countries belong to the highest.

However, my sketched blueprint for independence provides central bankers with more freedom than any central bank constitution to date; it even does not mention price stability as an official goal. Hence a few reflections may be in order.

First, under constitutional independence, central bankers will be free to set the expected rate of inflation at some positive number. Will they deviate from zero? The answer is *no*. The constitution of independence puts a Thomas Becket effect to work: upon appointment the governors are transformed into ultra-conservative bankers who lack the incentive to hunt for short-lived employment gains by generating inflation. They will enjoy the power of neither having to play the government's employment game nor having to satisfy the government's natural preference for collecting the inflation tax.

There is no reason to expect that independent central bankers will be less interested than dependent bankers in the appropriation of seigniorage for putting up architecturally stunning new buildings (Rogoff, 1985), but there is international evidence available that indicates that the zero-inflation return on central bank assets is sufficiently large to meet such preferences.

Second, what will hinder independent central bankers to choose a rate of deflation?

I do not see any incentive for them to do so. Moreover, there is a built-in threatpoint which rational bankers will take into account: they can be dismissed by a qualified majority in parliament.

To summarize, constitutional independence has the clear advantage over coercive rules that the expected rate of inflation will be equal to zero, hence be unaffected by changes in the trends of velocity or of output supply. The central bank's principal, the private sector, will not have to worry about an appropriate amendment of policy procedures because he knows that the self-interested conservative central bankers will take care of the problem. The worst that can happen will be that—for lack of better information or insight into changing economic trends—central bankers adopt Allan Meltzer's rule.

References

Bade, R., and Parkin, M. 1985. "Central Bank Laws and Monetary Policy." Unpublished.

Barro, R. J., and Gordon, D. B. 1983. "Rules, Discretion and Reputation in a Model of Monetary Policy." *Journal of Monetary Economics* (July):101–122.

Friedman, M. 1968. "The Role of Monetary Policy." *American Economic Review* 58 (March):1–17.

Hall, R. E. 1984. "Monetary Strategy with Elastic Price Standard." In *Price Stability and Public Policy*, Kansas City: Federal Reserve Bank of Kansas City, pp. 137–159.

McCallum, B. T. 1987. "The Case for Rules in the Conduct of Monetary Policy: A Concrete Example." *Weltwirtschaftliches Archiv* 123 (Heft 3):415–429.

Melzer, T. C. 1988. "A Proposal for the Adoption of Monetary Base Growth Constraints." Mimeo, Federal Reserve Bank of St. Louis.

Meltzer, A. H. 1984. "Overview." In *Price Stability and Public Policy*, Kansas City: Federal Reserve Bank of Kansas City, pp. 209–222.

Phelps, E. S. 1973. "Inflation in the Theory of Public Finance." *Swedish Journal of Economics* 75 (March):67–82.

Rogoff, K. 1985. "Can International Monetary Policy Cooperation be Counterproductive?" *Journal of International Economics* 18 (May):199–217.

SESSION III

4 MONITORING MONETARY AGGREGATES UNDER RISK AVERSION

William A. Barnett
Melvin Hinich
Piyu Yue

1. Introduction

1.1 Objectives

This article advocates a particular view regarding modeling aggregation methodology. That view is perhaps best represented within the federal government by the activities of the research staff at the Bureau of Labor Statistics (BLS). Within academic research circles, the view is maintained by aggregation and index number theorists as well as by a growing number of microfoundations and rational expectations theorists. The intent of the approach is to assure that the construction of data and its use within models are all internally consistent with rational optimizing behavior by economic agents. We advocate the application of this modern approach to data construction, model specification, and model estimation in monetary economics.

Since the BLS has adhered to this approach both internally and externally for years, the approach perhaps is best described in terms of BLS practice. The BLS, like most other governmental agencies, regularly publishes data produced from statistical (i.e., nonparametric) index numbers. For example, the BLS publishes the well-known and very important Consumer Price Index (CPI), which is a Laspeyres price index. In fact, most price and quantity indexes produced in Washington are Laspeyres-Paasche dual pairs. By their definition, statistical index numbers, such as the CPI, are nonparametric, and their construction requires no econometric estimation. Statistical index numbers are functions only of measurable variables. But the exact quantity and price indexes of economic theory are parametric. For example, the aggregator function that produces the true cost of living index is the cost function. To use that aggregator directly, one must specify the cost function and estimate its parameters.

Statistical index numbers, such as the Laspeyres and Paasche, are produced from approximation theorems to track the unknown aggregator function nonparametrically to within some specified order of approximation. For example, index numbers such as the Fisher Ideal or Törnqvist-Divisia are elements of Diewert's (1976) superlative class, defined to produce second order approximations to any unknown aggregator function. The Laspeyres and Paasche indexes are known to provide first order approximations. Rather than econometrically estimating the true cost of living index by specifying a cost function and estimating its parameters, the BLS publishes the CPI.

However, the research staff at the BLS are well aware of the second order remainder term in the CPI's Laspeyres approximation to the true cost of living index. That staff also are aware of the known upward bias in the Laspeyres index and the cumulative error produced by the failure to chain the index's weights continuously. Clearly some means is needed to assure that the convenient computation, interpretation, and use of the CPI statistical index number does not result in large errors relative to the underlying unknown true cost of living index. The BLS research staff historically have monitored this situation periodically by estimating the true cost of living index econometrically and publishing the resulting comparison between the CPI and the best available estimate of the true cost of living index. As new and more flexible specifications for the cost function become available and as improved econometric estimators become available, the BLS staff update their earlier research by adopting the latest methodology to estimate the true cost of living index.

This method is the best available one for walking the fine line between the convenience of statistical index numbers and the theoretical purity of estimated neoclassical aggregator functions. Even the third order remainder terms in superlative index numbers can become large, if the changes in component quantities or prices are large during a period. Only through the periodic estimation of the underlying aggregator function can the quality of a statistical index number be monitored. If the adequacy of the approximation is found to be deteriorating to an unacceptable degree, then the need arises for the adoption of a more sophisticated statistical index, or more frequent chaining, or more frequent collection of component data. To the end just described, there is a need for the existence of an economics research staff within data-generating government agencies to monitor the quality of the data and to publish papers containing estimated aggregator functions, so that the public can be kept informed of the prevailing quality of the available published statistical index numbers relative to the best available specification and estimation methodology.

We feel that the BLS over the years has admirably fulfilled this objective through the publications of its research staff in the Department of Labor's *Monthly Labor Review* and in various economics journals, such as the *Journal of Business and Economic Statistics*.[1] By doing so, the BLS has assured that data published by that agency not only adequately track the underlying economic aggregator functions but also are usable within economic models. Unless data track the relevant economic aggregator functions, the properties of the data are in conflict with the properties of the models within which they are used. An internal inconsistency arises.

In order for this method to be applied to monetary aggregation and to monetary modeling, there is a need for research in two related areas. One area is the specification and estimation of theoretical economic monetary aggregator functions. The other area is the derivation and computation of nonparametric monetary statistical index numbers. Ongoing research in the first area is needed to assure that monetary statistical index numbers being computed and published remain of adequate quality relative to the best available methods for specifying and estimating monetary aggregator functions. Observe that this is an ongoing process of continuous research, monitoring, and improvement. A procedure for adoption of this methodology within monetary economics was outlined by Barnett (1982) and was used by Barnett (1980, 1983a) in deriving and estimating monetary aggregator functions and in deriving and computing nonparametric monetary statistical index numbers, including both Divisia and Fisher Ideal monetary quantity and user cost index number. A large and growing empirical literature in monetary economics has been motivated by that approach. Much of that literature is surveyed in Barnett, Fisher, and Serletis (1989), and an especially interesting application recently was published by Belongia and Chalfant (1989). For a U.K. application, see Belongia and Chrystal (1990).

The state of the art in monetary aggregation and index number theory is synthesized in detail in Barnett (1987, 1989b), both in terms of the demand for monetary services by consumers and manufacturing firms and the production of monetary services by financial intermediaries. However, the approach to the derivation and specification of aggregator functions in that article implicitly assumes either perfect certainty or risk neutrality, as is the case in virtually all of the literature on economic aggregation and index number theory. The needed theorems on duality, two-stage budgeting, and nonparametric approximation to aggregator functions do not yet exist to extend that literature to the case of risk aversion. Nevertheless, although statistical index numbers with known properties are not yet available, Poterba and Rotemberg (1987) have demonstrated that estimation of theoretical economic monetary aggregator functions is presently possible under risk aversion.

1.2 Methodology

We therefore now advocate that the approach outlined by Barnett (1982) be updated in the following manner to make use of the Poterba and Rotemberg extension:

1.2.1. Step 1 (Admissibility). As originally proposed by Barnett (1982), the choice of component clusterings should be based upon testing for blockwise weak separability. But the testing should be conducted using models with intertemporal expected utility maximization or expected profit maximization, rather than utility or profit maximization. Such inference would have to be conducted from within Euler equations rather than from within money demand functions, since a closed form solution for demand functions typically is not available in the risk averse case. To our knowledge, no one has ever tested for weak separability from within Euler equations. A literature on conducting such tests needs to be developed and then applied with monetary data.[2]

1.2.2. Step 2 (Approximation). Once admissible separable component groupings are acquired, the best available statistical index number should be applied to aggregate over those components. The resulting monetary aggregates should be made publicly available. At present, the best available index numbers are those within Diewert's class of superlative index numbers, with prices measured by user costs. However, the approximation theorems used to derive the remainder terms of those index numbers assume perfect certainty or risk neutrality. Nothing is known about the rate at which the quality of the approximation is degraded as the degree of risk aversion is increased. Hence a literature needs to be produced on nonparametric approximations to aggregator functions under risk aversion. This direction of research is certain to be challenging and slow to appear. But clearly research in that direction would produce major advances in this literature. In fact, the entire literature on duality and functional structure, surveyed by Blackorby, Primont, and Russell (1978), would benefit from extension to the case of risk aversion. Two initial theorems have been proven in this new research in Barnett, Hinich, and Yue (1989).

1.2.3. Step 3 (Monitoring). Ongoing research is needed on the comparison of the quality of the monetary index numbers produced from step 2 versus estimated economic aggregator functions. To this end, the most flexible available specifications for tastes and technology should be used along with the best available estimators of the parameters of the Euler equations. As in the case of the monitoring of the CPI by the BLS through estimation of the true cost of living index, step 3 is a continuous process which should advance by adoption of the best modeling and estimation methods, as they become available.[3] However, we advocate the use of the most recent developments in econometric estimation and modeling to permit this monitoring function to be conducted in a manner consistent with risk aversion by economic agents. As has been pointed out by Poterba and Rotemberg (1987) and as we shall see below, the fact that interest rates are paid at the end of periods renders risk aversion especially important in money demand modeling and monetary asset aggregation.

1.2.4. Step 4 (Application). For policy purposes, monetary aggregates are introduced into demand for money functions, which in turn are introduced into macroeconometric models, such as the Federal Reserve's quarterly model. Those models then are used to run simulations made available to the Open Market Committee and Federal Reserve Board members. The simulations contain information regarding the response of final policy targets to various hypothesized paths for policy instruments. The approach to monetary aggregation advocated by Barnett (1980, 1982) assures that the resulting aggregates would be internally consistent with the theory used to produce demand for money functions, when the demand for money functions are derived under the assumption of risk neutrality.

At present, all of the widely known macroeconometric models, such as the Federal Reserve's MPS (MIT-Penn-SSRC) model, use demand for money functions produced under the assumption of risk neutrality. Those models typically are versions of the linear Goldfeld demand for money function. The use of integrable demand for money function systems in this context was introduced by Barnett (1980, 1983a) under risk neutrality. However, with the adoption of the modernized monitoring function in step 3, the generated aggregate data would be rendered consistent with risk aversion as well as integrability.

We therefore advocate that demand for money function modeling and estimation be conducted through the estimation of Euler equations under the assumption of risk aversion. Research is needed on the best means of introducing such estimated demand for money functions into macroeconometric models, given the difficulties in solving for demand for money functions in closed form in a rational expectations framework.

Although we shall maintain rational expectations in the research that follows, the four-step approach just outlined would be equally applicable under any other expectations formation hypothesis that is consistent with risk aversion.

1.3 A Moral of the Story

It is important to observe that each of the above four steps has its own appropriate purpose. Step 1 selects the clustering of components prior to aggregation. Step 2 produces the aggregation over the clustered components. Step 3 monitors the quality of the results from steps 1 and 2. Hence step 3 is relevant to the choice of method of aggregation, both in terms of the choice of clustering in step 1 and the choice of index number in step 2. In short, step 3 continually evaluates the results from steps 1 and 2. Step 4 assures that the data and their use are internally consistent and make the best use of available theoretical and econometric tools. If steps 1 and 2 produce aggregates at more than one level of aggregation, through acceptance of a recursively nested weakly separable blocking of components, such as M1, M2, M3, and so on, then the relative usefulness of the monetary aggregates at the different levels of aggregation in step 4 is relevant to the choice between those aggregates for any such use in step 4.

However, it is *very important* to observe that strict conformity with the principles just outlined would not permit step 4 to be used to evaluate different possible methods of aggregation over the same components, as, for example, simple sum versus Divisia aggregation over the components of M2. In valid statistical methodology, one is not permitted to select one's means of constructing data in a manner that considers its success in a possible application. Such a feedback from use to data construction method is among the most serious abuses of statistics. Unfortunately, that abuse is evident in many publications in monetary economics.

1.4 Illustration

Barnett, Hinich, and Yue (1989) illustrate the above four-step procedure by carrying out steps 2 and 3 with the monthly component data in Fayyad (1986). The economic theory on which that application is based is motivated by Poterba and Rotemberg (1987). In particular, Barnett, Hinich, and Yue (1989) estimated the economic aggregator function using generalized method of moments estimation and then used the resulting exact theoretical rational expectations monetary aggregate to monitor the tracking capabilities of two statistical index numbers—the simple sum and the Divisia—both in the time domain and in the frequency domain. We usually call the exact theoretical rational expectations aggregate simply the Theoretical aggregate.

In the frequency domain the approach used by Barnett, Hinich, and Yue (1989) to compare the dynamic properties of the three sets of aggregates is to test whether either of the statistical index numbers successfully extracts the nonlinearity from the path of the estimated theoretical aggregate. They conduct the comparisons at the M1 and M2 levels of aggregation. Although Barnett, Hinich, and Yue (1989) do not supply results relevant to step 4 in this article, results from cointegration tests between each monetary quantity index and Humphrey-Hawkins final targets are reported in Barnett and Serletis (1989).

In much of the following, we discuss the implications of the results in Barnett, Hinich, and Yue (1989).

2. Microfoundations for Consumer Demand for Money

2.1 Introduction

The model that Barnett, Hinich, and Yue (1989) estimate to acquire the exact theoretical rational expectations monetary aggregates is from Barnett and Yue (1989), which in turn is motivated by Poterba and Rotemberg (1987). The demand for money in Barnett and Yue's model is both by manufacturing firms and consumers. The supply of money is partially produced by financial intermediaries, which create the economy's inside money. Barnett and Yue model the stochastic decision problems of consumers, manufacturing firms, and financial intermediaries within a stochastic optimal control framework with Markov shocks to technology. Barnett and Yue's model produces a rational expectations equilibrium solution, which is recursive in the sense of Prescott and Mehra (1980). Using the first order conditions, Barnett and Yue prove the existence of a rational expectations equilibrium. Because of the model's recursive structure, the conditions for the use of Bellman's optimality principle are satisfied, and hence that principle is used in the solution procedure.

Barnett and Yue's model is functionally structured in a manner that produces the existence of an exact monetary aggregate for each economic agent.[4] In the current article, we provide results based only on the consumer's decision. In future research we plan similarly to operationalize Barnett and Yue's models of financial firms and of manufacturing firms to produce exact rational expectations aggregates for monetary services demanded by manufacturing firms and for monetary services supplied by financial intermediaries.

Unlike Barnett and Yue (1989) and Barnett, Hinich, and Yue (1989), Poterba and Rotemberg (1987) did not model decisions by manufacturing firms or by financial intermediaries. Their paper contains only a consumer model, and they did not produce the implied monetary aggregate data. However, in the current article we also use only a consumer model, and our expected utility function is exactly the same as Poterba and Rotemberg's. We use the more explicit stochastic optimal control modeling and solution procedure applied by Barnett and Yue (1989) along with their more explicit assumption structure. However, the first order conditions (Euler equations) derived by Barnett and Yue reduce to those produced in another manner by Poterba and Rotemberg, when Poterba and Rotemberg's choice of utility function specification is applied. Hence the exact theoretical rational expectations aggregates produced below could equivalently be viewed as Poterba and Rotemberg's—or, at the very least, strongly motivated by their work.

Aside from the more explicit theorizing involved in our work, our approach differs from Poterba and Rotemberg's only in our use of Hansen and Singleton's (1982) full generalized method of moments (GMM) estimator with iteration to convergence on the weight matrix. Poterba and Rotemberg used three stage least squares, sometimes called the "poor man's GMM estimator." However, the literature on GMM estimation is still evolving. The modeling approaches used by us and by Poterba and

Rotemberg are not inherently dependent upon any particular estimator. Any other researchers who may work in this area in the future surely will wish to use whatever may be the best available estimator at the time.

2.2 The Shocks

In accordance with Barnett and Yue (1989), we assume that all stochastic shocks are Markovian. Hence, at each time period economic agents make decisions regarding current and subsequent actions, given the current state of the economy and relevant information about the future. The past contains no information about the future.

As in Barnett and Yue (1989), the uncertainty in the economy is produced by a random vector of shocks, $\boldsymbol{\lambda}_t$. We assume that the vector of random shocks $\boldsymbol{\lambda}_t$ follows a stationary Markov process with the bounded ergotic realization set Λ defined by

$$\Lambda = \{\boldsymbol{\lambda}_t \in \mathrm{R}^K\colon P[\mathrm{Sup}\|\boldsymbol{\lambda}_t\| \leq D] \geq \beta\},$$

where D is a finite number, P is probability measure, R^K is K-dimensional Euclidean space, $\|\cdot\|$ is the Euclidean norm, and β is positive number less than one. Since $\boldsymbol{\lambda}_t$ follows a Markov process, the distribution of $\boldsymbol{\lambda}_t$ depends only upon the value of $\boldsymbol{\lambda}_{t-1}$. The dynamic properties of the random shocks are described by the transition function, $F(\boldsymbol{\lambda}_{t+1}|\boldsymbol{\lambda}_t)$, which is the conditional distribution of the random shocks. Since the shocks are stationary, the conditional distribution, F, is invariant to time, t. We assume that $F(\boldsymbol{\lambda}_{t+1}|\boldsymbol{\lambda}_t)$ is continuous in both of its arguments. As in Barnett and Yue (1989), the Markov stochastic shocks are assumed to be to technology, not to tastes. As a result, the shocks will not explicitly appear again in the following discussion, which will relate solely to consumer demand. However, the above assumptions have implications for the equilibrium stochastic behavior of the prices and interest rates that will be given to the consumer below.

2.3 Consumer Demand for Monetary Assets

In this section we describe the representative consumer's stochastic decision problem as formulated by Barnett, Hinich, and Yue (1989).[5] The consumer's decisions are made in discrete time over a finite planning horizon for the time intervals, $t, t+1, \ldots, s, \ldots, t+T$, where t is the current time period and $t+T$ is the terminal planning period. Hence the time interval s satisfies $s \in \{t, t+1, \ldots, t+T\}$. The variables used in defining the consumer's decision are as follows:

$\mathbf{x}_s$ = n dimensional vector of planned real consumption of goods and services during period s,
$\mathbf{p}_s$ = n dimensional vector of goods and services expected prices and of durable goods expected rental prices during period s,
$\mathbf{a}_s$ = k dimensional vector of planned real balances of monetary assets during period s,
$\boldsymbol{\rho}_s$ = k dimensional vector of expected nominal holding period yields of monetary assets,
A_s = planned holdings of the benchmark asset during period s,
R_s = the expected one-period holding yield on the benchmark asset during period s,
L_s = planned labor supply during period s,
w_s = the expected wage rate during period s,
I_s = the sum of all other sources of income during period s,
$p_s^* = p_s^*(\mathbf{p}_s)$ = the true cost of living index.

Under the assumption of rational expectations, $F(\boldsymbol{\lambda}_{t+1}|\boldsymbol{\lambda}_t)$ is known to the consumer. Since current period interest rates are not paid until the end of the period, they may be contemporaneously unknown to the consumer. Barnett, Hinich, and Yue (1989) assume that the consumer maximizes the expected value of intertemporal utility subject to a sequence of flow of funds constraints (one for each period of the planning horizon). The benchmark asset A_s provides no services other than its yield R_s. As a result, the benchmark asset does not enter the consumer's intertemporal utility function except in the last instant of the planning horizon. The asset is held only as a means of accumulating wealth to endow the next planning horizons. The consumer's intertemporal utility function is

$$U = U(\mathbf{a}_t, \ldots, \mathbf{a}_s, \ldots, \mathbf{a}_{t+T}; L_t, \ldots, L_s, \ldots, L_{t+T}; \mathbf{x}_t, \ldots, \mathbf{x}_s, \ldots, \mathbf{x}_{t+T}; A_{t+T}),$$

where U is assumed to be intertemporally additively (strongly) separable, such that

$$U = u(\mathbf{a}_t, L_t, \mathbf{x}_t) + \left(\frac{1}{1+\xi}\right) u(\mathbf{a}_{t+1}, L_{t+1}, \mathbf{x}_{t+1}) + \ldots$$

$$\ldots\ldots + \left(\frac{1}{1+\xi}\right)^{T-1} u(\mathbf{a}_{t+T-1}, L_{t+T-1}, \mathbf{x}_{t+T-1})$$

$$+ \left(\frac{1}{1+\xi}\right)^T u(\boldsymbol{a}_{t+T}, L_{t+T}, \boldsymbol{x}_{t+T}, A_{t+T})$$

$$= \sum_{s=t}^{t+T-1} \left(\frac{1}{1+\xi}\right)^{s-t} u(\boldsymbol{a}_s, L_s, X_s)$$

$$+ \left(\frac{1}{1+\xi}\right)^T u(\boldsymbol{a}_{t+T}, L_{t+T}, \boldsymbol{x}_{t+T}, A_{t+T}), \tag{2.2}$$

and the consumer's subjective rate of time preference, ξ, is assumed to be constant.[6]

Given the price, wage, and interest rate processes, the consumer selects the deterministic point $(\boldsymbol{a}_t, L_t, \boldsymbol{x}_t, A_t)$ and the stochastic process $(\boldsymbol{a}_s, L_s, \boldsymbol{x}_s, A_s)$, $s = t + 1, \ldots, t + T$ to maximize the expected value of U over the planning horizon, subject to the sequence of constraints.

2.4 Existence of a Monetary Aggregate for the Consumer

In order to assure the existence of a monetary aggregate for the consumer, Barnett, Hinich, and Yue (1989) partition the vector of monetary asset quantities, $\boldsymbol{a}_s$, such that $\boldsymbol{a}_s = (\boldsymbol{m}_s, \bar{\boldsymbol{m}}_s)$. They correspondingly partition the vector of interest rates of those assets, $\boldsymbol{\rho}_s$, such that $\boldsymbol{\rho}_s = (r_s, \bar{r}_s)$. They then assume that the utility function, u, is blockwise weakly separable in $\boldsymbol{m}_s$. Hence there exists a monetary aggregator ("category utility") function, M, and a utility function, u^*, such that

$$u(\boldsymbol{a}_s, L_s, \boldsymbol{x}_s) = u^*(M(\boldsymbol{m}_s), \bar{\boldsymbol{m}}_s, L_s, \boldsymbol{x}_s), \tag{2.5}$$

where u is the current period category utility function within the separable function U. Then it follows that the exact monetary aggregate, measuring the welfare acquired from consuming the services of $\boldsymbol{m}_s$, is

$$M_s = M(\boldsymbol{m}_s). \tag{2.6}$$

Note that Barnett, Hinich, and Yue (1989) assume only that there exists a partition, $\boldsymbol{a}_s = (\boldsymbol{m}_s, \bar{\boldsymbol{m}}_s)$, such that equation (2.5) holds. Testing for which partition satisfies the weak separability assumption (2.5) is the role of step 1 (Admissibility) in our advocated methodological approach. We define the dimension of $\boldsymbol{m}_s$ to be k_1, and the dimension of $\bar{\boldsymbol{m}}_s$ to be k_2, so that $k = k_1 + k_2$.

It is clear that equation (2.6) does define the exact monetary aggregate in the welfare sense, since M_s measures the consumer's subjective evaluation of the services that he receives from holding $\boldsymbol{m}_s$. However Barnett, Hinich, and Yue (1989, Theorem 1) also show that equation (2.6) defines the exact monetary aggregate in the aggregation theoretic sense.

Using Bellman's principle, Barnett and Yue (1989) derived the first order conditions for solving problems 1 and 2. Under the more restrictive conditions assumed by Poterba and Rotemberg (1987), the first order conditions derived by Barnett and Yue reduce to those acquired by Poterba and Rotemberg without the use of Bellman's method. Hence for their model, their Euler equations are confirmed.

3. The Risk Neutral Case

Under risk neutrality, the decision of each of the agents modeled in this section can be solved in two stages. In the first stage, expenditure is budgeted to aggregates. In the second stage, the budgeted expenditure on each aggregate is allocated over its components. For details of the two stage budgeting solutions, see Barnett (1987). For our purposes, only the contemporaneous second stage decision is relevant. For each of our economic agents, the contemporaneous second stage decision is to maximize the current period service flow produced from the components of the aggregate subject to the budgeted constraint on current period expenditure on those components. The service flow objective function is the agent's separable aggregator function over the components. Since that second stage decision has the same form for the various economic agents, (aside from a change in notation for variables and functions), we present the second stage decision only for one economic agent, the consumer.

In the perfect certainty case, Barnett (1978, 1980) proved that the nominal user cost of the services of m_{it} is π_{it}, where

$$\pi_{it} = p_t^* \frac{R_t - r_{it}}{1 + R_t}. \tag{3.1}$$

The corresponding real user cost is π_{it}/p^*. In the risk neutral case, the user cost formulas are the same as in the perfect certainty case, but with the interest rates replaced by their expected values. The second stage decision is to choose $\boldsymbol{m}_t \geq 0$ to maximize $M(\boldsymbol{m}_t)$ subject to $\boldsymbol{m}_t'\boldsymbol{\pi}_t = E_t$, where E_t is total expenditure budgeted to $\boldsymbol{m}_t$ in the first stage.

It can be shown that the solution value of the exact monetary aggregate $M_t = M(\boldsymbol{m}_t)$ can be tracked without error (see, e.g., Barnett (1983b)) by the Divisia index:[7]

$$d\log M_t = \sum_{i=1}^{k_1} s_{it}\, d\log m_{it}, \tag{3.2}$$

where the expenditure share of monetary asset i is $s_{it} = m_{it}\pi_{it}/E_t$. The flawless tracking ability of the index in the risk neutral case holds regardless of the form of the unknown aggregator function, M. However, under risk aversion the ability of equation (3.2) to track $M(\boldsymbol{m}_t)$ is compromised, and the rate at which that tracking ability deteriorates is unknown, as the degree of risk aversion increases above zero. Barnett, Hinich, and Yue (1989) investigate the magnitude of that error below by econometrically estimating $M(\boldsymbol{m}_t)$.

It should be observed that the monetary aggregate $M(\boldsymbol{m}_t)$ measures the flow of monetary services rather than the stock of monetary wealth. However, one can acquire the stock of monetary wealth by discounting to present value the monetary service flow expenditure stream. First observe that by Fisher's factor reversal test, we know that there must exist a user cost aggregate $\Pi(\boldsymbol{\pi}_t)$ dual to $M(\boldsymbol{m}_t)$ such that $M(\boldsymbol{m}_t)\Pi(\boldsymbol{\pi}_t) = \boldsymbol{m}_t'\boldsymbol{\pi}_t$. Hence expenditure on aggregate services $M(\boldsymbol{m}_t)$ must equal the sum of the user-cost evaluated expenditures on the components $\boldsymbol{m}_t$. As a result, we can derive monetary wealth by discounting to present value either the expenditure flow $\boldsymbol{m}_s'\boldsymbol{\pi}_s$ or the equal expenditure flow $M(\boldsymbol{m}_s)\Pi(\boldsymbol{\pi}_s)$ for $s \geq t$.

Barnett (1978, eq. 2, 1980, eq. 3.3; 1981, eq. 7.3) has derived that monetary capital stock by discounting to present value expenditure on the component flows $\boldsymbol{m}_s'\boldsymbol{\pi}_s$ for $s \geq t$. The resulting formula for the monetary stock, V_t, is:

$$V_t = \sum_{s=t}^{\infty} \sum_{i=1}^{n} \left[\frac{p_s^*}{\rho_s} - \frac{p_s^*(1 + r_{is})}{\rho_s + 1}\right] m_{is}. \tag{3.3}$$

The discount factors in that formula are:

$$\rho_s = \begin{cases} 1 & \text{for } s = t \\ \prod_{u=t}^{s-1}(1 + R_u) & \text{for } s > t. \end{cases}$$

In economics, variables in the structure of the economy usually are flows. The exceptions are the wealth variables that enter through intertemporal Fisherine wealth constraints, as appear on the right-hand-side of life-cycle consumption functions and in the monetary transmission mechanism, when it operates through a Pigou or real balance effect within the consumption function. In such cases, equation (3.3) can be used to measure monetary wealth conditionally upon assumptions regarding expectations formation. In principle one could use econometric methods to incorporate adaptive expectations or rational expectations into (3.3).

It would clearly be more convenient to have a nonparametric statistical means of computing (3.3) without the need to use parametric econometric estimators. But at present there are only two available nonparametric statistical means of computing (3.3).

1. One is to assume stationary expectations, so that $R_s = R_t$ and $r_s = r_t$ for all $s \geq t$. The result is the measure proposed by Rotemberg (1989) in this book. See Barnett (1989a) in this book for the proof that Rotemberg's money stock measure is correct under stationary expectations.

2. The other nonparametric method results from the implicit assumption made by the Federal Reserve in the production of its monetary aggregates: $r_s = 0$ for all $s \geq t$. Rotemberg's implicit assumption obviously is the one to be preferred. The days of noninterest-bearing money are long gone.

See Barnett (1989a) in this book for more discussion of money stock measures. In the general case of risk aversion and rational expectations, measurement of the economic stock of money is a complex capital asset pricing problem (see Merton, 1989).

4. Data and Specification

As in Barnett, Hinich, and Yue (1989), we first set $\boldsymbol{m}_s$ equal to those components of M1 found by Belongia and Chalfant (1989) to be weakly separable. We then repeat our analysis with $\boldsymbol{m}_s$ set equal to the components of M2, but with those components clustered into three groups with prior aggregation within groups, so that $\boldsymbol{m}_s$ contains three aggregated elements. Hence we implicitly assume that $\boldsymbol{a}_s$ is partitioned in accordance with a recursively nested two level separable blocking, such that the components of our M1 aggregate are separable within the components of our M2 aggregate, which in turn are separable within $\boldsymbol{a}_s$. Considering the little that is known about testing for separability in the risk averse case, the chosen clustering is hardly the last word on that subject. In short, we are not here seeking to advance the state of the art in step 1 Admissibility Testing, which nevertheless is an important part of proper aggregation.

Barnett, Hinich, and Yue (1989) assume that the monetary aggregator function, $M(\boldsymbol{m}_s)$, has the CES (constant elasticity of substitution) form, which then is nested into a Cobb-Douglas function of money and goods.[8]

That utility tree then is embedded in an expected utility function having constant degree of relative risk aversion.

5. Estimation

Barnett, Hinich, and Yue (1989) use Hansen and Singleton's (1982) generalized method of moments estimator to estimate the parameters of the Euler equations. Poterba and Rotemberg used three-stage least squares. In accordance with Hansen and Singleton's estimator, the weighting matrix is iterated on until convergence.

Using the parameter estimates and the components data, the estimated theoretical M1 monetary aggregate, $M_s = M(\mathbf{m}_s)$, was computed at each obervation. The Divisia quantity index and the simple sum index over the same components also were computed. The resulting nominal per capita time paths of these three M1 index numbers are supplied in table 4–2.

This procedure then was repeated with the M2 data. The components of M2 were clustered into three groups, and asset quantities within groups were aggreated by simple summation to produce three aggregated components over which we aggregate by the three methods. To identify the prior clustering of components, we list the components of M2 in table 4 – 1. The definition of the three aggregated monetary components, in terms of the numbered lines in table 4 – 1, is:

m_{1s} = (1) + (2) + (3) + (4) (real per capita during time period s),
m_{2s} = (5) + (6) + (7) + (8) + (9) + (10) + (11) + (12) + (13) + (14) + (15) (real per capita during the time period s)
m_{3s} = (16) + (17) + (18) (real per capita during time period s).

Using these parameter estimates and the component data, the estimated theoretical M2 monetary aggregate, $M_s = M(\mathbf{m}_s)$, was computed at each observation. The Divisia quantity index and the simple sum index over the same components also were computed. The nominal per capita time paths of these three M2 index numbers are supplied in table 4–2. See Barnett, Hinich, and Yue (1989) for the resulting parameter estimates and for the plots of the resulting estimated Theoretical aggregates. Central to the analysis of their data is the Hinich bispectrum test for nonlinearity. That test was used by Barnett, Hinich, and Yue (1989) to determine whether either of the statistical monetary indices (simple sum or Divisia) successfully extracts the nonlinear structure from the estimated Theoretical aggregate.

The Hinich test is a powerful and very general method for testing for

Table 4–1. M2 Components of Monetary Assets

Component	*Mnemonic*	*Asset Description*
1	CUR	currency and traveler checks
2	DDCON	demand deposits held by households
3	DDBUS	demand deposits held by business firms
4	OCD	other checkable deposits less Super NOW accounts
5	SNOWC	Super NOW accounts at commercial banks
6	SNOWT	Super NOW accounts at thrifts
7	ONRP	overnight repurchase agreements
8	ONED	overnight Eurodollars
9	MMMF	money market mutual fund shares
10	MMDAC	money market demand deposit accounts at commercial banks
11	MMDAT	money market demand deposit accounts at thrifts
12	SDCB	savings deposits at commercial banks less MMDAs
13	SDSL	savings deposits at savings and loans less MMDAs
14	SDMSB	savings deposits at mutual savings banks less MMDAs
15	SDCU	savings deposits at credit unions less MMDAs
16	STDCB	small-time deposits and retail repurchase agreements at commercial banks
17	STDTH	small-time deposits and retail repurchase agreements at thrifts
18	STDCU	small-time deposits at credit unions

Table 4–2. Monthly Growth Rates of Nominal Monetary Aggregate Indices of M1 and M2 (percent per month, per capita, not annualized)

Year	*Month*	$M1_{THEO}$	$M1_{SS}$	$M1_{DIV}$	$M2_{THEO}$	$M2_{SS}$	$M2_{DIV}$
1969	2	0.29	0.27	0.30	0.32	0.36	0.33
1969	3	0.25	0.27	0.25	0.11	0.16	0.15
1969	4	0.03	−0.03	0.02	0.00	0.06	0.03
1969	5	0.21	0.14	0.20	0.21	0.25	0.23
1969	6	0.14	0.10	0.14	−0.03	0.08	0.30
1969	7	0.02	−0.05	0.02	−0.09	0.01	−0.02
1969	8	0.11	0.07	0.11	0.16	0.24	0.21
1969	9	0.32	0.28	0.32	0.09	0.13	0.13
1969	10	0.28	0.23	0.28	0.48	0.56	0.53
1969	11	0.09	0.05	0.09	0.28	0.39	0.35
1969	12	0.98	1.05	0.97	0.22	0.10	0.16
1970	1	−0.50	−0.62	−0.49	−0.76	−0.56	−0.64
1970	2	0.32	0.31	0.33	−0.04	0.07	0.01

Table 4–2. (Continued)

Year	*Month*	$M1_{THEO}$	$M1_{SS}$	$M1_{DIV}$	$M2_{THEO}$	$M2_{SS}$	$M2_{DIV}$
1970	3	0.30	0.31	0.30	0.06	0.18	0.12
1970	4	0.25	0.17	0.26	0.22	0.40	0.31
1970	5	0.13	0.06	0.13	0.27	0.43	0.35
1970	6	0.14	0.09	0.15	0.30	0.44	0.37
1970	7	0.76	0.82	0.75	0.74	0.82	0.79
1970	8	0.74	0.79	0.74	0.87	0.93	0.90
1970	9	0.32	0.32	0.32	0.65	0.73	0.68
1970	10	0.31	0.30	0.31	0.53	0.65	0.58
1970	11	0.31	0.27	0.31	0.72	0.83	0.73
1970	12	0.38	0.36	0.37	0.66	0.85	0.73
1971	1	0.79	0.82	0.80	1.04	1.21	1.31
1971	2	0.53	0.56	0.54	1.11	1.28	1.10
1971	3	0.44	0.42	0.43	1.19	1.41	1.17
1971	4	0.77	0.84	0.80	1.04	1.12	1.06
1971	5	0.59	0.56	0.58	0.70	0.75	0.70
1971	6	0.56	0.50	0.54	0.76	0.86	0.78
1971	7	0.29	0.25	0.28	0.63	0.79	0.67
1971	8	0.31	0.28	0.30	0.74	0.90	0.77
1971	9	0.15	0.13	0.14	0.62	0.75	0.62
1971	10	0.21	0.21	0.21	0.64	0.83	0.68
1971	11	0.17	0.16	0.17	0.61	0.73	0.60
1971	12	0.64	0.65	0.64	0.74	0.90	0.82
1972	1	0.84	0.91	0.87	0.96	1.07	1.02
1972	2	0.74	0.79	0.77	0.95	1.00	0.94
1972	3	0.34	0.38	0.36	0.67	0.73	0.65
1972	4	0.18	0.11	0.15	0.42	0.55	0.44
1972	5	0.28	0.25	0.27	0.65	0.76	0.64
1972	6	0.71	0.76	0.73	1.05	1.20	1.09
1972	7	0.83	0.86	0.84	1.03	1.15	1.07
1972	8	0.82	0.83	0.82	0.96	1.08	1.01
1972	9	0.64	0.62	0.63	0.89	1.01	0.90
1972	10	0.56	0.52	0.55	0.73	0.82	0.74
1972	11	1.01	1.06	1.02	0.98	0.99	1.00
1972	12	0.84	0.87	0.84	0.81	0.99	0.90
1973	1	0.21	0.16	0.20	0.30	0.43	0.34
1973	2	−0.15	−0.27	−0.17	0.03	0.06	0.01
1973	3	0.39	0.30	0.39	0.44	0.52	0.45
1973	4	0.76	0.80	0.76	0.72	0.78	0.74
1973	5	0.71	0.69	0.71	0.71	0.73	0.71
1973	6	0.18	0.17	0.19	0.33	0.38	0.33
1973	7	0.12	0.05	0.13	0.02	0.20	−0.03

Table 4–2. (Continued)

Year	*Month*	$M1_{THEO}$	$M1_{SS}$	$M1_{DIV}$	$M2_{THEO}$	$M2_{SS}$	$M2_{DIV}$
1973	8	0.06	−0.05	0.07	−0.04	0.02	−0.07
1973	9	0.31	0.30	0.32	0.36	0.37	0.36
1973	10	0.71	0.72	0.70	0.56	0.64	0.47
1973	11	0.68	0.64	0.68	0.64	0.69	0.60
1973	12	0.39	0.33	0.39	0.32	0.47	0.19
1974	1	0.52	0.45	0.53	0.40	0.48	0.31
1974	2	0.53	0.48	0.54	0.62	0.65	0.62
1974	3	0.14	0.04	0.16	0.21	0.24	0.22
1974	4	0.22	0.13	0.24	0.17	0.19	0.16
1974	5	0.33	0.30	0.34	0.31	0.29	0.32
1974	6	0.20	0.17	0.20	0.28	0.31	0.29
1974	7	0.33	0.21	0.33	0.16	0.23	0.16
1974	8	0.34	0.29	0.35	0.29	0.36	0.31
1974	9	0.40	0.32	0.41	0.43	0.46	0.44
1974	10	0.53	0.46	0.54	0.50	0.51	0.51
1974	11	0.17	0.10	0.18	0.27	0.26	0.28
1974	12	−0.09	−0.21	−0.09	0.19	0.36	0.22
1975	1	0.27	0.22	0.26	0.67	0.79	0.69
1975	2	0.66	0.63	0.65	1.11	1.16	1.10
1975	3	−0.26	−0.30	−0.28	0.80	0.01	0.82
1975	4	0.95	0.93	0.94	1.24	1.30	1.25
1975	5	1.25	1.25	1.25	1.46	1.46	1.43
1975	6	0.13	0.07	0.11	0.89	1.13	0.95
1975	7	0.48	0.44	0.47	0.64	0.76	0.69
1975	8	0.19	0.20	0.19	0.66	0.78	0.69
1975	9	−0.14	−0.28	−0.18	0.37	0.53	0.41
1975	10	0.84	0.84	0.84	0.90	0.93	0.91
1975	11	−0.12	−0.22	−0.16	0.55	0.74	0.60
1975	12	0.38	0.32	0.36	0.82	0.99	0.88
1976	1	0.72	0.70	0.71	1.25	1.26	1.19
1976	2	0.40	0.33	0.37	0.86	0.80	0.76
1976	3	0.59	0.51	0.56	1.00	1.02	0.95
1976	4	0.61	0.56	0.59	1.09	1.21	1.10
1976	5	−0.07	−0.16	−0.10	0.21	0.31	0.23
1976	6	0.28	0.21	0.26	0.65	0.77	0.68
1976	7	0.52	0.52	0.52	0.99	1.11	1.01
1976	8	0.14	0.06	0.11	0.75	0.97	0.79
1976	9	0.92	0.95	0.93	1.21	1.27	1.21
1976	10	0.10	0.07	0.09	0.88	1.03	0.85
1976	11	0.78	0.81	0.79	1.19	1.24	1.17
1976	12	0.78	0.77	0.78	0.94	1.08	0.99

Table 4–2. (Continued)

Year	*Month*	$M1_{THEO}$	$M1_{SS}$	$M1_{DIV}$	$M2_{THEO}$	$M2_{SS}$	$M2_{DIV}$
1977	1	0.67	0.67	0.67	0.83	0.88	0.83
1977	2	0.52	0.52	0.52	0.84	0.86	0.81
1977	3	0.76	0.73	0.75	0.87	0.90	0.87
1977	4	0.13	0.08	0.11	0.64	0.79	0.63
1977	5	0.44	0.41	0.43	0.55	0.62	0.57
1977	6	0.66	0.60	0.64	0.74	0.79	0.75
1977	7	0.36	0.36	0.36	0.55	0.60	0.55
1977	8	0.59	0.55	0.58	0.64	0.69	0.65
1977	9	0.78	0.78	0.78	0.68	0.67	0.69
1977	10	0.43	0.40	0.42	0.52	0.57	0.52
1977	11	0.60	0.54	0.59	0.56	0.59	0.57
1977	12	0.85	0.91	0.86	0.62	0.66	0.65
1978	1	0.21	0.11	0.21	0.27	0.33	0.27
1978	2	0.42	0.37	0.41	0.52	0.48	0.50
1978	3	0.83	0.86	0.83	0.60	0.54	0.61
1978	4	0.84	0.87	0.84	0.63	0.61	0.65
1978	5	0.60	0.57	0.61	0.40	0.48	0.42
1978	6	0.43	0.41	0.43	0.36	0.54	0.35
1978	7	0.40	0.38	0.41	0.33	0.45	0.31
1978	8	0.98	0.98	0.98	0.77	0.87	0.72
1978	9	0.21	0.12	1.23	0.37	0.57	0.25
1978	10	0.13	0.03	0.16	0.20	0.44	−0.01
1978	11	0.23	0.12	0.26	0.42	0.63	0.20
1978	12	−0.38	−0.53	−0.33	−0.06	0.36	−0.46
1979	1	0.10	0.01	0.14	0.18	0.40	−0.09
1979	2	0.43	0.39	0.44	0.58	0.64	0.49
1979	3	1.00	1.04	0.98	0.79	0.85	0.64
1979	4	−0.13	−0.23	−0.08	0.29	0.48	0.12
1979	5	1.04	1.08	1.03	0.99	0.94	0.99
1979	6	0.71	0.72	0.70	0.75	0.74	0.75
1979	7	0.48	0.41	0.51	0.48	0.55	0.40
1979	8	0.45	0.38	0.48	0.50	0.69	0.36
1979	9	0.11	0.03	0.15	−0.08	0.27	−0.38
1979	10	0.03	−0.01	0.05	−0.38	0.10	−0.88
1979	11	0.16	0.12	0.18	0.24	0.41	0.06
1979	12	0.53	0.48	0.56	0.40	0.56	0.21
1980	1	0.85	0.87	0.85	0.68	0.79	0.54
1980	2	−0.18	−0.30	−0.11	−0.01	0.31	−0.29
1980	3	−1.58	−1.85	−1.45	−1.18	−0.42	−1.72
1980	4	−0.04	−0.16	−0.01	0.32	0.55	0.24
1980	5	0.93	0.97	0.93	1.55	1.20	1.61

Table 4–2. (Continued)

Year	*Month*	$M1_{THEO}$	$M1_{SS}$	$M1_{DIV}$	$M2_{THEO}$	$M2_{SS}$	$M2_{DIV}$
1980	6	0.71	0.70	0.71	1.60	1.23	1.63
1980	7	1.54	1.62	1.54	1.35	0.95	1.35
1980	8	0.88	0.96	0.87	0.94	0.82	0.95
1980	9	0.80	0.78	0.80	0.68	0.69	0.64
1980	10	0.17	0.02	0.24	0.41	0.74	0.15
1980	11	−1.04	−1.27	−0.92	−0.66	0.00	−1.06
1980	12	−3.09	−3.57	−2.84	−0.01	0.49	−0.42
1981	1	−1.43	−1.76	−1.21	0.53	0.66	0.41
1981	2	−0.29	−0.42	−0.19	1.14	0.99	1.29
1981	3	0.25	0.17	0.31	1.45	1.11	1.73
1981	4	−0.65	−0.80	−0.52	0.05	0.30	−0.06
1981	5	−0.48	−0.56	−0.41	0.27	0.46	0.21
1981	6	0.02	−0.07	0.10	0.70	0.61	0.77
1981	7	0.15	0.13	0.17	0.72	0.86	0.64
1981	8	−0.49	−0.56	−0.41	0.33	0.56	0.13
1981	9	−0.04	−0.09	0.01	0.43	0.70	0.09
1981	10	0.18	0.12	0.22	0.92	0.90	0.96
1981	11	0.42	0.34	0.46	1.06	0.89	1.18
1981	12	0.78	0.83	0.76	1.25	1.00	1.36
1982	1	−0.64	−0.80	−0.53	−0.15	0.10	−0.30
1982	2	−0.21	−0.30	−0.15	0.40	0.48	0.37
1982	3	0.28	0.19	0.35	0.53	0.52	0.53
1982	4	0.16	0.05	0.24	0.47	0.60	0.43
1982	5	−0.07	−0.15	−0.01	0.47	0.52	0.47
1982	6	−0.09	−0.17	−0.03	0.43	0.60	0.39
1982	7	0.53	0.53	0.53	1.05	0.93	1.06
1982	8	0.57	0.58	0.57	0.91	0.79	0.89
1982	9	0.83	0.83	0.83	1.05	0.65	0.95
1982	10	0.52	0.56	0.51	0.97	0.68	0.88
1982	11	0.39	0.35	0.41	1.28	0.72	1.00
1982	12	0.04	−0.02	0.05	3.90	2.71	2.84
1983	1	0.41	0.31	0.43	2.54	1.76	1.78
1983	2	0.72	0.68	0.74	1.27	0.75	0.94
1983	3	0.29	0.21	0.32	0.81	0.63	0.70
1983	4	0.86	0.87	0.85	0.93	0.70	0.86
1983	5	0.55	0.55	0.56	0.68	0.60	0.66
1983	6	0.49	0.47	0.50	0.45	0.53	0.47
1983	7	0.28	0.25	0.29	0.30	0.43	0.31
1983	8	0.21	0.12	0.27	0.37	0.53	0.38
1983	9	0.41	0.33	0.45	0.63	0.80	0.63
1983	10	0.20	0.12	0.25	0.38	0.56	0.39

Table 4–2. (Continued)

Year	*Month*	$M1_{THEO}$	$M1_{SS}$	$M1_{DIV}$	$M2_{THEO}$	$M2_{SS}$	$M2_{DIV}$
1983	11	0.26	0.20	0.30	0.34	0.42	0.34
1983	12	0.33	0.31	0.35	0.46	0.54	0.47
1984	1	0.44	0.42	0.45	0.59	0.59	0.58
1984	2	0.33	0.29	0.37	0.54	0.48	0.53
1984	3	0.29	0.26	0.32	0.47	0.47	0.46
1984	4	0.23	0.21	0.25	0.48	0.56	0.49
1984	5	0.94	0.95	0.93	0.48	0.55	0.50
1984	6	−0.21	−0.28	−0.15	0.13	0.40	0.14
1984	7	0.12	0.06	0.17	0.19	0.46	0.17
1984	8	0.23	0.21	0.25	0.38	0.58	0.34
1984	9	−0.71	−0.80	−0.62	0.12	0.36	0.06
1984	10	0.69	0.71	0.67	1.12	1.08	1.10
1984	11	0.61	0.62	0.60	1.08	1.02	1.05
1984	12	0.09	0.09	0.10	1.17	1.08	1.09
1985	1	0.89	0.91	0.89	1.09	0.85	1.01
1985	2	0.24	0.21	0.26	0.42	0.28	0.38

THEO—Growth rate of estimated theoretic index.
SS—Growth rate of simple sum index.
DIV—Growth rate of divisia index.

nonlinear structure in a time series, and hence can be useful for comparing the dynamic structures of any two time series. As a result, we present the relevant theory required for the use of the Hinich test in the Appendix. We present the background and methodology in a self-contained form to make the use of the test available to others in any relevant applications. For a related survey and application of methods of testing for chaos (a form of deep nonlinearity), see Barnett and Chen (1988).

6. Results

Barnett, Hinich, and Yue (1989) found at both the M1 and M2 levels of aggregation that the Divisia monetary aggregate tracks the estimated Theoretical aggregate well, while the simple sum aggregate does not. The few exceptional cases were during periods of unusually high economic uncertainty within the economy, so that the Theoretical index's ability to incorporate risk aversion became particularly important. In general, the risk neutrality assumption implied by the Divisia index was found to be an adequate approximation for purposes of monetary aggregation.

7. Another Example

In this article we have emphasized one application of monitoring in monetary economics. However, it should be observed that another exists. Since monitoring is by definition a means of verifying robustness of the tracking ability of an index to variations in the underlying economic model's specification, the monitoring role can be applied to check robustness to any aspect of that specification. Barnett, Hinich, and Weber (1986) have checked for robustness to the rate of taxation on interest. In particular, they observed that many financial intermediaries are subject to required reserves, which pay no interest. The result is an implicit tax on financial intermediaries. That tax is seen on the supply side of money markets, since financial intermediaries supply monetary services. However, that implicit tax is not seen on the demand side of money markets by the consumers and firms that demand monetary services.

As a result of this regulatory wedge, the user cost of produced monetary services by financial intermediaries is not equal to the user cost of demanded monetary services. The reason is that the interest rates that appear in the user cost formula, (3.1.), are holding period yields and hence are after-tax yields. Hence the supply side Divisia index may be different from the demand side Divisia index. This conclusion should not be viewed as a defect of the Divisia index, since the exact economic aggregate produces the same paradox. Even if all component markets are cleared, the exact demand side aggregate may not be equal to the exact supply side aggregate, when a regulatory wedge exists. See Barnett, Hinich, and Weber (1986, figure 2) for a demonstration of that fact in terms of exact economic aggregator functions in economic equilibrium. In effect, when a regulatory wedge exists, the suppliers of services believe that the total quantity of services that they are producing is different from the quantity of services that demanders perceive themselves to be receiving. As a result, the demand side and supply side aggregates *should not* be equal.

Although it is perhaps comforting to know that the difference between the demand side and supply side Divisia index is no error, in practice we usually must choose between the demand and supply side aggregate, since joint use of both defeats the informational simplification that is the primary justification for the use of aggregates. As a result, Barnett, Hinich, and Weber (1986) used a Hilbert transform method and a spectral method to test the significance of the difference in growth rates between the demand and supply side Divisia monetary aggregates. The conclusion is that no statistical significance exists, except perhaps at very high frequency (i.e., in the very short run). Hence the choice between the demand side and supply side Divisia aggregate is of no consequence.

8. Conclusions

The Bureau of Labor Statistics has adopted data construction procedures and data quality monitoring methods which use the available literature on index number and aggregation theory extensively. We advocate analogous procedures in the production and monitoring of monetary data. However, the fact that interest rates are not paid until the end of the period increases the importance of risk in estimating money demand and supply functions and in aggregating over component monetary assets. With many non-monetary goods, prices are paid at the start of the period, so that the assumption of perfect certainty need not be a serious issue in applying index number theory. But as pointed out by Poterba and Rotemberg (1987), the lack of perfect certainty regarding contemporaneous interest rates raises a serious complication for index number theory when applied to monetary data.

We advocate modeling, estimation, testing, and monitoring procedures that are analogous to those used by the Bureau of Labor Statistics, but which are rendered necessarily more complex in monetary economics as a result of the problems raised by risk. We believe that these procedures not only could produce immediate improvement in the quality of existing monetary data but also would encourage and promote much deep new research in the area. For example, much research is needed on duality theory and functional structure and on nonparametric statistical approximations to aggregator functions under risk. Barnett, Hinich, and Yue (1989) have provided two such theorems. Those theorems demonstrate the role in aggregation theory of the Theoretical aggregate, and hence capture the potential usefulness of the Theoretical aggregate in modeling and in policy. Much more research in that direction is needed.

The two existing theorems in Barnett, Hinich, and Yue (1989) demonstrate that under rational expectations the Theoretical aggregate can be used either as an indicator or as an intermediate target. The simple sum monetary aggregates, on the other hand, do not enter into the economy's structure and hence cannot be used either as an indicator or as an intermediate target. We see no useful role for the simple sum monetary aggregates in modeling or in policy.

In conclusion, it should be observed that the particular results discussed in this article are of less importance than the methodology. In the monitoring function that is emphasized in this article, an estimated aggregator function is used to monitor the tracking ability of a statistical index, in a manner analogous to the periodic use by BLS staff of estimated cost functions to monitor the tracking ability of the CPI, which is a Laspeyres price index. However, it should be observed that the estimation of only one aggregator function cannot adequately serve that role. Hence the results in Barnett, Hinich, and Yue (1989), which we emphasize, should be viewed only as an illustration. Fully adequate monitoring of a statistical index can be accomplished only by continuous research demonstrating its *robustness* as a tracking tool relative to many specifications for the aggregator function and many estimators of the parameters of the aggregate.

In fact, if one were faced with a choice between any one estimated parametric aggregator function and a high quality "superlative" statistical index, such as the Törnqvist-Divisia, one should prefer the index. The reason is that a superlative index, at least under risk neutrality, will track any aggregator function up to a third order remainder term *in the changes*. The fact that the order of the remainder is in the changes, rather than in the levels, results from the chaining of the index. However, estimated aggregator functions, including those produced from flexible function forms, produce approximations that are no better than those of fixed base indexes, since the parameters of an estimated aggregator function are not re-estimated at each observation. Hence it is hardly reasonable to view a single estimated aggregator function as a standard against which to compare a chained superlative index number, when in fact the index should be viewed as preferable to any such single estimated aggregator function.

The monitoring role can only be accomplished in a satisfactory manner when viewed as a check on robustness. At present, we have two such studies: Barnett, Hinich, and Weber's (1986) study of robustness to taxation, and Barnett, Hinich, and Yue's (1989) test of robustness to one specification of tastes under risk aversion. In this article we report only upon those two illustrations of monitoring. Many more such studies are needed.

Notes

1. In fact, there recently has even been some research within the BLS on monetary aggregation. See, for example, Fixler (1988) and Fixler and Zieschang (1989a, 1989b, 1989c).

2. This is despite the fact that even in the perfect certainty case, testing for weak separability is very difficult. See Barnett and Choi (1989a, 1989b) for the results of a Monte Carlo study investigating the relative merits of various available weak separability tests in the

perfect certainty case. For relevant theory, see Russell (1975) and Blackorby, Primont, and Russell (1977).

3. The need for monitoring increases as the Divisia variance increases. Hence monitoring the Divisia variance is useful for that purpose. See Barnett and Serletis (1990).

4. That is, the relevant blockwise weak separability conditions are satisified.

5. In later research we plan to delete the representative consumer assumption and aggregate over consumers by weaker means. See Barnett (1981, appendix B1.2), Barnett (1987, section 9), and Barnett and Serletis (1990).

6. Although money may not exist in the elementary utility function, there exists a derived utility function that contains money, so long as money has positive value in equilibrium. See, for example, Arrow and Hahn (1971), Phlips and Spinnewyn (1982), and Feenstra (1986). We implicitly are using that derived utility function.

7. In discrete time, the index's Törnqvist approximation is used by replacing s_{it} by its average s_{it}^* over the discrete time interval, where $s_{it}^* = (1/2)(s_{it} + s_{i,t-1})$, and by replacing the differential log changes by discrete log changes.

8. In later research, we plan to extend the model to the case of AIM preferences and technology, in accordance with Barnett, Geweke, and Wolfe (1989) and Barnett, Geweke, and Yue (1989).

References

Arrow, K. J., and Hahn, F. 1971. *General Competitive Analysis*. San Francisco: Holden-Day.

Ashley, Richard, Patterson, Douglas M., and Hinich, Melvin. 1986. "A Diagnostic Test for Nonlinear Serial Dependence in Time Series Fitting Errors." *Journal of Time Series Analysis* 7(3):165–178.

Barnett, William A. 1978. "The User Cost of Money." *Economics Letters* 1:145–149.

Barnett, William A. 1980. "Economic Monetary Aggregates: An Application of Index Number and Aggregation Theory." *Journal of Econometrics* 14:11–48.

Barnett, William A. 1981. *Consumer Demand and Labor Supply: Goods, Monetary Assets, and Time*. Amsterdam: North-Holland.

Barnett, William A. 1982. "The Optimal Level of Monetary Aggregation." *Journal of Money, Credit and Banking*, 14:687–710.

Barnett, William A. 1983a. "New Indices of Money Supply and the Flexible Laurent Demand System." *Journal of Business and Economic Statistics* 1:7–23.

Barnett, William A. 1983b. "Understanding the New Divisia Monetary Aggregates." *Review of Public Data Use* 11:349–355.

Barnett, William A. 1987. "The Microeconomic Theory of Monetary Aggregation." In William A. Barnett and Kenneth J. Singleton (Eds.), *New Approaches to Monetary Economics*, Proceedings of the Second International Symposium in Economic Theory and Econometrics. Cambridge: Cambridge University Press.

Barnett, William A. 1990. "A Reply to Julio J. Rotemberg." In Michael T. Belongia (Ed.). *Monetary Policy on the 75th Anniversary of the Federal Reserve System*. Boston: Kluwer Academic Publishers, pp. 233–244.

Barnett, William A. 1989. "Developments in Monetary Aggregation Theory." *Journal of Policy Modelling*, forthcoming.

Barnett, William A., and Serletis, Apostolos. 1990. "A Dispersion-Dependency Diagnostic Test for Aggregation Error: with Applications to Monetary Economics and Income Distribution." *Journal of Econometrics*, 43 (January/February): 5–34.

Barnett, William A., and Serletis, Apostolos. 1989. "Prices, Output, and Money: An Application of Co-Integration Techniques." University of Texas at Austin.

Barnett, William A., Fisher, Douglas, and Serletis, Apostolos, 1989. "Consumer Theory and the Demand for and Measurement of Money. University of Texas at Austin, North Carolina State University, and University of Calgary.

Barnett, William A., Geweke, John, and Wolfe, Michael. 1989. "Seminonparametric Bayesian Estimation of the Asymptotically Ideal Production Model." *Journal of Econometrics*, forthcoming.

Barnett, William A., Geweke, John, and Yue, Piyu. 1989. "Seminonparametric Bayesian Estimation of the Asymptotically Ideal Model: The AIM Demand System." *Nonparametric and Semiparametric Methods in Econometrics and Statistics*. In William A. Barnett, George Tauchen, and James Powell (Eds.), Cambridge: Cambridge University Press, forthcoming.

Barnett, William A., Hinich, Melvin, and Weber, Warren. 1986. "The Regulatory Wedge between the Demand-Side and Supply-Side Aggregation-Theoretic Monetary Aggregates." *Journal of Econometrics* 33:165–185.

Barnett, William A., Hinich, Melvin, and Yue, Piyu. 1989. "Monetary Policy with the Exact Theoretical Rational Expectations Monetary Aggregates." University of Texas at Austin.

Barnett, William A., and Chen, Ping. 1988. "The Aggregation-Theoretic Monetary Aggregates are Chaotic and Have Strange Attractors: An Econometric Application of Mathematical Chaos." In William Barnett, Ernst Berndt, and Halbert White (Eds.), *Dynamic Econometric Modeling*, Proceedings of the Third International Symposium in Economic Theory and Econometrics. Cambridge: Cambridge University Press, pp. 199–246.

Barnett, William A., and Yue, Piyu. 1989. "Monetary Aggregation with Risk Aversion." University of Texas at Austin.

Barnett, William A., and Choi, Seungmook S. 1989a. "A Comparison between the Conventional Econometric Approach to Structural Inference and the Nonparametric Chaotic Attractor Approach." In William Barnett, John Geweke, and Karl Shell (Eds.), *Economic Complexity: Chaos, Sunspots, Bubbles, and Nonlinearity*, Proceedings of the Fourth International Symposium in Economic Theory and Econometrics. Cambridge: Cambridge University Press, pp. 141–212.

Barnett, William A., and Choi, Seungmook, S. 1989b. "A Monte Carlo Study of Tests of Blockwise Weak Separability." *Journal of Business and Economic Statistics* 7 (July):363–377.

Belongia, Michael, and Chalfant, James. 1989. "The Changing Empirical Definition of Money: Some Estimates from a Model of the Demand for Money Substitutes." *Journal of Political Economy* 97(April): 387–398.

Belongia, Michael, and Chrystal, K. Alec. 1990. "An Admissible Monetary Aggregate for the United Kingdom." Federal Reserve Bank of St. Louis, Working paper No. 90–01.

Blackorby, Charles, Primont, Daniel, and Russell, R. Robert. 1977. "On Testing Separability Restrictions with Flexible Functional Forms." *Journal of Econometrics* 5: 195–209.

Blackorby, Charles, Primont, Daniel, and Russell, R. Robert. 1978. *Duality, Separability, and Functional Structure: Theory and Economic Applications*. New York: North-Holland.

Box, G. E. P., and Jenkins, G. M. 1970. *Time Series Analysis—Forecasting and Control*. San Francisco: Holden-Day.

Brillinger, David R. 1965. "An Introduction to Polyspectrum." *Annals of Mathematical Statistics*. 36:1351–1374.

Brock, W. A., and Dechert, W. D. 1988. "Theorems on Distinguishing Deterministic from Random Systems." In William Barnett, Ernst Bernett, and Halbert White (Eds.), *Dynamic Econometric Modeling*, Proceedings of the Third International Symposium in Economic Theory and Econometrics. Cambridge: Cambridge University Press, pp. 247–268

Brockett, P. L. Hinich, Melvin, and Patterson, Douglas. 1988. "Bispectral-Based Test for the Detection of Gaussianity and Linearity in Time Series." *Journal of the American Statistical Association* 83(403): 657–664.

Brockett, P. L., Hinich, Melvin, and Wilson, Gary R. 1987. "Nonlinear and Non-Gaussian Ocean Noise." *Journal of the Accoustical Society of America* 82(4):1386–1394.

Diewert, W. Erwin. 1976. "Exact and Superlative Index Numbers." *Journal of Econometrics* 4:115–145.

Fayyad, Salam K. 1986. "Monetary Asset Component Grouping and Aggregation: An Inquiry into the Definition of Money." Ph.D. dissertation, University of Texas, Austin.

Feenstra, Robert C. 1986. "Functional Equivalence Between Liquidity Costs and the Utility of Money." *Journal of Monetary Economics* March:271–291.

Fischer, Stanley. 1974. "Money and the Production Function." *Economic Inquiry* 12:517–533.

Fixler, Dennis. 1988. "Measuring Financial Service Output and Prices in Commerical Banking." Division of Price and Index Number Research, Bureau of Labor Statistics, August.

Fixler, Dennis, and Zieschang, Kimberly. 1989a. "Measuring the Nominal Value of Financial Services in the National Income Accounts." Bureau of Labor Statistics Working Paper 193; *Economic Inquiry*, forthcoming.

Fixler, Dennis, and Zieschang, Kimberly. 1989b. "Output and Price Measurement in Commercial Banking." Division of Price and Index Number Research, Bureau of Labor Statistics, August.

Fixler, Dennis, and Zieschang, Kimberly. 1989c. "User Costs, Shadow Prices, and the Real Output of Banks." Division of Price and Index Number Research, Bureau of Labor Statistics, August.

Hansen, Lars Peter, and Sargent, Thomas J. 1980. "Formulating and Estimating Dynamic Linear Rational Expectations Models." *Journal of Economic Dynamics and Control* 2(1):7–46.

Hansen, Lars Peter, and Sargent, Thomas J. 1981. "Linear Rational Expectations Models for Dynamically Interrelated Variables." In R.E. Lucas, Jr., and T. J. Sargent (Eds.), *Rational Expectations and Econometric Practice*. Minneapolis: University of Minnesota Press, pp. 127–156.

Hansen, Lars Peter, and Singleton, Kenneth J. 1982. "Generalized Instrumental Variables Estimation of Nonlinear Rational Expectations Models." *Econometrica* 50:1269–1286.

Hinich, Melvin J. 1982. "Testing for Gaussianity and Linearity of a Stationary Time Series." *Journal of Time Series Analysis* 3(3):169–176.

Hinich, Melvin J., Patterson, Douglas. 1985. "Identification of the Coefficients in a Non-Linear Time Series of the Quadratic Type." *Journal of Econometrics* 30:269–288; reprinted in William Barnett and Ronald Gallant (Eds.), *New Approaches to Modelling, Specification Selection, and Econometric Inference*, Proceedings of the First International Symposium in Economic Theory and Econometrics. Cambridge: Cambridge University Press, 1989.

Hinich, Melvin J., Patterson, Douglas. 1989. "Evidence of Nonlinearity in the Trade-by-Trade Stock Market Return Generating Process." In William Barnett, John Geweke, and Karl Shell (Eds.), *Economic Complexity: Chaos, Sunspots, Bubbles, and Nonlinearity*, Proceedings of the Fourth International Symposium in Economic Theory and Econometrics. Cambridge: Cambridge University Press, pp. 383–409.

Jenkins, G., and Watts, D. 1968. *Spectral Analysis and Its Applications*. San Francisco: Holden-Day.

Merton, Robert C. 1989. "Capital Market Theory and the Pricing of Financial Securities." Working Paper 90–024, Harvard Business School, September.

Phlips, Louis, and Spinnewyn, Frans. 1982. "Rationality versus Myopia in Dynamic Demand System." In R. L. Basmann and G. F. Rhodes (Eds.), *Advances in Econometrics*. New York: JAI Press, pp. 3–33.

Poterba, James M., and Rotemberg, Julio J. 1987. "Money in the Utility Function: an Empirical Implementation." In William Barnett and Kenneth Singleton (Eds.), *New Approaches to Monetary Economics*, Proceedings of the Second International Symposium in Economic Theory and Econometrics. Cambridge: Cambridge University Press, pp.219–240.

Prescott, Edward C., and Mehra, Rajnish. 1980. "Recursive Competitive Equilibrium: The Case of Homogeneous Households." *Econometrica* 48(6): 1365–80.

Priestley, M. 1981. *Spectral Analysis and Time Series*, 2. New York: Academic Press.

Rotemberg, Julio. 1990. "Monetary Aggregates and their Uses." Michael T. Belongia

(Ed.). *Monetary Policy on the 75th Anniversary of the Federal Reserve System*. Boston: Kluwer Academic Publishers, pp. 242–232.

Russell, R. R. 1975. "Functional Separability and Partial Elasticities of Substitution." *Reveiw of Economic Studies* 42:79–86.

Sargent, Thomas J. 1987. *Dynamic Macroeconomic Theory*. Cambridge, Mass.: Harvard University Press.

Ullah, A., and Vinod, H. D. 1988. "Flexible Production Function Estimation by Nonparametric Kernel Estimators." In G. F. Rhodes and T. B. Fomby (Eds.), *Nonparametric and Robust Inference: Advances in Econometrics* 7: 139–162.

APPENDIX: THE HINICH BISPECTRAL APPROACH

A.1 Definitions and Background

If $\{x(t)\}$ is a zero mean third order stationary time series, then the mean $\mu_x = E[x(t)] = 0$, the covariance $c_{xx}(m) = E[x(t+m)x(t)]$, and the general third order moments $c_{xxx}(s, r) = E[x(t+r)x(t+s)x(t)]$ are independent of t. If $c_{xx}(m) = 0$ for all non-zero m, the series is white noise. Priestly (1981) and Hinich and Patterson (1985) stress that, although a series may be white noise, $x(n)$ and $x(m)$ may be stochastically dependent unless $\{x(t)\}$ is multivariate Gaussian. Only under multivariate Gaussianity are lack of correlation (whiteness) and stochastic independence the same. If the distribution of $\{x(n_1), \ldots, x(n_N)$ is multivariate normal for all $n_1, \ldots, n_N$, then the series is defined to be Gaussian, where N is the sample size.[1] Hinich and Patterson (1985, p. 70) fault Box and Jenkins (1970, p. 8 vs. p. 46) and Jenkins and Watts (1968, p. 149 vs. p. 157) for blurring the definitions of whiteness and independence.

We define a pure white noise series as one in which $x(n_1), \ldots, x(n_N)$ are independent random variables for all values of $n_1, \ldots, n_N$. All pure white noise series are white. All white noise series are not pure white noise unless, in addition, they are Gaussian.

In addition to stationarity, whiteness, and pure whiteness, another often assumed property of a time series is linearity. Many researchers implicitly assume the errors of their models are Gaussian, and test for pure white noise by using the covariance function $c_{xx}(m)$, but ignore the information regarding possible nonlinear relationships which are found in the third order moments $c_{xxx}(s, r)$.

The above discussion suggests the need to test for both nonlinearity and Gaussianity, in addition to testing in the usual manners for whiteness.

A.2 The Test Method

Hinich (1985) argues that the bispectrum in the frequency domain is easier to interpret than the multiplicity of third order moments $\{c_{xxx}(r,s): s \leq r, r = 0, 1, 2, \ldots\}$ in the time domain. For frequencies f_1 and f_2 in the principal domain

$$\Omega = \{(f_1, f_2): 0 < f_1 < .5, f_2 < f_1, 2f_1 + f_2 < 1\},$$

the bispectrum, $B_{xxx}(f_1, f_2)$, is defined by

$$B_{xxx}(f_1, f_2) = \sum_{r=-\infty}^{\infty} \sum_{s=-\infty}^{\infty} c_{xxx}(r, s) \exp[-i2\pi(f_1 r + f_2 s)]. \quad \text{(A.1)}$$

The bispectrum is the double Fourier transformation of the third order moments function.[2]

The statistical tests based on the sample bispectrum that we briefly discuss in this section were applied with success to the study of acoustic signals and noise by Brockett, Hinich, and Wilson (1987) and to stock prices and exchange rates by Hinich and Patterson (1985, 1989) and Brockett, Hinich, and Patterson (1988).

The skewness function $\Gamma(f_1, f_2)$ is defined in terms of the bispectrum as follows:

$$\Gamma^2(f_1, f_2) = |B_{xxx}(f_1, f_2)|^2 / S_{xx}(f_1) S_{xx}(f_2) S_{xx}(f_1 + f_2), \quad \text{(A.2)}$$

where $S_{xx}(f)$ is the (ordinary power) spectrum of $x(t)$ at frequency f. Since the bispectrum is complex valued, the absolute value (vertical) lines in equation (7.2) designate modulus. Brillinger (1965) proves that the skewness function $\Gamma(f_1, f_2)$ is constant over all frequency pairs $(f_1, f_2) \in \Omega$, if $\{x(t)\}$ is linear, while $\Gamma(f_1, f_2)$ is zero over all frequencies, if $\{x(t)\}$ is Gaussian. Linearity and Gaussianity can be tested using a sample estimator of the skewness function $\Gamma(f_1, f_2)$. We now outline the procedure we use to obtain the bispectrum.

A.3 Computation of the Test Statistics

Let $f_k = k/N$ for each integer k. *For the sample* $\{x(0), x(1), \ldots, x(N-1)\}$, define $F_{xxx}(f_j, f_k)$ to be an estimate of the bispectrum of $\{x(t)\}$ at the frequency pair (f_j, f_k) such that:

$$F_{xxx}(f_j, f_k) = Z(f_j)Z(f_k)Z^*(f_j + f_k)/N, \tag{A.3}$$

where

$$Z(f_j) = \sum_{t=0}^{N-1} x(t)\exp(-i2\pi f_j t).$$

The asterisk in equation (A.3) designates complex conjugate.

The function $F_{xxx}(f_j, f_k)$ must be smoothed as follows to form a consistent estimator. Let $\langle B_{xxx}(f_m, f_n)\rangle$ denote a smoothed estimate of $B_{xxx}(f_m, f_n)$, which is obtained by averaging over values of $F_{xxx}(f_j, f_k)$ at adjacent frequency pairs such that

$$\langle B_{xxx}(f_m, f_n)\rangle = M^{-2} \sum_{j=(m-1)M}^{mM-1} \sum_{k=(m-1)M}^{nM-1} F_{xxx}(f_j, f_k). \tag{A.4}$$

This estimator, $\langle B_{xxx}(f_m, f_n)\rangle$, is the average of the $F_{xxx}(f_j, f_k)$ over a square on M^2 points. It is a consistent and asymptotically complex normal estimator of the bispectrum, $B_{xxx}(f_1, f_2)$, if the sequence (f_m, f_n) converges to (f_1, f_2) (see Hinich, 1982).

As discussed earlier, the estimated skewness function, $\Gamma(f_m, f_n)$, will not be significantly different from a constant at any frequency pair in Ω under the null hypothesis of linearity. If the null hypothesis is Gaussianity as well as linearity, then that constant will be zero. The skewness function can be used to motivate construction of the normalized test statistic, $2|\delta(f_m, f_n)|^2$, where

$$\delta(f_m, f_n) = \langle B_{xxx}(f_m, f_n)\rangle/[(N/M^2)\langle S_{xx}(f_m)\rangle \langle S_{xx}(f_n)\rangle \langle S_{xx}(f_m + f_n)\rangle]^{1/2}. \tag{A.5}$$

In this formula, $\langle S_{xx}(\cdot)\rangle$ is defined to be a consistent and asymptotically normal estimator of the power spectrum $S_{xx}(\cdot)$, and f_m is defined by $f_m = (2m-1)M/2N$ for each integer m. Hinich has shown that $2[\delta(f_m, f_n)]^2$ is approximately distributed as an independent noncentral chi-squared variate with two degrees of freedom at frequency pair (f_m, f_n).

The larger M, the less the finite sample variance and the larger the sample bias. Because of this tradeoff, there is no one unique M that is appropriate to use for performing nonlinearity and Gaussianity tests based upon the estimated statistics given by equation (A.5). When M is large, the bandwidth is large, the variance is reduced, and the resolution of the tests is small, since there are too few terms for the linearity test. If M is small, there is a large number of terms to sort for the linearity tests, the variance may be too large, and the chi-square approximation used for the linearity test may not be good. Hinich (1982) has suggested that M should be selected to be approximately the square root of the number of observations, N.

Let P denote the number of frequency pairs in the principal domain, Ω, and let

$$D = \{(m, n): (f_m, f_n) \in \Omega\},$$

so that P is the cardinal number of the set D. Hinich (1982) has shown that the P values of $2|\delta(f_m, f_n)|^2$ for $(m, n) \in D$ are approximately distributed as independent, noncentral chi-square variates with noncentrality parameter $\lambda(f_m, f_n)$, where

$$\begin{aligned}\lambda(f_m, f_n) &= (2\,M^2/N)\,|B_{xxx}(f_m, f_n)|^2/S_{xx}(f_m)S_{xx}(f_n)S_{xx}(f_m + f_n)\\ &= (2M^2/N)\Gamma^2(f_m, f_n). \qquad \text{(A.6)}\end{aligned}$$

Define the test statistic

$$CHISUM = 2 \sum_{(m,n)\in D}\sum |\delta(f_m, f_n)|^2. \qquad \text{(A.7)}$$

The distribution of $CHISUM$ is approximately a noncentral chi-square with $2P$ degrees of freedom with a noncentrality parameter that is the sum of the $\lambda(f_m, f_n)$ over all $(m, n) \in D$.

Under the null hypothesis that $\{x(t)\}$ is Gaussian and thus the skewness function, $\Gamma(f_m, f_n)$, is identically zero over all $(m, n) \in D$, $CHISUM$ is approximately a central chi-square $2P$ variate. Equation (A.7) gives us an asymptotic chi-square test of the Gaussianity hypothesis. If the time series is linear but not necessarily Gaussian, then the skewness function is constant, which implies from (A.6) that the noncentrality parameters are constant. The Hinich linearity test uses the emprical distribution function of $\{2|\delta(f_m, f_n)|\}$ in the principal domain to test the null hypothesis that the $\lambda(f_m, f_n)$'s are all the same. A robust single test statistic for this dispersion is the 80th quantile of these statistics.

For details of the test, see Hinich (1982), Hinich and Patterson (1985, 1989), and Ashley, Patterson, and Hinich (1986). In particular, the final transformed test statistics are distributed as standard normal random variates under the respective null hypotheses. When the null is Gaussianity, the resulting test statistic is denoted by H. When the null is linearity, the test statistic is denoted by Z. In both cases, the distribution of the standard normal is used to produce a one-sided test, in which the null is rejected if the test statistic is large.

Ashley, Patterson, and Hinich (1986, p. 174) presented an equivalence theorem which proves that the Hinich bispectral linearity test statistic is invariant to linear filtering of the data. This important result proves that *the linearity test can be applied either to the raw series or to the residuals of a linear model fitted to the data.* Hence there is no need to choose between possible linear methods of detrending or prefiltering the data. An additional important implication of the theorem is that if $x(t)$ is found to be nonlinear, then the residuals of a linear model of the form $y(t) = f(x(t))$ will also be nonlinear, since the nonlinearity in $x(t)$ will pass through any linear filter, f. The above article further reported tables on the power of the Hinich linearity test for detecting violations of the linearity and Gaussianity hypotheses for a number of sample sizes and M values. The table indicates substantial power for both tests, even when N is as small as 256, if the value of M used is between 12 and 17. For this sample size, the power of the test falls off as M increases above 17.

Notes

1. In accordance with time series conventions, we equate Gaussianity of the process with multivariate Gaussianity.

2. The bispectrum is the third order polyspectrum, while the ordinary power spectrum is the second order polyspectrum. Strictly speaking, the polyspectrum of order k is the Fourier transform of the cumulant function (not the moment function) of order k.

Cumulants are defined to be the coefficients of the terms in the power series expansion of the *logarithm* of the characteristic function of a distribution, while the moments are the coefficients of the terms in the power series expansion of the *level* of the characteristic function of the distribution. Unlike the moments, the cumulants have the merit of being semi-invariants. However, for a stationary time series with zero mean, the second and third order cumulant functions are identical to the second and third order moment functions. Only at the fourth and higher orders do the cumulant functions differ from the moment functions. But since we here use only the second and third orders under the assumption of stationarity and zero mean, we need draw no distinction between moments and cumulants.

Commentary: Monetary Aggregates and Their Uses

by Julio J. Rotemberg

I agree completely with the thrust of the article by William Barnett, Melvin Hinich, and Piyu Yue (BHY). In common with earlier work by Barnett, they suggest that the widely used monetary aggregates M1 through L be replaced by aggregates which take into account the different "money-ness" of different monetary assets. Moreover, they recommend that these new aggregates be anchored in notions of money that make economic sense. To me these ideas seem unimpeachable, and my main question is why traditional aggregates remain so popular in the face of superior alternatives.

Barnett has long been on a campaign against the standard, numbered monetary aggregates. This is a good campaign; the use of M1, M2, M3, and L is indefensible. These standard aggregates are obtained by adding together things that clearly should not be a added together. Kuznets did not obtain a Nobel prize for suggesting that GNP be measured by adding together the tons of output produced in different industries. Nor did he have to come up with GNP1 through GNP20 to denote aggregates in which tons of ever more types of goods are added together.

Kuznets reasoned that it would be more economically meaningful to add together the tons of apples and raspberries by weighting them by the amount people are willing to pay for them. In the case of monetary assets, what people pay for them is the interest foregone from holding a relatively liquid asset. People give up more interest when they hold one additional dollar of currency than when they hold one additional dollar in a money market account. Currency costs more which, if people are rational, means that it performs some other service better. It is more "liquid" or "money-like." This suggests that simply adding together currency and money market accounts will give a misleading measure of the amount of liquidity services that people are purchasing.

Let m_t^i denote the units (dollars) of monetary asset i that people hold at t. Let r_t^i be the interest rate earned on asset i at t. More precisely, let $(1 + r_t^i)$ denote the total return (in dollars) at $t + 1$ from holding one unit of asset i at t. Finally, let r_t^b be the interest earned on a benchmark asset. This benchmark asset is one that provides no liquidity services. Because it provides fewer such services, this interest rate must exceed those on monetary assets. Following Kuznets, a naive measure of nominal expenditure on liquidity service at t is then:

$$\sum_i (r_t^b - r_t^i)m_t^i. \tag{1}$$

Note that this measures nominal $t+1$ expenditure on monetary assets held at t.

To obtain an index of quantity (or more accurately of change in quantity), Kuznets proposed that expenditure be computed also at the prices in some base period. Let r_0^i denote interest rates in the base period. Then, a Laspeyres index of monetary assets (which corresponds to measurements of GNP at base prices) is:

$$\sum_i (r_0^b - r_0^i)m_t^i. \tag{2}$$

This Laspeyres index was used in Barnett (1983).

These indices measure flows of expenditure on assets. Note that we are not measuring directly the flows of services provided by these assets. Measuring the services provided by a durable presents certain well-known difficulties. Even in the case of a physical asset such as an airplane the income produced by the asset is generally not a satisfactory measure of the service flow. The reason is that even an idle airplane offers some services by being available should the need arise. A more satisfactory measure of services can be obtained if one imagines that people equate (at least at the margin) the services they obtain to the cost of holding the durable. Then, one can measure the services by the amount foregone in order to hold the asset. That is what the indices advocated by Barnett achieve.

The indices (1) and (2) as well as the Divisia indices I discuss below measure flows, not stocks. Their dimension is dollars spent on assets (or percent changes of dollars spent on assets) as opposed to dollars of monetary assets. This does not seem like a big problem as long as one knows the prices (difference in returns) that convert stocks of assets into expenditures. In any event, it is easily remedied. Consider in particular the following index:

$$\mathrm{CE} \equiv \sum_i \frac{r_t^b - r_t^i}{r_t^b} m_t^i, \tag{3}$$

a stock measure which I call the currency equivalent (CE) measurement of liquidity. I give it this name because, as long as currency gives no interest, units of currency are added together with a weight of one. Other assets are added to currency but with a weight that declines toward zero as that asset's return increases. Assets whose return equals that of the benchmark return get a weight of zero as in (1) and (2). One advantage of CE over (2) is that the latter is sensitive to the choice of the base period if the level of the benchmark return varies over time. Since the CE measure does not involve a base period, it has the additional advantage that it is straightforward to add new monetary assets to the measure as these are created.

For many years, Barnett has advocated the use of Divisia aggregates. The Divisia aggregate at t can be approximated by D_t:

$$\log D_t = \log D_{t-1} + \left(\sum_i \frac{(r_t^b - r_t^i)m_t^i}{\Sigma_j(r_t^b - r_t^j)m_t^j}[\log m_t^i - \log m_{t-1}^i]\right). \quad (4)$$

Like its more naive counterparts (1), (2) and (3), the Divisia index gives more weight to the rate of growth of those monetary assets whose return is relatively low. The advantage of the Divisia index over the others is that, under certainty, it approximates well the change in the utility derived from monetary assets. For this approximation to be useful, the demand for monetary assets must be well approximated by the behavior of a representative individual whose utility function is given by:

$$E_t\sum_j \rho^j U\left(C_{t+j}, V\left(\frac{m_{t+j}^1}{P_{t+j}} \cdots \frac{m_{t+j}^n}{P_{t+j}}\right)\right) \quad (5)$$

where E_t takes expectations conditional on information available at t, C_t represents consumption at t and P_t represents the dollar price of a unit of the aggregate consumption good at t.

Much has been written on the merits of the representative agent in macroeconomics, and here I can do little to advance this debate. I should mention however, that the fact that monetary assets are held for payment *between* agents may mean that distributional considerations are important and that aggregation of individual asset demands into the behavior of a representative individual is problematical.[1] Nonetheless, the only behavior-based currently available model of demand for liquid assets that is tractable and relatively general involves assets in the utility function of the representative agent.[2]

Under certainty, the Divisia index approximates (to third order) the changes in the V. This is an attractive feature because, as BHY show, changes in V have important consequences for individual behavior.

Unfortunately, these approximation properties appear to be lost when there is uncertainty and individuals are risk averse. Suppose that asset returns are random. Then, the ex post returns do not measure the expected opportunity cost of holding monetary assets. So, it is not appropriate to use ex post returns in (1), (3), and (4). Under risk neutrality, one could replace these ex post returns with the corresponding ex ante returns and I return to this idea below. First, I illustrate the problems introduced by risk aversion.

Consider an individual who maximizes (5) subject to the usual lifetime budget constraint. If the individual holds one more unit of monetary asset i (and one less unit of the benchmark asset), he will have to reduce his consumption at some point. Randomness in returns precludes reducing consumption only at t and leaving future consumption unaffected. Because the returns are random, the individual must wait until $t + 1$ to learn by how much consumption must be reduced. On the other hand, if the individual is optimizing, he is indifferent between reducing consumption only at $t + 1$ (the first time that he knows by how much consumption must fall) or reducing it partially in future periods as well. This means that the individual must be indifferent between holding one additional unit of asset i at t and consuming $(r_t^b - r_t^i)P_t/P_{t+1}$ less at $t + 1$. In other words:

$$\frac{\partial V}{\partial m_t^i/P_t} = E_t \frac{(r_t^b - r_t^i)P_t}{P_{t+1}} \frac{\partial U}{\partial C_{t+1}}. \tag{6}$$

The left-hand side of (6) gives the benefit from holding an additional unit of the monetary asset while the right-hand side gives the cost. The problem is that, with risk aversion, the ex post return on the benchmark asset is generally correlated with the marginal utility of consumption at $t + 1$. This means that the cost of holding monetary assets does not depend only on the expected return on the various assets. It also depends on their consumption "betas."

As a result formulae such as (1), (3), and (4) with expected returns substituted for ex post returns cannot approximate well the change in utility V. While this is a weakness, it is apparent even from (6) that the basic principle of more heavily weighting assets whose rate of return is lower in monetary aggregates is sound. Changes in these assets have a bigger effect on total utility because, as their cost is larger, their marginal utility must be larger as well.

An alternative solution is to estimate a parametric version of the utility function V directly. Estimation of such utility functions has a long history (see Chetty, 1969) though uncertainty and risk aversion have been incorporated only recently (Poterba and Rotemberg, (1987). This estimation involves fitting equations such as (6). After estimation of the utility function's parameters it is a simple matter to compute estimates of the monetary aggregate V.

Here I want to record two quibbles with the way the estimation is actually carried out by BHY. The first concerns their choice of benchmark return. They use the maximum ex post return among the assets included in the aggregate L. However, there is no asset in existence that actually has this pattern of returns. More seriously, the assets in L all provide some liquidity services. It would be better to use the return on an asset that provides no such services. It is also important that the asset that is chosen be one for which returns are easily observable. This led Poterba and me to chose the returns on common stocks.

The second quibble is that BHY have not completely abandoned the use of numbered aggregates. They construct a utility-based measure for M1 and one for M2. In other words, they are still arbitrarily including and excluding assets from their measures. I would prefer that, once a benchmark asset is chosen, the utility be specified so that essentially all assets be permitted to contribute to utility directly. If an asset provides no liquidity services, that will be picked up in the estimation. Inspection of (6) reveals that estimation of these first order conditions implies that assets whose return is similar to that of the benchmark return will be deemed to provide no liquidity services.

Monetary aggregates have at least two uses. The first is as an input into elaborate forecasting models. Models such as these are used in practice to predict the effect of various monetary policies. The second is to convey a sense of the monetary stance to a vast audience of relatively informed observers of the economy. This vast audience does not rely on elaborate parametric models. Members of this audience gather a relatively small number of aggregate statistics on the economy and use either simple models or their intuition to interpret these aggregates. This audience seeks at least two properties of monetary aggregates. The first is that there be a relatively small number of aggregates that convey a relatively large fraction of monetary information. The second is that the numbers be relatively easy to interpret.

I agree with BHY that, for this second audience, aggregates of the form (1), (2), (3), or (4) are likely to be much superior to current monetary aggregates. I also agree that these aggregates should be monitored by estimation of utility functions. Big departures of the aggregates from estimated versions of V should lead to revisions in the compilation of the aggregates.

The main mystery here is why the existing monetary aggregates have proved so durable in spite of Barnett's demonstration that Divisia aggregates are more useful in forecasting, say, changes in income.[3] My own interpretation is that virtues of the new aggregates have not been contrasted sufficiently to the deficiencies of the old.

The deficiencies of the old are not just theoretical. Because essentially irrelevant compositional shifts affect the traditional measures, intelligent

Table 1. Monetary Indicators and Short-Term Inflation; Log Change in CPI Is Dependent Variable

Independent Variable			
Log change in CPI(−1)	0.407 (0.042)	0.429 (0.049)	0.431 (0.050)
Log change in CPI(−2)	0.325 (0.049)	0.347 (0.049)	0.347 (0.050)
Log change in Base(−1)	0.177 (0.042)		
Log change in M1(−1)		0.056 (0.024)	
Log change in M2(−1)			0.043 (0.037)

Notes: Monthly data from February 1959 to June 1989. Standard errors in parentheses. Constants omitted.

observers must keep track of several monetary aggregates at once. They cannot afford to focus on just one monetary aggregate. I will illustrate this by looking at the prediction of inflation.

People are interested in predicting inflation in the next month and also in getting a sense of the long-term trend in inflation. Ideally a single monetary aggregate would convey information about both. Unfortunately, of the current aggregates some are better for short-term forecasting, others for long-term forecasting. Table 1 reports regressions of the monthly inflation in the CPI on two lags of inflation and the lagged value of three monetary aggregates. Of these three, the base has the biggest and most significant coefficient followed by M1 with M2 performing poorest.

For long-term forecasting, it is better to look at the stability of velocity. This is the basis of the P^* method of Hallman, Porter, and Small (1989) who recommend using M2 velocity for long-term inflation forecasting. If velocity is stable and one has some confidence in one's long-run forecast for output, then long-term inflation can be predicted from monetary growth numbers. If velocity is unstable then, even if one is certain of long-term output growth, long-term inflation has little to do with long-term trends in money.

The velocity of M2 is more stable than either that of the base or of M1. If one divides monthly observations of personal income by monthly observations of the three aggregates, one obtains an estimate of the three

Table 2. Long-Term Stability of Velocity; Log Velocity Is Dependent Variable

Independent Variable	*Base Velocity*	*M1 Velocity*	*M2 Velocity*
Velocity(−1)	0.996 (0.006)	0.997 (0.004)	0.981 (0.008)
Change in velocity(−1)	0.011 (0.053)	0.131 (0.052)	0.179 (0.052)
Change in velocity(−1)	0.083 (0.052)	0.137 (0.053)	0.171 (0.052)
Trend	6.2e–7 (1e–5)	1.8e–6 (1e–5)	5.9e-6 (3.2e-6)

Notes: Monthly data from April 1959 to June 1989. Standard errors in parentheses. Constants omitted.

velocities. The standard deviation of the logarithm of the level of velocity is 0.19, 0.24, and 0.04 when one uses the base, M1, and M2, respectively. Not surprisingly, given this fact, M2 velocity also returns fastest to its normal value. This is demonstrated in table 2.

This table reports regressions of each (logarithmic) level of velocity on a constant, a linear trend, the lagged level of velocity, and two lags of the changes in velocity. A random walk (which never returns to normal) would involve a coefficient of 1 on the lagged dependent variable. It is apparent from the table that M2 velocity has the smallest coefficient on the lagged dependent variable so that it returns to normal fastest. Thus the evidence for a unit root in the velocity series is weakest in the case of M2. This and the low variance of M2 velocity both suggest that M2 is indeed the most attractive measure if one is to adopt the P^* method.

My interpretation for the differing behavior of the aggregates for short-term and long-term prediction is the following. What matters for inflation is the amount of liquidity in the economy. Because assets with low interest rates are more liquid, the changes in these assets convey most information about short-term inflation. Unfortunately, there exist also essentially irrelevant compositional shifts like the shift (for those with large savings accounts) from super NOW accounts at commercial banks to money market accounts at commercial banks. These shifts affect the base and M1 but occur sufficiently slowly that they do not degrade very much their usefulness for short-term forecasting. On the other hand, because these shifts are long lasting, they make aggregates such as the base and M1 very poor at predicting long-term trends in inflation. For that purpose, it is better to use broader aggregates which are less affected by compositional shifts.

The major advantage of the aggregates given in (1) through (4) is that, while they are affected mostly by changes in the assets with zero interest, they are also less likely to be affected by irrelevant compositional shifts. Thus, a single aggregate of this type might end up conveying useful information about *both* short-term and long-term inflation.

In terms of leading to a stable level of velocity there is some reason to expect the CE index to behave better than the Divisia index if both are measured using expected returns. It is impossible to measure expected returns perfectly. Such measures will contain some error. Unfortunately, any error in measuring expected returns at time t affects the level of the Divisia index forever. The reason is that the Divisia index is a chained index; current measurements affect only the change in the index. By contrast, any measurement error affects the CE index only during the interval where the measurement error actually occurs. This suggests that the need for checking that the measured indices do not drift apart from the underlying theoretical aggregate V is particularly acute in the case of Divisia aggregates.

One additional advantage of the CE index is that it involves one less measurement. While the Divisia requires that we measure the expected nominal return on all assets, the CE index requires only that we measure the expected values of the relative returns r^i/r^b. These considerations as well as its ease of interpretation suggest that the CE measure deserves further study even though, under certainty, its use would be less justifiable than that of the Divisia aggregate.

So far I have only discussed the use of monetary aggregates by the informed public at large. I now turn to their use by those who employ elaborate econometric models. Such models are regularly used to inform monetary policy. Should such models use the new aggregates? Certainly, this seems appropriate if these models are to consist of a series of equations only loosely related to economic behavior. Such models are best interpreted as reduced forms and the new monetary aggregates are likely to be more closely related to the variables economic agents actually care about.

But, once the process of monitoring the behavior of monetary aggregates involves the estimation of parametric utility functions, it is hard to see why these estimated utility functions are not used directly for forecasting. In other words, like the usual econometric models, the estimated utility function is parametric. These parameters are not just useful for obtaining monetary aggregates. They also can be used to derive coherent systems of asset demand equations.[4] These coherent systems of demand equations can be used directly to gauge the effect of open market operations and the like. My hope is that, as the utility approach to thinking about the aggregation of liquid assets comes to be accepted, its usefulness for obtaining estimates that are useful in gauging the effects of monetary policy will come to be appreciated as well.

Notes

1. See Grossman and Weiss (1983) and Rotemberg (1984) for models where these distributional considerations are important.
2. Or equivalently, assets that affect the transactions cost of the representative agent. See Feenstra (1986).
3. See, for instance, Barnett, Spindt, and Offenbacher (1984).
4. They are coherent in that they embody the restrictions stressed by Tobin and Brainard (1968).

References

Barnett, William A. 1983. "New Indices of Money Supply and the Flexible Laurent Demand System." *Journal of Business and Economic Statistics* 1:7–23.

Barnett, William A., Offenbacher, Edward K., and Spindt, Paul A. 1984. "The New Divisia Monetary Aggregates." *Journal of Political Economy* 92:1049–1086.

Chetty, V. Karuppan. 1969. "On Measuring the Nearness of Near-Moneys." *American Economic Reveiw* 59:270–281.

Feenstra, Robert C. 1986. "Functional Equivalence between Liquidity Costs and the Utility of Money." *Journal of Monetary Economics*: 271–291.

Grossman, Sanford J., and Weiss, Laurence. 1983. "A Transactions Based Model of the Monetary Transmission Mechanism." *American Economic Review* 73: 871–880.

Hallman, Jeffrey J., Porter, Richard D., and Small, David H. 1989. "M2 per unit of Potential Output as an Anchor for the Price Level." Staff Study 157, Board of Governors of the Federal Reserve System.

Poterba, James, and Rotemberg, Julio J. 1987. "Money in the Utility Function: An Empirical Implementation." In William Barnett and Kenneth Singleton (Eds.), *New Approaches to Monetary Economics*. Cambridge: Cambridge University Press.

Rotemberg, Julio J. 1984. "A Monetary Equilibrium Model with Transactions Costs." *Journal of Political Economy* 92:40–58.

Tobin, James, and Brainard, William. 1968. "Pitfalls in Financial Model Building." *American Economic Review* 58:99–122.

A Reply to Julio J. Rotemberg

by William A. Barnett

1. Introduction

Among the many excellent ideas contained in Rotemberg's comments is a proposed new monetary aggregate, which Rotemberg calls the CE (currency equivalent) index. My reply consists primarily of the proof of a theorem regarding that index. The theorem supports Rotemberg's index by providing a derivation of his index directly from economic theory, when the index is treated as a measure of the economic stock of money under stationary expectations.

Rotemberg argues for his index largely on the basis of the intuitive appeal of its "weights." However, I feel that the greatest contribution of that index can be found in Rotemberg's observation that the index is measured in units of *stock* and therefore seems to measure the monetary capital stock, while the estimated Theoretical and Divisia aggregates considered in Barnett, Hinich, and Yue (1989) are measures of service *flow*. As a result, I shall refer to the CE index as the "Rotemberg Money Stock." I prove that Rotemberg is indeed correct in viewing his index as a measure of the economic stock of money. The Rotemberg Money Stock is a special case of the money stock measure derived in Barnett (1978, eq. 2, p. 148; 1980, eq. 3.3; 1981, eq. 7.3, p. 196). In particular, my measure of the stock of money reduces to the Rotemberg Money Stock under the assumption of stationary expectations.

As a result, the indexes considered in Barnett, Hinich, and Yue (1989, 1990) and in Rotemberg are tied together through discounting. The indexes in Barnett, Hinich, and Yue (1989, 1990) measure the service flow, while the Rotemberg Money Stock discounts that service flow to present value, if expectations are stationary. The Rotemberg Money Stock is produced from a particularly useful special case, since stationary expectations require no parametric modeling of expectations formation, and hence the Rotemberg Money Stock can be constructed directly from current period data.

2. The Economic Stock of Money

Barnett (1987, sec. 12, p. 160; 1990) defined the economic stock of money to be the discounted present value of expenditure on the services of monetary assets. Barnett (1978, eq. 2, p. 148; 1980, eq. 3.3; 1981, eq. 7.3, p. 196) derived that discounted present value in the form that we display below. Also see Barnett, Hinich, and Yue (1989, section 3) in this book for the same result, but with less discussion. During period s, let p^*_s be the true cost of living index, let M_{is} be nominal balances of monetary asset i, let r_{is} be the nominal expected holding period yield on monetary asset i, and define $m_{is} = M_{is} / p^*_s$ to be real balances of monetary asset i. The current period is defined to be period t, so that $s \geq t$. Define the discount rate for period s to be

$$\rho_s = \begin{cases} 1 & \text{for } s = t \\ \prod_{u=t}^{s-1}(1 + R_u) & \text{for } s > t. \end{cases} \tag{2.1}$$

By letting the planning horizon, T, go to infinity in the second term of Barnett (1978, eq. 2, p. 148; 1980, eq. 3.3; 1981, eq. 7.3, p. 196), we immediately acquire the following definition for the Economic Stock of Money.

Definition 1: Under risk neutrality, The Economic Stock of Money during period t is

$$V_t = \sum_{s=t}^{\infty} \sum_{i=1}^{n} \left[\frac{p^*_s}{\rho_s} - \frac{p^*_s(1 + r_{is})}{\rho_{s+1}}\right] m_{is}. \tag{2.2}$$

Also see Barnett, Hinich, and Yue (1989, eq. 3.3) in this book for the same result. The concept of economic stock used to produce definition 1 is the user-cost evaluated expenditure on the services of the n component monetary assets. It should be observed that the procedure used in Barnett (1978, eq. 2, p. 148; 1980, eq. 3.3; 1981, eq. 7.3, p. 196) to acquire that discounted present value was just back substitution and algebraic manipulation of the sequence of flow of funds identities to collapse the sequence of flow of funds identities into a single Fisherine discounted wealth constraint. Hence our conclusion is produced entirely from accounting identities.

If we now substitute (2.1) and $m_{is} = M_{is}/p^*_s$ into equation (2.2), we acquire the following result:

$$V_t = \sum_{s=t}^{\infty}\sum_{i=1}^{n}\left[\frac{R_s - r_{is}}{\prod_{u=t}^{s}(1 + R_u)}\right]M_{is}. \tag{2.3}$$

Our problem is to determine the conditions under which (2.3) reduces to the Rotemberg Money Stock, which is the following.

Definition 2: The Rotemberg Money Stock is

$$V_t = \sum_{i=1}^{n}\frac{R_t - r_{it}}{R_t}M_{it}. \tag{2.4}$$

We seek to find conditions under which equation (2.4) will equal (2.3). To that end, suppose that expectations are stationary in the sense that $r_{is} = r_{it}$ and $R_{is} = R_{it}$ for all $s \geq t$, and consider the static portfolio, $(M_{1s}, M_{2s}, \ldots, M_{ns}) = (M_{1t}, M_{2t}, \ldots, M_{nt})$ for all $s \geq t$. Equation (2.3) reduces to

$$V_t = \sum_{i=1}^{n}\sum_{s=t}^{\infty}\left[\frac{R_t - r_{it}}{(1 + R_t)^{s-t+1}}\right]M_{it}. \tag{2.5}$$

However, observe that

$$\sum_{s=t}^{\infty}\frac{R_t - r_{it}}{(1 + R_t)^{s-t+1}} = \frac{R_t - r_{it}}{R_t}, \tag{2.6}$$

since the left-hand side of equation (2.6) is a convergent geometric series (minus the first term in the series). Substituting (2.6) into (2.5), we acquire our result:

Theorem 1: Under stationary expectations, the Rotemberg Money Stock is equal to the Economic Money Stock.

3. Implications for Simple Sum Aggregation

Theorem 1 is especially interesting as a means of illustrating the source of confusion that has existed in recent years regarding the role of the official simple sum monetary aggregates. In particular, it is sometimes argued that the simple sum monetary aggregates measure the stock of money, while the Divisia monetary aggregates measure the service flow. Hence the use of the simple sum aggregates sometimes is defended on the grounds that stock measures are needed in some uses of monetary data. For example, monetary wealth is relevant to modeling the real balance effect, which is intended to explain the monetary transmission mechanism through a wealth effect.

However, it is evident both from the Rotemberg Money Stock and from the more general money stock formula in definition 1 that the simple sum aggregates do not measure the economic stock of money. In this section I consider why it is that the accounting stock does not equal the economic stock.

It is perhaps worth observing that at one time the use of the simple sum aggregates as measures of the money stock may have been justified. The reason is that up until recent decades, the only assets that were viewed as candidates for inclusion in monetary assets were assets yielding zero own rates of return.[1] Consideration of broad monetary assets has been a relatively recent phenomenon within the central banks of the world and has largely resulted from the expanded role of financial intermediation along with the increased nominal yield on money substitutes in the inflationary environment of recent decades. Inspection of the Rotemberg Money Stock reveals immediately that simple sum aggregation is correct when $r_{it} = 0$ for all i.[2]

While this observation may provide a comforting explanation for the historical use of simple sum monetary aggregation by central banks, we still are left with a paradox. In order to acquire the services of the nominal portfolio $(M_{1t}, M_{2t}, \ldots, M_{nt})$, we must pay $\Sigma_{i=1}^{n} M_{it}$, although under stationary expectations the economic value of the money stock is (2.4). How can that be?

The answer is acquired by discounting to present value the portfolio's investment yield as well as expenditure on the service flow. In particular, under the stationary expectations assumption, we easily can discount to present value the expected investment yield flows, $r_{is}M_{is} = r_{it}M_{it}$ for $s \geq t$ to get the following capitalized value:

$$V_t^* = \sum_{s=t}^{\infty} \sum_{i=1}^{n} \left[\frac{r_{it}M_{it}}{(1 + R_t)^{s-t+1}} \right]. \tag{3.1}$$

Again we have a convergent geometric series in the summation over s at any given i, so that we find:

$$V_t^* = \sum_{i=1}^{n} \frac{r_{it}}{R_t} M_{it}. \tag{3.2}$$

Adding equation (3.2) to (2.4), we find that

$$V_t + V_t^* = \sum_{i=1}^{n} M_{it}. \tag{3.3}$$

The conclusion is clear. The simple sum monetary aggregates measure the stock of money only if the investment (interest) yield of the monetary components is treated as a monetary service. Yet it is difficult to think of any macroeconomic school of thought which has *ever* viewed the interest yield on monetary assets to be a monetary service. In fact, that possibility was considered carefully and rejected unequivocally in Pesek and Saving (1967).

4. The Economic Stock of Money and the Divisia Monetary Aggregate

Expenditure on the monetary service flow was evaluated in definition 1 by summing the user-cost evaluated expenditures over individual monetary assets. We now shall ask whether there exists a connection between that monetary stock aggregate and the aggregation-theoretic aggregator function, $M(m_t)$, which measures the service flow. I have long advocated the use of the Divisia monetary aggregate or any other element of Diewert's superlative index number class (with user costs as prices), since such index numbers track the aggregator function $M(m_t)$ to within a third order remainder term, regardless of the form of the unknown aggregator function, M. See Diewert (1976).

But by Fisher's factor reversal test, we know that there must exist a user-cost price aggregate $\Pi(\pi_t)$ dual to the exact service quantity aggregate $M(m_t)$, such that $M(m_t)\,\Pi(\pi_t) = m_t'\pi_t$. Hence expenditure on aggregate monetary services $M(m_t)$ must equal the sum of the user-cost evaluated expenditures on the components m_t. As a result, we can derive monetary wealth by discounting to present value either the expenditure flow $m_s'\pi_s$ for $s \geq t$ or the exactly equal aggregate expenditure flow $M(m_s)\,\Pi(\pi_s)$ for $s \geq t$. In fact, if the user costs are themselves already computed as discounted present values, we need only sum the expenditure flow to get:

$$V_t = \sum_{s=t}^{\infty} \Pi(\pi_s) M(m_s). \tag{4.1}$$

It is clear from equation (2.3) above that the discounted user costs π_s in (4.1) must be

$$\pi_{is} = \frac{R_s - r_{is}}{\prod_{u=t}^{s}(1 + R_u)},$$

as has explicitly been derived by Barnett (1978, p. 148; 1980, eq. 3.4; 1981, eq. 7.4, p. 196).

If we impose the stationarity assumption used to acquire the Rotemberg Money Stock in definition 2 above, we find that

$$V_t = M(m_t)\sum_{s=t}^{\infty}\Pi(\pi_s),$$

where

$$\pi_{is} = \frac{R_t - r_{it}}{(1 + R_t)^{s-t+1}} .$$

Hence we see that under the implicit stationary expectations assumption, the Rotemberg Money Stock is proportional to the monetary service flow $M(m_t)$, which is measured by the Divisia monetary index. But the proportionality factor $\Sigma_{s=t}^{\infty}\Pi(\pi_s)$ need not be a constant over time, when actual ex post data on the interest rates is used. In any case, it is clear from (4.1) that the Economic Stock of Money equals the discounted present value of expenditure on the aggregate service flow $M(m_s)$, $s \geq t$, regardless of whether or not expectations are stationary; and the Divisia index tracks that aggregate flow $M(m_s)$, $s \geq t$, very accurately (to within a third order remainder term in the changes).

5. Uses of the Stock and the Flow Monetary Aggregates

As we have seen, a clear economic connection exists between the stock and flow monetary aggregates. Rotemberg has emphasized some practical matters regarding the choice between them. I would like to emphasize that in theory the service flow and the stock are not substitute methods of measuring the same variable. On the contrary, they are separate variables, and both may exist within the structure of the economy simultaneously. Hence I am inclined to suggest that both be used, but only for the purposes that are relevant in theory.

Most variables appearing in structural economic theory are flows. However, stocks do appear through Fisherine discounted intertemporal wealth constraints. For example, demand and supply functions are demands and supplies for flows. Flow index numbers (such as Divisia, Laspeyres, etc.) with user-cost prices should be used to measure such flows. On the other hand, life-cycle consumption functions typically have wealth variables as explanatory variables. Hence consumption functions containing Pigou or real balance effects should contain stock measures as explanatory variables.

My position on this subject seems to be somewhat different from Rotemberg's. He appears to argue that there is a greater need to monitor the tracking ability of the Divisia index than the Rotemberg Money Stock. I do not agree. That which is tracked by the Rotemberg Money Stock is the capital value of the stock of money. Under risk aversion and rational expectations, measuring that stock is a complex capital asset pricing problem.[3] The tracking error produced by the Rotemberg Money Stock's implicit stationary expectations assumption is undoubtedly formidable. On the other hand, the tracking error of the Divisia index (actually we use its Törnqvist discrete time approximation) is third order in the changes, as has been proven by Diewert (1986). Furthermore, Barnett, Hinich, and Yue (1989, 1990) have shown that tracking ability is usually not badly compromised by risk aversion. In fact investigation of robustness to the degree of relative risk aversion is the primary purpose of Barnett, Hinich, and Yue (1989, 1990).

The chaining property that Rotemberg criticizes is necessary for the third order remainder to be in changes (rather than in levels). Unchained indexes have remainder terms defined in differences from the fixed base. Those changes are far greater than the discrete time changes between succeeding periods. Hence fixed base indexes are very much inferior to chained indexes in measuring flows.[4] Again, see Diewert (1986). However, Rotemberg is correct in observing that there is no need to choose between chaining or fixed base with the Rotemberg Money Stock, since his stock index has no "base" to chain, as also is true of my more general Economic Stock of Money in definition 1.

Although the tracking problems of the Rotemberg Money Stock are undoubtedly many orders of magnitude greater than those of the Divisia index, I do not view that as being a reason to prefer the Divisia index over the Rotemberg Money Stock (and certainly not vice versa). As I already have pointed out, the two indexes measure different variables, and therefore neither is a substitute for the other. Each can serve its own purpose. I agree with Rotemberg that his stock index "deserves further study." In fact as a measure of the stock of money, the Rotemberg Money Stock would surely be a major advance over the official simple sum aggregates.

Under no circumstances should the simple sum monetary aggregates be used to measure either the flow or stock, except perhaps in investigating the distant economic past, when money maybe did not yield interest. The simple sum monetary aggregates are an anachronism.

6. Other Comments

Rotemberg offers a number of other comments, on which I have little to offer, other than the following brief observations—largely because I agree with nearly all of those comments.

6.1 Nested Hierarchies of Aggregates

Rotemberg feels that the use of a recursively nested tree of aggregates, such as M1, M2, M3, and L, should be abandoned, and only the broadest of aggregates should be used. His point is that a properly weighted index captures the contribution of each component to the total service flow, so that there remains no reason to impute zero weights to some components. In fact I tend to lean in that same direction, as is evident from the conclusion in Barnett (1982), in which I find that Divisia L should be favored both on theoretical and empirical grounds.

However, I am probably somewhat less militant about that conclusion than Rotemberg appears to be. For example, Rotemberg states that Barnett, Hinich, and Yue (1989) include and exclude components "arbitrarily." Actually there is a rigorous criterion for including components in an aggregate: blockwise weak separability. As made clear in Barnett (1982), blockwise weakly separable nesting is the uniquely correct method of clustering components in aggregation theory. Hence, I do not oppose in principle the use of multiple clusterings in producing aggregates, so long as each is blockwise weakly separable and so long as aggregation over the components is accomplished by the use of a competent index number, such as the Laspeyres, Divisia, or Rotemberg Money Stock indexes mentioned by Rotemberg. Such multiple levels of aggregation are admissible in aggregation theory. The clusterings used in Barnett, Hinich, and Yue (1989) were the ones that resulted from weak separability testing in Belongia and Chalfant (1989), and hence were hardly arbitrary.

Nevertheless, I do share Rotemberg's preference for the broadest weakly separable component clustering. In addition, the reliability of the available tests for weak separability is currently in question, as a result of Barnett and Choi's (1989) recently published Monte Carlo results.

Under risk aversion, the state of the art in separability testing is even more unsettled.

6.2 Benchmark Rate

Rotemberg observes that Poterba and Rotemberg (1987) use the return on common stock as the benchmark rate, while Barnett, Hinich, and Yue (1989a, 1989b) use the maximum ex post yield-curve-adjusted rate of return among all assets in the aggregate L. In fact, the rate of return on common stocks cannot be used in the computation of any of the monetary indexes, (1), (2), (3), or (4), in Rotemberg. The reason is that the ex post rate of return on common stock is not always greater than the rate of return on all monetary components. As a result, the weights on some of the monetary components in each of those aggregates would sometimes be negative. However, it should be observed that while such indexes (in particular the Divisia) were used in Barnett, Hinich, and Yue (1989, 1990), no such indexes were used in Poterba and Rotemberg (1987), so the problem of negative weights did not arise in their article.

The subject of measurement of the benchmark rate merits more research. In theory, the benchmark asset is the rate of return on human capital, which is the least liquid of all assets (in a world without slavery). Without frequent direct measurements on that rate of return, one can only construct proxy measures, which need not be acquired from the rate of return on only one other asset. We believe that the procedure used in Barnett, Hinich, and Yue (1989, 1990) provides the best currently available proxy, although we have no doubt that better proxies could be generated. In any case, since the benchmark yield enters symmetrically in all of the index numbers under consideration here, the conclusions reached in Barnett, Hinich, and Yue (1989, 1990) and in Poterba and Rotemberg (1987) can be shown to be robust to variations in the benchmark yield within plausible limits, as has been shown in some of my earlier research on robustness to the benchmark yield.

6.3 Long-Run versus Short-Run Applications

Rotemberg argues very convincingly that a broad monetary index should be able to do well both in long-run and short-run applications (especially forecasting), while each simple sum aggregate is applicable to only one time horizon. As a result, he argues that the hierarchy of increasingly broad aggregates could be replaced by one aggregate, if it were constructed as a proper index number.

There is, in fact, now a large literature demonstrating that the Divisia monetary index does better in applications than the simple sum index in monetary aggregation. For a survey of those empirical results, see Barnett, Fisher, and Serletis (1989). Rotemberg's intriguing observation may go a long way toward explaning that growing body of empirical results.

6.4 Aggregation over Economic Agents

Rotemberg observes correctly that distributional effects could become important, if Gorman's conditions for the existence of a representative consumer are not satisified. Barnett and Serletis (1989) have, in fact, extended Divisia monetary aggregation to include a Divisia second moment capturing such potential distribution effects. At present, we do not find much evidence for important distribution effects, since the Divisia second moments usually are far less statistically significant in applications than the Divisia first moments (i.e., the Divisia index, which itself is a first moment). However, in any applications in which such distribution effects might become important, Barnett and Serletis's (1989) procedure for including Divisia second moments would permit inclusion and use of those distribution effects.

6.5 The Use of Coherent Demand Systems

Rotemberg concludes by observing that the coherent approach to money demand modeling based upon integrable models should be used in policy. I agree. The approach to generating and applying money demand models in Poterba and Rotemberg (1987) and Barnett (1983) is far preferable to the incoherent linear modeling procedure that is so common in monetary economics. However, the use of well-structured models is not a substitute for aggregation (as seems to be implied in Rotemberg's concluding paragraph). It is inconceivable that every disaggregated component of the broadest monetary aggregate, L, could be included as a separate good in the model developed by Poterba and Rotemberg (1987) or the model developed by Barnett (1983). In fact, a primary objective of aggregation theoretic indexes is to permit the construction of aggregated data that are internally consistent with the assumptions on which coherent models are based, so that the data construction is not in conflict with the models within which the data are used.

In other words, the aggregator functions tracked by the aggregated data and the model in which the data are used should be jointly coherent. For further discussion of that connection between model and data and the critical role of robustness, see the conclusion in Barnett, Hinich, and Yue (1990, section 7) in this book.

7. Conclusion

As perhaps is evident from the length of this reply, I found Rotemberg's (1989) comments to be filled with interesting and often important ideas, as also was the case with Poterba and Rotemberg's (1987) earlier article.

Notes

1. Some economists believe that demand deposits have always yielded a positive implicit rate of return. If so, then the simple sum aggregates have never measured the economic stock of money.

2. Actually the same is true for the Divisia index of monetary services, when own rates are all zero, although the demonstration is less transparent than with the Rotemberg Money Stock index.

3. See, for example, Merton (1989).

4. In that regard, it perhaps should be observed that the Laspeyres index displayed in Barnett (1983) was a chained index, rather than the fixed base Laspeyres index defined in Rotemberg's (1989) equation 2. I did try the fixed base Laspeyres index in that research, but did not supply the fixed base plot in the article, since I found that the well-known substitution bias of the unchained Laspeyres index accumulated alarmingly rapidly. In short, fixing the base—far from being a means of solving the problem of biased drift—is its cause. Chaining is the remedy.

References

Barnett, William A. 1978. "The User Cost of Money." *Economics Letters* 1:145–149.

Barnett, William A. 1980. "Economic Monetary Aggregates: An Application of Index Number and Aggregation Theory." *Journal of Econometrics* 14:11–48.

Barnett, William A. 1981. *Consumer Demand and Labor Supply:Goods, Monetary Assets, and Time*. Amsterdam: North-Holland.

Barnett, William A. 1982. "The Optimal Level of Monetary Aggregation." *Journal of Money, Credit, and Banking* 14:687–710.

Barnett, William A. 1987. "The Microeconomic Theory of Monetary Aggregation." In William A. Barnett and Kenneth J. Singleton (Eds.), *New Approaches to Monetary Economics*. Proceedings of the Second International Symposium in Economic Theory and Econometrics. Cambridge: Cambridge University Press.

Barnett, William A. 1990. "Developments in Monetary Aggregation Theory." *Journal of Policy Modeling* 12 No. 2 (September):205–257.

Barnett, William A., and Choi, Seungmook S. 1989. "A Monte Carlo Study of Tests of Blockwise Weak Separability." *Journal of Business and Economic Statistics* 7 (July):363–377.

Barnett, William A., Fisher, Douglas, and Serletis, Apostolos. 1989. "Consumer Theory and the Demand for and Measurement of Money." University of Texas at Austin, North Carolina State University, and University of Calgary.

Barnett, William A., Hinich, Melvin, and Yue, Piyu. 1989. "Monetary Policy with the Exact Theoretical Rational Expectations Monetary Aggregates." University of Texas at Austin.

Barnett, William A., Hinich, Melvin, and Yue, Piyu. 1990. "Monitoring Monetary Aggregates under Risk Aversion." Michael T. Belongia (Ed.). *Monetary Policy on the 75th Anniversary of the Federal Reserve System*. Boston: Kluwer Academic Publishers, pp. 189–223.

Belongia, Michael, and Chalfant, James. 1989. "The Changing Empirical Definition of Money: Some Estimates from a Model of the Demand for Money Substitutes." *Journal of Political Economy* 97 (April):387–398.

Diewert, W. Erwin. 1976. "Exact and Superlative Index Numbers." *Journal of Econometrics* 4:115–145.

Merton, Robert C. 1989. "Capital Market Theory and the Pricing of Financial Securities." Working Paper #90–024, Harvard Business School, September.

Pesek, B. P., and Saving, T. R. 1967. *Money, Wealth, Economic Theory*. New York: Macmillan.

Poterba, James M., and Rotemberg, Julio J. 1987. "Money in the Utility Function: An Empirical Implementation." In William Barnett and Kenneth Singleton (Eds.), *New Approaches to Monetary Economics*, Proceedings of the Second International Symposium in Economic Theory and Econometrics. Cambridge: Cambridge University Press, pp. 219–240.

Rotemberg, Julio J. 1990. "Monetary Aggregates and their Uses." Michael T. Belongia (Ed.). *Monetary Policy on the 75th Anniversary of the Federal Reserve System*. Boston: Kluwer Academic Publishers, pp. 224–232.

5 MONEY AND BUSINESS CYCLES: A REAL BUSINESS CYCLE INTERPRETATION

Charles I. Plosser

1. Introduction

Money serves some very important functions in a market economy. Money undoubtedly improves economic efficiency by economizing on the costs of information (e.g., Brunner and Meltzer, 1971; King and Plosser, 1986). Money, without question, plays the dominant role in determining the rate of inflation. It also may be true that the Federal Reserve can and does manipulate the federal funds market on a day-to-day basis, although there is considerable question as to its ability to do so for sustained periods and what the consequences are. Yet it does not necessarily follow that money must be the prime impulse to business cycles. Nevertheless, a significant portion of the research in monetary economics over the past 25 years has

---

Support for this article has been provided by the John M. Olin Foundation and the Bradley Policy Research Center. This article is part of the NBER's research programs in Financial Markets and Monetary Economics. Any opinions expressed are those of the author and not of the NBER. The comments of Gerald Dwyer, Thomas Cooley, Robert King, and Gregory Mankiw are appreciated.

been devoted to developing and exploring a monetary theory of the business cycle. These models seek to explain business cycles as arising from independent variations in the nominal quantity of money.

In recent years, however, there has been a resurgence of interest in real theories of the cycle. This class of models, summarized recently by Plosser (1989), are distinguished from pre-Keynesian real theories by their emphasis on the dynamic equilibrium behavior of market economies. They are also purely real models in that variation in nominal quantities is ignored. These models, of course, have been critized for the absence of a role for money in the model's environment. Yet these models are not intended to address those issues raised by Brunner and Meltzer (1971), but to address the dynamic character of market economies and how it pertains to business cycles. By some standards these models have been fairly successful in replicating many features of the business cycle.

King and Plosser (1984) expand the class of real business cycle models by explicitly incorporating a financial or banking industry and positing a demand for real currency. The nominal quantity of fiat currency is supplied by a central monetary authority. The basic implication of this framework is that, under a variety of conditions, variation in the nominal quantity of outside money (either currency or the monetary base) is neutral. Furthermore, variation in the real quantity of inside or bank money is determined by the real supply and demand for transaction services: the nominal quantity of outside money plays no particular role. Although independent variation in the nominal quantity of outside money is neutral, monetary aggregates such as M1 or M2 may indeed be systematically related to real activity because of the endogeniety of inside money.

Distinguishing real theories of the business cycle from monetary theories requires a more careful analysis of Federal Reserve actions than is typically offered. The reason is that the Federal Reserve plays two important but—for the question at hand—distinct roles. One is as a central bank charged with regulating the nominal quantity of money in the economy primarily through open market operations. The second is as a regulator of commercial banking activity. This role includes, for example, the setting of reserve requirements on deposits and, in the not-too-distant past, the setting of interest rate ceilings on deposits. In its role as regulator, the Federal Reserve can clearly be a source of real shocks to the banking system and thus to the economy as a whole. On this point, real theories and monetary theory should agree. What makes a monetary theory of the cycle distinctive is that it assigns an important and independent role to variations in some *nominal* quantity controlled by the central bank in initiating significant fluctuations in real economic activity.

In this article I survey some of the evidence that has been used to support the importance of money as an impulse to business cycles and reinterpret it in the context of the framework proposed in King and Plosser (1984). I conclude that neither statistical evidence—nor the historical record—provides a convincing case for the dominant role of nominal money in the business cycle. Consistent with the work of Cagan (1965), I find that to the extent that monetary measures are correlated with real activity, it is variation in endogenously determined magnitudes that is most important.

2. A Brief Overview of the Evidence

The evidence that movements in the nominal quantity of money are an important impulse to business cycles can be classified as falling into one of three broad categories. The first category includes analyses of specific historical episodes and is most notably associated with the pioneering work of Friedman and Schwartz (1963a). The second category is the systematic analysis of the cyclical behavior of money using the methods established by Burns and Mitchell (1946). Finally, the last category includes all the more traditional statistical approaches based on some form of regression or correlation analysis.[1]

2.1 Historical Episodes

Perhaps the most famous and influential work in this category is the seminal contribution of Friedman and Schwartz (1963a), *A Monetary History of the United States, 1867–1960*. They conclude, from their analysis of the historical record, that independent movements in the stock of money have played a major role in causing business cycles. In summarizing their findings, they emphasize six historical episodes of "deep depression" that support their view that independent movements in the quantity of money have important real effects (see Friedman and Schwartz, 1963a, pp. 686–695; 1963b, pp. 217–218). In their view the key periods were: (1) 1875–1878—a decline in high-powered money preceded the banking crisis of 1873 which in turn led to a reduction in the money stock as the public shifted from deposits to currency; (2) 1892–1894—an outflow of gold combined with the banking panic of 1893 once again reduced the deposit to currency ratio and the money stock; (3) 1907–1908—the banking panic of 1907 precipitated a contraction in the stock of money; (4) 1920–1921—a significant increase in the Federal Reserve discount rate was followed by a sharp contraction in Federal Reserve credit and the money stock, albeit with some lag; (5) 1929–1933—the Federal Reserve's failure to respond to widespread banking failures and the increase in demand for currency resulted in a dramatic decline in the money stock; and (6) 1937–1938—the Federal Reserve doubled legal reserve requirements.

Each of these episodes closely corresponded to a major contraction. Friedman and Schwartz (1963b, pp. 60–61), however, acknowledge that in four of these six episodes (1875–1878, 1892–1894, 1907–1908, and 1929–1933) a banking crisis played an important role in altering the deposit-currency ratio. Thus the independent role of movements in the quantity of money is not easily isolated.[2] Therefore, there are two critical episodes where bank failures played no role, the discount rate changes of 1920 and the increase in required reserves in 1937. Based on these two episodes and their attempts to isolate independent movements in the quantity of money from feedback in the circumstances associated with the banking crises, they conclude that the money stock is an important, but highly irregular in timing, impulse to business cycles.

Recently, Romer and Romer (1989) have attempted to follow the spirit of the analysis of Friedman and Schwartz by studying specific historical episodes of postwar U.S. monetary experience in order to investigate the real effects of autonomous monetary disturbances. Their strategy was to look for times when the Federal Reserve, as expressed in official documents, discussed a desire or a willingness to tolerate a recession to curb inflation.

The Romers' reading of Federal Reserve documents leads them to isolate six episodes when Federal Reserve officials indicated their desire to restrain the economy. Their description of those episodes are roughly as follows: (1) October 1947—the Federal Reserve began a series of open market purchases, an increase in the discount rate, and an increase in reserve requirements in an effort to reduce inflation; (2) September 1955—once again the Federal Open Market Committee (FOMC) expressed the desire to maintain "restraint" through open market operations even in the event of a downturn; (3) December 1968—continuing concern over inflation and inflationary expectations led to "restraint" despite signs of an economic slowdown; (4) April 1974—experiencing very rapid inflation following the end of wage and price controls and the oil embargo, the Federal Reserve repeatedly pushed for contraction through higher interest rates; (5) August 1978—once again concern over inflation resulted in more restrictive policies including increases in the discount rate and reserve requirements; and (6) October 1979—recognizing that the efforts in 1978 were unsuccessful, the FOMC switched to a policy that it anticipated would raise interest rates by limiting the expansion of money.[3]

The next step in the Romers' analysis is a statistical investigation of industrial production and unemployment. They conclude that the growth rate of industrial production for the three-year period following five of the six selected episodes is lower than otherwise might have been predicted from a univariate autoregression.[4] The Romers conclude that efforts to curb inflation through contractionary monetary actions have important and persistent effects on real output.

2.2 Business Cycle Analysis

The second category of evidence that supports the importance of changes in the money stock for business cycles is based on systematic study of the cyclical behavior of money. The pioneering work of Burns and Mitchell (1946) changed dramatically the way economists think about business cycles. Probably the most important feature of their methodological contribution was to think not in terms of calendar time, but in business cycle time. Their strategy of treating the business cycle as a unit of measurement and of investigating the common characteristics of these units was both controversial and influential.

The methods developed by Burns and Mitchell have been used by several authors, most notably Friedman and Schwartz (1963b), to study the behavior of money over the business cycle (i.e., reference cycle analysis in the terminology of Burns and Mitchell). They conclude that the rate of change in the money stock displays positive conformity to the reference cycle with a long lead. Moreover, the amplitude in the money stock rates of change is much larger for deep contractions than mild contractions.

Cagan (1965) also studied the reference properties of the money stock and some of the key determinants such as the monetary base, deposit-currency ratio, and the deposit-reserve ratio. He concluded that the deposit-currency ratio was the most important single contributor to the cyclical behavior of the money stock.

2.3 Regression Evidence

The last category is intended to encompass the wide variety of empirical studies that have attempted to isolate the statistical link between movements in money and economic activity. The seminal work of Friedman and Schwartz provided the initial impetus to a generation of research into monetary theories of the business cycle. To summarize over 20 years of empirical work is not the task of this article. I simply try to highlight examples of the sort of evidence that have been produced in support of the importance of monetary impulses for the business cycle.

One of the early studies in this tradition was by Friedman and Meiselman (1963). They focused on the relative importance of money and investment. Using standard regression techniques, they found that the relation between money and income was more significant and stable than the relation between autonomous expenditures and income. Like the earlier work of Friedman and Schwartz, Friedman and Meiselman focused on nominal income as the dependent variable to be explained. This was also the case for many of the empirical studies in the 1960s. The general view at the time seemed to be that inflation was not a significant factor for most of the sample and, therefore, money income and real income moved together.

The 1960s ended with the influential and controversial empirical work of Andersen and Jordan (1968) and their estimates of what became known as the "St. Louis" equation. Andersen and Jordan regressed various measures of money and fiscal variables on nominal GNP and concluded that the influence of the money stock on nominal GNP was larger and more significant than the influence of fiscal actions.

Sims (1972) further intensified the controversies by arguing that "Granger causality tests" indicated a one-way temporal ordering from money to nominal income. The debate as to whether money helps predict output or not has continued for some 15 years. More recently the attention has shifted to real output instead of nominal income. The approach has been to focus on the predictive content of money for real output in the context of bivariate or multivariate autoregressions (VAR's). Examples, in addition to Sims (1972), are Sims (1980a, 1980b), Litterman and Weiss (1985), Eichenbaum and Singleton (1986), and recently Stock and Watson (1989).

The results of these studies are mixed. The statistical significance of money appears sensitive to the method of detrending and to the other variables included in the system. The results are also subject to different interpretations since the methods are not based on any structural model.[5] As representative of the current state of this literature, I cite the recent contribution of Stock and Watson (1989). They conclude that innovations in the growth of nominal M1 are statistically significant for forecasting industrial production in both bivariate money-output specifications and those that include prices and interest rates.

Another line of empirical work on money and real output was stimulated by the work of Lucas (1972), Barro (1976), and others who incorporated rational expectations into monetary models of the business cycle. The empirical work of Barro (1977a, 1978) was particularly influential in this regard. Barro's empirical work focused on unanticipated monetary growth and its impact on unemployment and real output. He concluded that not only were unanticipated money shocks important but that the unanticipated part of monetary growth was empirically significant.[6] These results led to an explosion of studies relating unanticipated and anticipated money to almost every conceivable variable.

3. The Elusive Transmission Mechanism

The sort of evidence summarized in the previous section has led many economists to conclude that variations in the stock of money play an important role in business fluctuations. Yet without the theory and supporting evidence for the mechanism by which nominal money disturbances are transmitted to the real economy, there is little reason for complacency. After all, the neoclassical model with flexible prices exhibits the dichotomy of real and nominal magnitudes so that changes in the money stock are neutral.

> Of course, it is one thing to assert that monetary changes are the key to major movements in money income; it is quite a different thing to know in any detail what is the mechanism that links monetary change to economic change.... We have little confidence in our knowledge of the transmission mechanism.... Indeed, this is the challenge our evidence poses...(Friedman and Schwartz, 1963a, p. 227).

Unfortunately, it seems that over 25 years after Friedman and Schwartz laid out this "challenge," we are no closer to having a coherent theoretical or empirical understanding of the transmission mechanism of money shocks to real economic activity than they were. Indeed, Friedman and Schwartz (1982, p. 462) conclude:

> ...we have not succeeded, as we had hoped we would, in giving satisfactory empirical content...bearing on the division over short periods of a change in nominal income between prices and output.

If we are to stress the importance of changes in nominal stock of money for fluctuations in real economic activity, we must come up with an empirically satisfactory explanation of how movements in the nominal quantity of money produce changes in real output. There are numerous mechanisms that researchers have employed to generate monetary non-neutrality. I classify the attempts to explain monetary non-neutrality into three broad categories: (1) sticky prices, (2) nominal wage contracts, and (3) imperfect information.

3.1 Sticky Price Models

Many of the rationales for monetary non-neutrality can be classified under the heading of sticky price models. In these models, changes in the nominal quantity of money are translated into changes in real output because the nominal price level (or its constituent parts) does not adjust or adjusts only very slowly. Many different types of models resort to nominal price rigidities of this sort. Some of them are equilibrium rational expectations models that exhibit monetary non-neutrality but provide little scope for exploitation by policymakers. Other models employ sticky prices but retain the necessary elements that permit policymakers to vary systematically the quantity of money to target real output (e.g., Gordon, 1982).

Recently, for example, McCallum (1986) has stressed that firms acting to economize on costs optimally choose to set a nominal price over some period. The price-setting process incorporates the firms' anticipations of inflation and monetary policy. The implication is that monetary shocks will have real effects within the interval when prices are fixed. Firms and other participants presumably find the gains to indexing or more frequently adjusting prices sufficiently small that they do not have the private incentive to do so. If the private costs are small, it remains to be explained why these sorts of rigidities should be the key to understanding large economic fluctuations.

In an effort to develop the foundations of sticky price models many authors have recently stressed "menu costs" in the adjustment of prices. This line of research (see Ball, Mankiw, and Romer, 1988, for a survey), argues that in models with monopolistically competitive firms facing menu costs, monetary disturbances can result in social costs that are large even though private costs of price adjustment may be small. Many economists point out, however, that prices do change, sometimes very quickly; consumers bargain over price, sales occur, and so on. Moreover, when reported or quoted prices do change, their changes are sometimes very small in magnitude. Thus, despite the recent flurry of interest in these models and the claim to have revitalized "Keynesian economics," the majority of economists remain unconvinced that small menu costs are the primary reason why money affects real output and thus the rationale behind major economic contractions.

3.2 Nominal Wage Contracts

Another line of research has focused on "sticky wages" as opposed to "sticky prices" as a source of monetary non-neutrality. For example, Fischer (1977) and Taylor (1980) have stressed the importance of long-term nominal wage contracts as a source of nominal rigidity and thus monetary non-neutrality. Both of these models admit the possibility of a stabilizing role for monetary policy.

The attempts to isolate the transmission mechanism of changes in the money supply via stickiness in the nominal wage have met with two sorts of criticism. First, at the theoretical level, Barro (1977b), for example, stresses that these models lack a microeconomic foundation for why labor contracts exist in the form hypothesized in the models and why, if such contracts are socially costly, they persist. Most attempts to develop the foundations for the existence of long-term labor contracts pertain to contracting for real wages and do not really explain nominal wage stickiness.

A second criticism of these models is empirical. A key prediction of this class of models is that the greater the degree of indexing of wage contracts, the less sensitive the economy should be to monetary disturbances. Ahmed (1987) studies the sensitivity of 19 Canadian industries to monetary disturbances. The wage contracts in these industries exhibit varying degrees of indexation. Ahmed finds no relation between the degree of indexation and the sensitivity of industry-specific output to monetary shocks. This raises important doubts about the relevance of the mechanisms emphasized by these models.

3.3 Imperfect Information Models

For over a decade, the most controversial and most investigated model of monetary non-neutrality stemmed from the work of Lucas (1972, 1973). Lucas' explanation, building on the earlier work of Friedman (1968) and Phelps (1967), stressed the idea that there were informational frictions that resulted in the inability of agents to distinguish changes in relative prices from changes in the absolute price level. Suppliers, when faced with an unanticipated monetary disturbance that raised the general price level, generally attributed some of the rise in price to a shift in the relative price of their good and hence chose to supply more output. A key feature of Lucas' model was that agents' expectations were rational so that anticipated changes in the price level or money supply were entirely neutral. Thus unanticipated movements in money could be a significant business cycle impulse. This type of model received initial empirical support from the work of Barro (1977a, 1978) and Sargent (1976). Barro, as noted previously, found empirical support for the proposition that only unanticipated money was important for explaining real magnitudes. Later, Mishkin (1982) and others claimed to find evidence that anticipated money does matter.

An important line of criticism of this class of models was that monetary statistics and price level statistics are readily available to the public, so why are they so frequently misperceived by agents? Boschen and Grossman (1982), for example, found that contemporaneous perceived monetary movements were correlated with real activity in contradiction to the theory. Additional empirical evidence questioning the appropriateness of the Lucas transmission mechanism was reported by King and Plosser (1986). They found that, although unanticipated movements in M1 are correlated with output, the same doesn't hold for surprise movements in the monetary base. Moreover, they found that there is little correlation between price surprises and real output. The absence of important correlations between price surprises and output casts doubt on the channels stressed by Lucas.

4. A Real Business Cycle Interpretation

The inability of economists to develop a theoretically and empirically coherent mechanism for explaining why movements in the nominal quantity of money alter real output has, in part, resulted in a renewed interest in alternative theories of the business cycle. One line of research has followed the work of Kydland and Prescott (1982) and Long and Plosser (1983) in stressing the important role of real shocks as impulses to the business cycle.[7] These models are purely real economic models driven by shocks to productivity and thus admit no role for nominal measures of money as an impulse for business cycles.

King and Plosser (1984) integrate money and banking into the real business cycle model. The result is a class of models that predicts a positive correlation between money and real activity but the causation runs from real activity to money and the banking sector. In this section I briefly summarize the arguments of King and Plosser and their implications and predictions for the relation between nominal measures of money and business cycles. Next I discuss the empirical evidence and its potential relevance for this real business cycle view of money.

4.1 *Money in a Real Business Cycle*

King and Plosser incorprate money and banking into a real business cycle model by introducing a financial or banking industry that supplies an intermediate good called transaction services to a final goods industry. The demand for transaction services arises from the desire to economize on time and other inputs in the exchange of goods. The output of the transactions or financial industry depends on the real costs of providing the services. In the presence of a positive productivity shock to the final goods industry, the production of transaction services rises as well. To relate the flow of transaction services to the stock of deposits, it is assumed that the stock of deposits is related to the flow of services by a monotonic increasing function. Thus, the model implies that the volume of real deposits, or real bank money, is positively correlated with output.

The economy just described is completely real with no nominal quantities. To incorporate a pure nominal quantity we simply posit a real demand for a non-interest-bearing fiat currency. Deposit or transaction services and real currency are assumed to be substitutes but not perfect substitutes for one another. The demand for currency depends on both a nominal interest rate and the cost of financial services. If, for example, banks are required to hold non-interest-bearing reserves, this raises the cost of bank supplied transaction services and reduces its demand while increasing the demand for currency services.

In an unregulated banking environment the price level is determined by the interaction of the demand and supply of currency. What is significant is that bank or inside money plays no role in this model in the determination of the price level. The only way that developments in the financial sector are relevant to price level determination is through variations in the cost of financial services which alters the relative demands for inside and outside money. Thus changes in the quantity of nominal currency are completely neutral. The volume of real deposits is determined solely by variation in the real economy. Assuming that prices are not too counter-cyclical, the nominal quantity of deposits will also be procyclical. An important implication of this framework is that broad measures of money like M1 or M2 are likely to be procyclical because of the endogeneity of bank money. On the other hand, variations in a measure of outside money like currency or the monetary base are neutral.

Another important characteristic of this model is that it highlights the possibility that important real variations in the banking sector may be a source of fluctuations in real output. For example, in a regulated banking environment, a change in reserve requirements alters real opportunities in that it changes the real tax on deposit services. Other real shocks to the financial industry may also arise. The important role played by banking panics in the 19th and early 20th century are another example. The financial system has played an important role in economic fluctuations in the work of Bernanke (1983) and, more recently, Stiglitz and Weiss (1988).

The real business cycle view forces one to think carefully about what is meant by a monetary theory of the business cycle and how it is different from a real theory. The distinction must be that a monetary theory stresses the importance of independent or exogenous changes in some nominal quantity of money as opposed to variations in banking policies (e.g., changes in reserve requirements) that alter real opportunities. Friedman and Schwartz (1963a) recognized this problem at one level by stressing that in some episodes, like banking panics, variation in the deposit-currency ratio was likely to be demand determined. Thus such episodes did not represent a clean example of independent movements in the money stock. They also stress as important evidence the nearly doubling of reserve requirements in 1937–1938. Yet such changes in the tax on banks are a real disturbance and cannot effectively be used to argue for a monetary explanation of fluctuations in preference to a real theory of fluctuations. In the discussion that follows I reinterpret some of the evidence highlighted in section 3 in an attempt to see if it provides the compelling evidence, sometimes ascribed to it, that changes in the nominal quantity of money are the major impulses to business cycles.

4.2 Historical Episodes

Friedman and Schwartz (1963a) and Romer and Romer (1988) stress a number of historical episodes that, to them, provide convincing evidence that variations in the quantity of money are the most important impulse to business cycles. How convincing is this collection of episodes when viewed from a real business cycle perspective? In attempting to distinguish monetary from real explanations of the cycle, it is important to keep in mind two things: first, the key factor that distinguishes a monetary theory of the cycle from a real theory is that the monetary theory assigns the primary impulse to independent variations in the nominal quantity of money. Thus, as stressed by Friedman and Schwartz, variations in money that are attributable to feedback from the real economy cannot be relied upon for strong support of monetary explanations. Perhaps just as important is to stress that changes in "monetary policy" that alter real opportunities, perhaps through changes in bank regulation, cannot be used to argue for a theory that assigns a major role to nominal variations in money.[8] As discussed above, examples can most frequently be found in changes in regulatory policy by the Federal Reserve such as changes in reserve requirements which alter the tax rate on certain forms of financial intermediation.

The second point to keep in mind is that real theories of the cycle do not stress that every business cycle must be initiated by the same easily identifiable impulse. Variations in real opportunities can arise from many sources, including changes in tax rates; real government spending; changes in the terms of trade brought about through tariffs or import-export restrictions; changes in regulations, in addition to more general changes in productivity or preferences, just to name a few. Of course, this is part of the theory's strength and weakness. Since there is no single, always easily observable impulse that initiates the cycle, systematic empirical investigations are difficult to conduct. Such difficulties, however, cannot be used as prima facie evidence that the theory is wrong.

Romer and Romer (1989) discuss in some detail the episodes designated by Friedman and Schwartz as important independent monetary shocks. They argue that there is evidence of selection bias in the choice of episodes by Friedman and Schwartz. For example, the Romers cite the banking panic in early 1933 when the money stock declined 12% in just two months as an important monetary disturbance. This was the largest two-month decline during the entire period of 1929–1933. Yet, despite this dramatic shock to the money stock, the economy bottomed out in March 1933 and began a recovery. The Romers argue that Friedman and Schwartz do not emphasize this episode as evidence in conflict with their hypothesis regarding the importance of monetary disturbances.

The Romers also question the role of monetary shocks in those episodes that were stressed by Friedman and Schwartz. Of particular interest are the contractions of 1920–1921 and 1936–1937. The Romers suggest that non-monetary factors in the downturn of 1920 were potentially important, including declining government spending following the war. Another non-monetary influence was identified by Loungani (1986) in the form of a large rise in the relative price of fuels and power in late 1919 and 1920.

The Romers also cite non-monetary factors influencing the downturn of 1936–1937. In addition to their concerns, Friedman and Schwartz emphasize that the important initial shock involved a doubling of reserve requirements. As discussed previously, such an event should be construed as a real shock to the banking industry and not as a nominal disturbance. Friedman and Schwartz (1963a, p. 218) acknowledge that the decline in the money stock was largely the result of a decline in the deposit-reserve ratio.

The conclusion reached by the Romers is that the interwar episodes stressed by Friedman and Schwartz are not particularly supportive of the hypothesis that nominal monetary disturbances are important for economic fluctuations. In a curious twist, Romer and Romer go on to conclude from their own analysis of U.S. postwar data that monetary disturbances (in particular, anti-inflationary rhetoric) provide "decisive evidence of the importance of monetary policy" (p. 36).

In contrast to their analysis of the important interwar episodes of Friedman and Schwartz, the Romer and Romer narrative of the six episodes that they isolate contains almost no discussion of non-monetary events. For example, they do not seem to see the potential relevance of the major oil shocks of 1948, 1953, 1957, 1973, 1979, and 1980 for the subsequent contractions as stressed by Hamilton (1983). They do not entertain the notion that the major temporary income tax increases from 1968–1970, the sharp reductions in government spending, and the elimination of the investment tax credit were relevant at all for the recession of 1970.

In addition, Romer and Romer make no distinction between monetary policy and banking or regulatory policy. For example, in the nine months prior to the onset of the recession in November of 1948, the Federal Reserve raised required reserves by 30% from 20% to 26%. While such a significant increase in the tax on banks was caused by Federal Reserve policy, it is not a nominal disturbance but a change in real opportunities. Similarly in October 1979 reserve requirements were again raised significantly and expanded to include a broader range of bank liabilities. In April 1980 these reserve requirements were raised again when credit controls were adopted. Another factor sometimes cited as important in the 1981–1982 recession is the intertemporal substitution that occurred, after the passing of the Tax Reform Act, because the tax cuts were phased in over several years.

It is also interesting to note that Romer and Romer offer no evidence that the nominal quantity of any money bore any correspondence to the verbal behavior of the Federal Reserve authorities. It is most unlikely that many economists are prepared to believe that the Federal Reserve can talk the economy into a recession. The only evidence they offer in passing is that interest rates rose around the dates of their events. This is not terribly convincing since the short-term nominal interest rate has been procyclical over this period, rising during virtually every expansion. It would not be hard to pick a date at random during any expansion and observe the nominal rate higher on average after the date than before. It is also interesting to note that the average length of postwar expansions is about 39 months. Assuming that recessions are unpredictable based on a univariate autoregression of industrial productivity, it does not seem too surprising that by selecting some date during an expansion that in the subsequent three years a recession could occur. Thus the Romers' narrative and their subsequent statistical tests offer little or no discriminating evidence in support of a monetary theory of the cycle.

4.3 Business Cycle Analysis

Friedman and Schwartz (1963b) and Cagan (1965) applied the method of analysis developed by Burns and Mitchell (1946) to study the business cycle patterns of the money stock. Friedman and Schwartz focused on the behavior of the growth rate of the money stock and concluded that it conforms positively to the reference cycle with a long lead. I have applied the Burns and Mitchell methodology to the growth rate of various measures of money and plotted the average behavior for the seven complete reference cycles since 1948 in figure 5–1.[9] Also plotted is the cyclical pattern of real GNP growth.[10] There are several points to make about these patterns. First, unlike the findings of Freidman and Schwartz, there is very little evidence of a procyclical pattern to broad measures such as M1 or M2. To the extent that they follow any cyclical pattern it is because of the sharply lower growth rates midway between the peak and the terminal trough. The monetary base, on the other hand, shows even less evidence of systematic cyclical behavior.

Second, and probably most important, is that figure 5–1 confirms the finding of Cagan (1965). In his investigations of the source of cyclical variability of M1, he found that variation in the deposit-currency ratio was the single most important contributor to the cyclical variation in the money stock. In the figure, it is apparent that the dramatic decline in the growth rate of M1 and M2 during the contraction is closely matched by the pattern of cyclical variability of the respective deposit-currency ratios. Moreover, the pattern of declining deviations from average cycle growth throughout the expansion appears largely a phenomenon driven by the deposit-currency ratios.

Friedman and Schwartz, and Cagan, acknowledge that variation in the

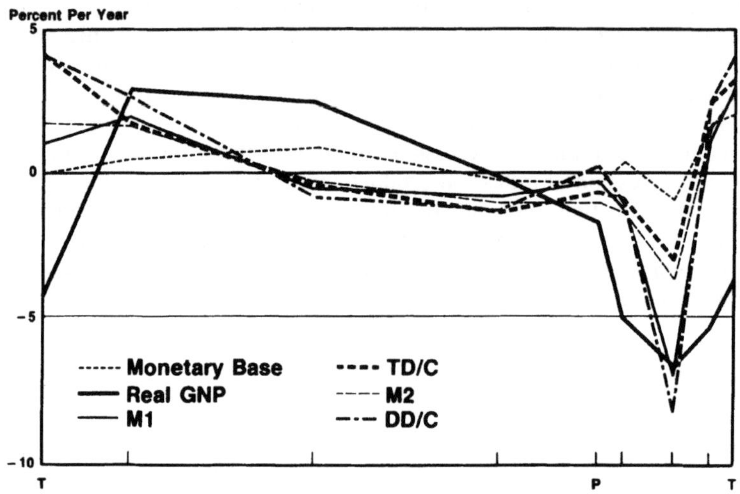

Figure 5–1. Average reference cycle patterns, 1947–1988: averages of seven cycles *Note*: Annual Rates of change are expressed as deviations from cycle averages.

deposit-currency ratio is a component of monetary growth that is attributable to the real economy feeding back into the determination of the money stock. The chart clearly shows that the bulk of the cyclical variability of M1 and M2 can be associated with cyclical variability in their respective deposit-currency ratios. Thus cyclical variation in nominal M1 and M2 growth can be interpreted as largely endogenous as predicted in the real business cycle model of King and Plosser.

4.4 Regression Results

The model developed by King and Plosser stresses the distinction between inside or bank money and outside money. In particular, an important implication is that the endogenous factors influencing the growth of money should be more closely correlated with real output fluctuations than exogenous factors. Cagan (1965) decomposed movements in money into three basic components: (1) movements in high-powered money or monetary base which in the postwar period have been under the control of the

Federal Reserve; (2) the ratio of deposits to currency which is determined by private agents; and (3) the ratio of deposits to reserves which is determined by banks and legal reserve requirements. The two ratios can be viewed as key determinants of the money multiplier. As noted previously, Cagan concluded that the monetary base and the deposit-to-currency ratio were the most important sources of variability in the money stock. In the empirical analysis I follow Cagan in focusing on the deposit-to-currency ratio and the monetary base, investigating how they behave relative to movements in real output.

Table 5–1 presents the summary statistics of the data for five different time periods: 1948–1988, 1948–1979, 1948–1969, 1959–1988, and 1959–1979. Although there are some differences, the data display similar properties in all the periods. Several points are worth noting. First, the standard deviation of output is higher than any of the monetary measures. Second, all the monetary growth measures exhibit more persistence than the growth in real output. Finally, the growth rate of the ratio of the non-currency portion of M1 to currency (DD/C) is not much different from zero in the early part of the sample whereas it displays some negative growth particularly in the 1970s and 1980s. The growth rate of the non-currency portion of M2 to currency ratio (TD/C) exhibits positive growth in all periods, although it appears to be smaller in the later periods.

The monetary base numbers are a peculiar mixture of real and nominal elements of monetary policy. The practice of adjusting the base figures for reserve requirement changes confuses real and nominal disturbances. For example, if reserve requirements are lowered (reducing the tax on banks), then the reserve adjustment increases the adjusted base, thus inducing a positive correlation between changes in real opportunities and the nominal monetary base. More generally, this happens anytime the public alters its mix of assets among deposits with different reserve requirements. I have attempted to look at this distinction by reporting the percentage change in the adjusted base attributable to changes in the source base ($\Delta SB/B$) and that attributable to changes in the reserve adjustment ($\Delta RAM/B$).[11] These data cover the period 1959–1988. The summary measures of these series are also reported in table 5–1.

Table 5–2 presents the cross-correlations of each of the variables with the growth rate of real output. For the period 1948–1988 broad measures of money exhibit some correlation with real output, while the monetary base and the source base show almost no correlation. On the other hand, the two deposit-to-currency ratios show more correlation with output than any of the other variables. Across the different time periods the results are broadly similar. Depending on the sample, sometimes M1 growth is more

Table 5–1. Summary Statistics

Variable	*Mean*	*Std. Dev.*	ρ_1	ρ_2	ρ_4
		A: 1948–1988			
Δlog(Y)	3.24	4.40	.37	.25	−.10
Δlog(M2)	7.03	3.29	.68	.48	.31
Δlog(M1)	4.76	4.07	.58	.43	.37
Δlog(B)	4.95	3.42	.76	.68	.63
Δlog(TD/C)	2.15	3.58	.71	.50	.23
Δlog(DD/C)	−0.47	4.42	.48	.29	.16
Δlog(P)	4.10	3.04	.65	.60	.47
		B: 1948–1979			
Δlog(Y)	3.40	4.47	.37	.24	−.15
Δlog(M2)	6.77	3.24	.79	.58	.35
Δlog(M1)	3.84	3.12	.64	.47	.39
Δlog(B)	4.24	3.33	.78	.70	.66
Δlog(TD/C)	2.71	3.40	.76	.54	.19
Δlog(DD/C)	−0.67	3.43	.58	.40	.26
Δlog(P)	3.94	3.14	.61	.55	.40
		C: 1948–1969			
Δlog(Y)	3.69	4.46	.43	.25	−.22
Δlog(M2)	5.58	2.41	.71	.43	.29
Δlog(M1)	2.69	2.79	.56	.34	.23
Δlog(B)	2.67	2.77	.63	.50	.50
Δlog(TD/C)	3.44	2.86	.72	.43	.10
Δlog(DD/C)	0.22	3.25	.53	.30	.06
Δlog(P)	2.57	2.51	.28	.20	−.06
		D: 1959–1988			
Δlog(Y)	3.12	3.94	.25	.22	.02
Δlog(M2)	7.94	3.15	.60	.34	.11
Δlog(M1)	5.82	4.00	.50	.30	.23
Δlog(B)	6.32	2.58	.67	.52	.41
Δlog(TD/C)	1.33	3.59	.66	.43	.15
Δlog(DD/C)	−1.17	4.60	.43	.22	.14
Δlog(P)	4.73	2.81	.76	.72	.66
ΔSB/B	5.98	3.39	.60	.48	.42
ΔRAM/B	0.40	2.50	.32	−.03	.11
		E: 1959–1979			
Δlog(Y)	3.32	3.86	.19	.20	−.01
Δlog(M2)	7.94	3.09	.75	.48	.13
Δlog(M1)	4.88	2.85	.60	.37	.28
Δlog(B)	5.83	2.52	.77	.65	.54

Table 5–1. (Continued)

Variable	*Mean*	*Std. Dev.*	ρ_1	ρ_2	ρ_4
Δlog(TD/C)	1.84	3.53	.75	.50	.14
Δlog(DD/C)	−1.79	3.01	.46	.19	.16
Δlog(P)	4.75	2.93	.73	.69	.61
ΔSB/B	5.64	3.68	.67	.50	.43
ΔRAM/B	0.25	2.48	.42	−.04	.03

Notes: The data are quarterly and defined as follows: Y is real GNP; M1 and M2 are consistent money stock series constructed by Rasche (1988); B is the monetary base as constructed by the Federal Reserve Bank of St. Louis; TD/C is the ratio of the non-currency to currency components of M2; DD/C is the ratio of the non-currency to currency components of M1; and P is the GNP price deflator. The last two variables ΔSB/B and ΔRAM/B decompose the base growth into that attributable to changes in the source base (ΔSB/B) and that attributable to the reserve adjustment (ΔRAM/B). All growth rates are expressed at annual rates. ρ_1, ρ_2, and ρ_4 are the first, second, and fourth sample autocorrelations.

Table 5–2. Cross-Correlations with Real Output

	Cross-Correlations with $\Delta log(Y_{t-j})$								
Variable	*−4*	*−3*	*−2*	*−1*	*0*	*1*	*2*	*3*	*4*
				A: 1948–1988					
Δlog(M2)	.02	.07	.17	.19	.11	−.08	−.13	−.13	−.18
Δlog(M1)	−.07	−.02	.15	.16	.17	−.02	−.03	−.09	−.05
Δlog(B)	−.07	−.05	−.01	.04	.06	−.03	.02	.02	−.04
Δlog(TD/C)	.24	.25	.29	.23	.08	.08	−.10	−.15	−.15
Δlog(DD/C)	.12	.13	.30	.23	.19	−.06	−.05	−.13	−.04
Δlog(P)	−.10	−.11	−.06	−.05	−.08	−.09	−.15	−.25	−.24
				B: 1948–1979					
Δlog(M2)	−.00	.13	.20	.21	.18	.03	−.09	−.12	−.16
Δlog(M1)	−.12	.02	.17	.19	.28	.15	.04	−.01	.01
Δlog(B)	−.11	−.06	−.03	−.01	−.08	.03	.08	.09	.03
Δlog(TD/C)	.26	.33	.36	.29	.15	−.08	−.19	−.23	−.25
Δlog(DD/C)	.14	.25	.37	.31	.29	.05	−.07	−.13	−.07
Δlog(P)	−.15	−.20	−.09	−.02	−.02	−.02	−.01	−.06	−.07
				C: 1948–1969					
Δlog(M2)	−.05	.09	.20	.22	.18	.00	−.07	−.07	−.07
Δlog(M1)	−.10	.08	.25	.30	.37	.24	.11	−.02	.00
Δlog(B)	−.07	−.03	.04	.09	.19	.16	.22	.28	.13
Δlog(TD/C)	.24	.28	.31	.12	−.05	−.32	−.34	−.39	−.32
Δlog(DD/C)	.18	.28	.40	.24	.19	−.07	−.15	−.30	−.24
Δlog(P)	−.21	−.19	.07	.19	.23	.24	.21	−.03	−.04

Table 5–2. (Continued)

Variable	−4	−3	−2	−1	0	1	2	3	4
			Cross-Correlations with $\Delta log(Y_{t-j})$						
			D: 1959–1988						
Δlog(M2)	.15	.15	.26	.26	.15	−.05	−.10	−.13	−.23
Δlog(M1)	−.03	−.04	.16	.14	.13	−.10	−.06	−.13	−.07
Δlog(B)	.01	−.01	.06	.12	.08	−.08	−.00	−.09	−.14
Δlog(TD/C)	.21	.24	.29	.25	.14	−.02	−.09	−.06	−.12
Δlog(DD/C)	.03	.03	.22	.16	.14	−.10	−.05	−.09	.01
Δlog(P)	−.25	−.33	−.30	−.29	−.27	−.22	−.22	−.11	−.09
ΔSB/B	−.13	−.14	−.11	−.25	.07	.10	.10	.05	−.02
ΔRAM/B	.19	.18	.21	.20	−.01	−.22	−.14	−.16	−.12
			E: 1959–1979						
Δlog(M2)	.13	.27	.33	.33	.29	.13	−.05	−.14	−.24
Δlog(M1)	−.13	−.02	.13	.10	.21	.12	.10	−.04	−.02
Δlog(B)	−.10	−.05	.01	−.01	.09	−.01	.06	−.04	−.07
Δlog(TD/C)	.23	.37	.40	.38	.29	.08	−.09	−.11	−.20
Δlog(DD/C)	−.01	.14	.27	.23	.29	.10	−.05	−.01	.03
Δlog(P)	−.09	−.29	−.25	−.27	−.26	−.18	−.18	−.06	−.05
ΔSB/B	−.19	−.18	−.09	−.15	.08	.11	.20	.04	−.00
ΔRAM/B	.29	.22	.14	.21	−.03	−.18	−.23	−.11	−.07

Notes: All variables are defined in table 5–1. The cross-correlations are between the column variable at time t and Δlog (Y) at time t-j. The large sample standard error for the cross-correlations is .08 in panel A, .09 in panels B and D, and .11 in panels C and E.

correlated with real output growth than M2, and in other periods the reverse is true. The monetary base appears consistently unrelated to real economic activity. The only possible exception is during the 1948–1969 period when real activity seems to help predict the monetary base. In no period does the monetary base appear correlated with future real activity.

Another interesting feature of table 5–2 is the correlation between inflation and real activity. Except for the 1948–1969 sample, the correlation between output and inflation is negative. Dividing the sample up into seven nonoverlapping periods beginning with 1948–1953 and ending with 1983–1989, the correlation is negative in five of the seven samples (1948–1953 and 1960–1965 being the exceptions). Others have noted this phenomenon as well. Friedman and Schwartz (1982, pp. 399–400) conclude from phase-averaged data that prices or inflation are procyclical only for the interwar period. In the postwar period the average rate of inflation during expansions is actually lower than during contractions. Cooley and

Table 5–3. Summary of the Regressions for Real Output in Bivariate VAR's

	Sample Period				
Variable	*1948–1988*	*1948–1979*	*1948–1969*	*1959–1988*	*1959–1979*
	A. Exclusion Restrictions: F-statistics and *p*-values[a]				
Δlog(M2)	1.95(.10)	1.51(.21)	0.67(.61)	2.46(.05)	3.52(.01)
Δlog(M1)	2.35(.06)	1.71(.15)	1.20(.32)	2.29(.06)	1.99(.10)
Δlog(B)	0.67(.61)	0.10(.98)	0.42(.79)	1.11(.36)	0.17(.95)
Δlog(TD/C)	2.34(.06)	1.95(.11)	1.59(.19)	2.20(.07)	3.11(.02)
Δlog(DD/C)	2.58(.04)	2.85(.03)	2.43(.05)	1.93(.11)	1.76(.15)
ΔSB/B	—	—	—	0.32(.86)	1.30(.28)
ΔRAM/B	—	—	—	2.78(.03)	2.03(.10)
	B. Three-Year-Ahead Forecast Error Variance Decomposition[b]				
Δlog(M2)	7.6(5.7)	13.4(8.5)	11.1(4.4)	11.3(10.5)	20.9(18.3)
Δlog(M1)	16.7(6.1)	24.9(7.2)	23.8(8.4)	13.6(7.1)	22.4(7.5)
Δlog(B)	6.5(1.8)	8.5(0.5)	12.6(2.8)	6.7(4.7)	5.6(1.1)
Δlog(TD/C)	8.0(8.2)	9.7(9.7)	7.6(7.4)	10.6(10.6)	17.5(17.4)
Δlog(DD/C)	11.1(7.3)	20.4(13.4)	20.0(15.7)	9.9(6.5)	18.5(7.9)
ΔSB/B	—	—	—	4.3(2.0)	14.3(7.2)
ΔRAM/B	—	—	—	12.4(12.7)	13.9(13.4)

[a] The bivariate VAR includes four lags of Δlog(Y), four lags of the appropriate money or ratio growth rate variable, and a time trend. The F-tests are for the hypothesis that the coefficients on the four lags of the money or ratio growth rate variable are jointly equal to zero. The corresponding p values are in parentheses.

[b] The forecast error variance decompositions are in percent. The first number places real output growth second in the variance decomposition, and the number in parentheses places output first, which is the more usual practice.

Ohanian (1989) have also documented this finding and conclude, based on methods much different from those employed by Friedman and Schwartz, that the interwar period is the only period for which inflation or prices can be viewed as systematically procyclical.[12]

Table 5–3 summarizes some of the characteristics of several bivariate autoregressions of real output growth and various measures of money and of the deposit-currency ratio. The specification of the regression follows that suggested by Stock and Watson (1989). All variables are expressed as growth rates, and a time trend is included. They found that this specification consistently yielded significant results in their study of monthly industrial production. In order to give money the maximum opportunity to predict output, I have not included interest rates or other variables. If the transmission mechanism is through price surprises or through interest rates, including those variables may diminish the importance of money.[13]

Panel A of table 5–3 presents the F-statistics and *p*-values of the hypothesis that the variables specified in the first column can be omitted from the equation for real output growth. As can be seen, the degree of significance varies with the time period. Both M1 and M2 have statistically significant (at the 10% level) predictive content for real activity for the overall period. Curiously enough, the evidence is stronger for the post-1959 period than the earlier period. More importantly for a real business cycle interpretation is that the monetary base is not significant in any period. The F-statistic is above 1.0 only in the 1959–1988 sample.[14] As noted previously, the monetary base represents a mixture of banking policy and monetary policy. Interestingly enough, the reserve adjustment component of the base seems to be marginally significant, while the source base does not. The two deposit-to-currency ratios have a much greater tendency to have significant predictive content for real activity. The same qualitative results show up when deposits or the money multipliers are used instead of the deposit-to-currency ratio.[15]

In the lower panel of table 5–3, the three-year ahead forecast error variance decomposition is presented. The first number presented orders the column variable first and real output second in the decomposition of the contemporaneous covariance matrix. This practice attributes all contemporaneous covariance between the variables to the money or ratio variable and so produces a higher contribution to the forecast error variance. The second number (in parentheses) places real output first in the ordering and thus leads to a lower contribution of the variables to output. In periods when M2 exhibits statistically significant predictive value, it accounts for between 7.6% and 20.9% of the forecast error variance three years out. For M1 the numbers range from 13.6% to 22.4%. Note, however, that these values are sensitive to whether they are placed first or second in the ordering. In some cases the number is reduced by as much as two-thirds. These results confirm a statiscally significant role for broad measures of money in predicting real output. Whether one wants to consider the magnitudes of the variance decompositions economically significant is open to debate.

As might be guessed from panel A, the monetary base plays virtually no role in explaining real output three years ahead. The only period when the point estimate is above 10% is 1948–1969. The deposit-to-currency ratios, on the other hand, are more similar to the broad money aggregates than to the monetary base. One interesting observation is that the growth rate in TD/C is less sensitive to the ordering of the variables. Regardless of whether it is ordered before or after real output, its explanatory power for real output is little changed. In addition, while the growth in DD/C is more sensitive than TD/C to the ordering, DD/C is somewhat less sensitive than M1 is to the ordering. The source base appears to play a small role in the 1959–1979 period, but it is sensitive to the ordering.

Table 5–4 reports the results of three variable systems that include the monetary base and the deposit ratios. As might be anticipated from the bivariate results, the growth rate of the deposit-to-currency ratio is always more significant than the base. The lower panel of table 5–4 summarizes the three-year-ahead forecast error variance decompositions. The first number is based on ordering the base first, the deposit-currency ratio second, and output last. This ordering maximizes the opportunity for the base to play an important role. The number in parentheses places output first, the base second, and the deposit-to-currency ratio third. There is another ordering issue that is relevant. As discussed previously, the monetary base figures, by construction, are influenced by changes in reserve requirements and changes in the public's mix of bank deposits that are subject to different reserve requirements. As a consequence there is an induced positive correlation between the ratios and the base. Although not reported here, I have computed the forecast error variance decompositions placing the deposit ratio before the base in an effort to account for the feedback. The results are similar to those reported except that the contribution of the base to future output is reduced in every case, sometimes substantially, while the contribution of the ratios rises. For example, in the 1948–1969 period ordering the demand deposit-to-currency ratio before the base reduces the base's contribution to output from 14.2% to 7.8% and increases the demand-deposit-to-currency ratio's from 18.0% to 24.4%.

Overall, these results in table 5–4 confirm the general view that endogenous elements of money are the major contributors to the predictive value of money to real activity. The evidence that exogenous variations in the nominal quantity of outside money is important for subsequent movements in real output is very weak. These findings are consistent with the work of others. For example, Rush (1985) estimates regressions similar to Barro (1978) for the period when the United States was on the gold standard from 1880–1913. He found that neither expected nor unexpected movements in base money affect real output. He also showed that variations in the money multiplier were significantly correlated with real activity. King and Plosser (1984, 1986) have also noted that fact that the monetary base and currency seem unrelated to real activity. Boschen and Mills (1988) have reported similar results. They attempt to identify additional real shocks and to hold them fixed to see if money is important for predicting

Table 5–4. Summary of the Regressions for Real Output in Three and Four Variable VAR's

Variable	1948–1988	1948–1979	Sample Period 1948–1969	1959–1988	1959–1979
	A. Exclusion Restrictions: F-statistics and *p*-values[a]				
System: Δlog(B), Δlog(TD/C)					
Δlog(B)	.75(.56)	.26(.90)	.51(.73)	1.24(.30)	.26(.90)
Δlog(TD/C)	2.39(.05)	2.09(.09)	1.64(.18)	2.30(.06)	3.05(.02)
System: Δlog(B), Δlog(DD/C)					
Δlog(B)	.69(.60)	.27(.89)	.48(.75)	.79(.53)	.25(.91)
Δlog(DD/C)	2.56(.04)	2.95(.02)	2.39(.06)	1.58(.19)	1.76(.15)
System: ΔSB/B,ΔRAM/B, Δlog(TD/C)					
ΔSB/B	—	—	—	1.36(.25)	.47(.76)
ΔRAM/B	—	—	—	2.61(.04)	.54(.70)
Δlog(TD/C)	—	—	—	.76(.55)	1.38(.25)

	B. Three-Year-Ahead Forecast Error Variance Decomposition[b]				
System: $\Delta\log(B)$, $\Delta\log(TD/C)$					
$\Delta\log(B)$	4.8(1.2)	8.7(0.5)	13.1(3.4)	3.5(2.7)	7.5(1.0)
$\Delta\log(TD/C)$	9.1(8.9)	10.9(10.9)	10.9(10.5)	12.5(12.3)	17.9(17.3)
System: $\Delta\log(B)$, $\Delta\log(DD/C)$					
$\Delta\log(B)$	7.7(2.3)	8.4(0.8)	14.2(4.0)	7.0(4.2)	10.0(1.5)
$\Delta\log(DD/C)$	10.0(7.4)	19.2(13.4)	18.0(16.1)	8.5(5.6)	15.9(6.8)
System: $\Delta SB/B$, $\Delta RAM/B$, $\Delta\log(TD/C)$					
$\Delta SB/B$	—	—	—	4.2(2.9)	13.1(4.6)
$\Delta RAM/B$	—	—	—	12.1(10.3)	6.0(2.9)
$\Delta\log(TD/C)$	—	—	—	6.9(6.9)	16.4(14.9)

[a] The data are all quarterly and defined in table 5–1. The three-variable system includes four lags of $\Delta\log(Y)$, four lags of $\Delta\log(B)$, and four lags of either $\Delta\log(TD/C)$ or $\Delta\log(DD/C)$, and a time trend. The F-tests are for the hypothesis that the coefficients on the indicated variable are jointly equal to zero. The corresponding *p*-values are in parentheses.

[b] The forecast error variance decompositions are in percent. The first number is based on an orthogonalization that orders the variables $\{\Delta\log(B), \Delta\log(TD(\text{or } DD))/C, \Delta\log(Y)\}$. The second number is based on the ordering. $\{\Delta\log(Y), \Delta\log(B), \Delta\log(TD(\text{or } DD))/C)\}$. In the four-variable system $\Delta\log(B)$ is replaced by $\{\Delta SB/B, \Delta RAM/B\}$ so that variation due to the source base is always placed first relative to the reserve adjustment component.

output. Their real variables include oil prices, real government purchases, population, real exports, and changes in the marginal tax rate. They find that while the role of noncurrency components of M1 and M2 are sometimes important, currency never plays a significant role. Manchester (1989) reports results based VARs that focus on the role of the money multiplier instead of the deposit ratios. Her results are similar to those reported here in that the money multiplier appears to play a much more important role than the monetary base.

5. Conclusion

In this article I have focused on the role of money in economic fluctuations. While money may play an important role in market economies, its role as an important impulse to business cycles remains a highly controversial hypothesis. For years economists have attempted to construct monetary theories of the business cycle with only limited empirical success. Alternatively, recent real theories of the cycle have taken the view that to a first approximation independent variations in the quantity of outside money are neutral. These models, however, do not necessarily deny the possibility of important real affects arising from real shocks to the financial sector nor that the Federal Reserve can be the initiator of those shocks.

The conclusion of this brief look at some of the various forms of evidence pertaining to money and business cycles is that the case for a monetary theory of the cycle that relies on independent variations in the nominal quantity of money as an important business cycle impulse is weak. Not only do variations in nominal money explain very little of subsequent movements in real activity, but what explanatory power exists arises from variations in endogenous components of money. These characteristics are perfectly compatible with the implications of a class of real business cycle models proposed by King and Plosser (1984). Real business cycle models clearly have a long way to go before they offer a complete testable theory of the business cycle. However, their emphasis on real rather than monetary impulses as the primary source of shocks to the business cycle seems appropriate.

Notes

1. In the discussions that follow, the references to over a generation of work by dozens of authors is grossly inadequate. The references cited are only meant to be representative of the work or results, not an exhaustive bibliography.

2. Although they argue that in 1875–1878 and 1892–1894 the decline in the deposit-currency ratio was most likely attributable to a prior monetary disturbance.

3. The recent desire of the Federal Reserve to reduce inflation would appear to represent another episode based on the Romers' selection criteria. The results of this most recent autonomous change in money have yet to be played out.

4. The growth rate over a two- to two-and-one-half-year period is below expected in all six episodes. At a one-year horizon the growth rate appears lower than expected in only three of the six cases. Thus there appear to be "long and variable lags."

5. See Bernanke (1986) for one effort to impose some structure on these methods.

6. There developed an extended debate as to whether anticipated money growth was important or not. At this level of discussion this issue is not particularly relevant.

7. See King, Plosser, and Rebelo (1988a, 1988b) for a more general development of this class of models and Plosser (1989) for a less technical discussion.

8. See Goodfriend and King (1988) for a recent discussion pertaining to the distinction between monetary policy and banking policy functions of the central bank.

9. See Burns and Mitchell (1946) or, more recently, King and Plosser (1989) for a detailed description of the methodology. Generally, the procedure treats the cycle (trough-peak-trough) as a unit and partitions the series into nine stages: three stages of expansion, three stages of contraction, and a stage at each of the three turning points.

10. All data are quarterly with growth rates expressed at annual rates. The data are as follows: real GNP; M1 and M2 are consistent money stock series constructed by Rasche (1988); the monetary base is constructed by the St. Louis Federal Reserve Bank; TD/C is the ratio of the non-currency component of M2 to currency; and DD/C is the ratio of the non-currency component of M1 to currency.

11. The basic data for the source base and reserve adjustment components of the monetary base were kindly provided by Mike Belongia of the St. Louis Federal Reserve Bank.

12. Mankiw (1989) has argued that real business cycle models such as developed in King and Plosser (1984) are seriously deficient because, without a systematic feedback rule for monetary policy, they deliver a counter-cyclical price level. It would appear, however, that the evidence tends to suggest that counter-cyclical prices are the more frequently observed phenomenon.

13. McCallum (1983) has suggested that the observation of Litterman and Weiss (1985) and others subsequently that including interest rates eliminates the predictive role of money is irrelevant. He argues that the Fed has usually employed interest rates as a target. Thus movements in interest rates may in fact represent variations in money. While this argument may have some merit, more recent results reported by Friedman and Kuttner (1989) and Stock and Watson (1990) find that the spread between the commercial paper rate and the Treasury bill rate also eliminates the role of money and the role of individual interest rates. Since this default spread is not generally considered to be a target of monetary policy, it would seem that McCallum's argument may be moot. In any event, I do not include interest rates in any form in order to give variation in money the most opportunity to play a role.

14. Recently Stock and Watson (1990) have investigated the bivariate relation between industrial production and 157 series. In terms of predictive content, the monetary base ranked among the bottom 10 to 15 series.

15. Interestingly, the regressions that use the ratios exhibit a somewhat better fit than those using either the non-deflated deposits or the money multipliers.

References

Ahmed, A. 1987. "Wages Stickiness and the Nonneutrality of Money: A Cross Industry Analysis." *Journal of Monetary Economics* 20:25–50.

Andersen, L., and Jordan, J. 1968. "Monetary and Fiscal Actions: A Test of Their Relative Importance in Economic Stabilization." Federal Reserve Bank of St. Louis Review 50:11–24.

Ball, L., Mankiw, G., and Romer, D. 1988. "The New Keynesian Economics and the Output-Inflation Tradeoff." *Brookings Papers on Economic Activity* 1:1–66.

Barro, R. 1976. "Rational Expectations and the Role of Monetary Policy." *Journal of Monetary Economics* 2:1–32.

Barro, R. 1977a. "Unanticipated Money Growth and Unemployment in the United States." *American Economic Review* 67:101–115.

Barro, R. 1977b. "Long-Term Contracting, Sticky Prices and Monetary Policy." *Journal of Monetary Economics* 3:305–316.

Barro, R. 1978. "Unanticipated Money, Output and the Price Level in the United States." *Journal of Political Economy* 86:549–580.

Bernanke, B. 1983. "Nonmonetary Effects of The Financial Crisis in Propagation of the Great Depression." *American Economic Review* 73:257–276.

Bernanke, B. 1986. "Alternative Explanations of the Money-Income Correlation." In K. Brunner and A. Meltzer (Eds.), *Carnegie- Rochester Conference Series on Public Policy,* 25. Amsterdam: North-Holland, pp. 49–99.

Brunner, K., and Meltzer, A. 1971. "The Uses of Money: Money in the Theory of an Exchange Economy." *American Economic Review* 61:784–805.

Boschen, J., and Grossman, H. 1982. "Tests of Equilibrium Macroeconomics Using Contemporaneous Monetary Data." *Journal of Monetary Economics* 10:309–334.

Boschen, J., and Mills, L. 1988. "Tests of the Relation Between Money and Output in the Real Business Cycle Model." *Journal of Monetary Economics* 22:355–374.

Burns, A., and Mitchell, W. 1946. *Measuring Business Cycles*. New York: NBER.

Cagan, P. 1965. *Determinants and Effects of Changes in the Stock of Money 1875–1960*. New York: NBER.

Cooley, T., and Ohanian, L. 1989. "The Cyclical Behavior of Prices." Working Paper, University of Rochester.

Eichenbaum, M., and Singleton, K. 1986. "Do Equilibrium Real Business Cycle Theories Explain Post-War U.S. Business Cycles?" *NBER Macroeconomics Annual 1986*. Cambridge, Mass.: MIT Press, pp. 91–134.

Friedman, B., and Kuttner, K. 1989. "Money, Income and Prices after the 1980's." NBER Working Paper 2852.

Friedman, M., and Meiselman, D. 1963. "The Relative Stability of Monetary Velocity and the Investment Multiplier in the United States, 1897–1958." In *Stabilization Policies*. Englewood Cliffs, N.J.: Prentice Hall.

Friedman, M., and Schwartz, A. 1963a. *A Monetary History of the United States, 1867–1960*. Princeton: Princeton University Press.

Friedman, M., and Schwartz, A. 1963b. "Money and Business Cycles." *Review of Economics and Statistics* 45:32–64.

Friedman, M., and Schwartz, A. 1982. *Monetary Trends in the United States and the United Kingdom*. Chicago: University of Chicago Press.

Fischer, S. 1977. "Long-Term Contracts, Rational Expectations, and the Optimal Money Supply Rule." *Journal of Political Economy* 85:191–205.

Gordon, R. 1982. "Price Inertia and Policy Ineffectiveness in the U.S. 1890–1980." *Journal of Political Economy* 90:1087–1117.

Hamilton, J. 1983. "Oil and the Macreoconomy Since World War II." *Journal of Political Economy* 91:228–248.

King, R., and Goodfriend, M. 1988. "Financial Deregulation, Monetary Policy, and Central Banking." Federal Reserve Bank of Richmond, *Economic Review* (May/June):3–22.

King, R., and Plosser, C. 1984. "Money, Credit and Prices in a Real Business Cycle." *American Economic Review* 74:363–380.

King, R., and Plosser, C. 1986. "Money as the Mechanism of Exchange." *Journal of Monetary Economics* 17:93–115.

King, R., and Plosser, C. 1987. "Nominal Surprises, Real Factors, and Propagation Mechanisms." In W. Barnett and K. Singleton (Eds.), *New Approaches to Monetary Economics*. Cambridge: Cambridge University Press, pp. 273–292.

King, R., and Plosser, C. 1989. "Real Business Cycles and the Test of the Adelmans." Working Paper, University of Rochester.

King, R., Plosser, C., and Rebelo, S. 1989a. "Production, Growth and Business Cycles I: The Basic Neoclassical Model." *Journal of Monetary Economics* 21:195–232.

King, R., Plosser, C., and Rebelo, S. 1989b. "Production, Growth and Business Cycles II: New Directions." *Journal of Monetary Economics* 21:309–341.

Kydland, F., and Prescott, E. 1982. "Time to Build and Aggregate Fluctuations." *Econometrica* 50:1345–1370.

Litterman, R., and Weiss, L. 1985. "Money, Real Interest Rates and Output: A Reinterpretation of Postwar U.S. Data." *Econometrica* 53:129–156.

Long, J., and Plosser, C. 1983. "Real Business Cycles." *Journal of Political Economy* 91:39–69.

Loungani, P. 1986. "Oil Price Shock and the Dispersion Hypothesis, 1900–1980." Rochester Center for Economic Research Working Paper 33.

Lucas, R. 1972. "Expectations and the Neutrality of Money." *Journal of Economic Theory*, 4:103–134.

Lucas, R. 1973. "Some International Evidence on Output-Inflation Tradeoffs." *American Economic Review* 63:326–334.

Manchester, J. 1989. "How Money Affects Real Output." *Journal of Money, Credit and Banking* 21:16–32.

Mankiw, G. 1989. "Real Business Cycles: A New Keynesian Perspective." *Journal of Economic Perspectives* 3 (Summer):79–90.

McCallum, B. 1983. "A Reconsideration of Sims' Evidence Concerning Monetarism." *Economic Letters* 13:167–171.

McCallum, B. 1986. "On 'Real' and 'Sticky-Price' Theories of the Business Cycle." *Journal of Money Credit and Banking* 18:397– 414.

Mishkin, F. 1982. "Does Anticipated Monetary Policy Matter?: An Econometric Investigation." *Journal of Political Economy* 90:22–51.

Phelps, E. S. 1967. "Phillips Curves, Expectations of Inflation and Optimal Employment over Time." *Economica* 34 (August):254–281.

Plosser, C. 1989. "Understanding Real Business Cycles." *Journal of Economic Perspectives* 3 (Summer):51–78.

Rasche, R. 1988. "Demand Functions for U.S. Money and Credit Measures." Michigan State University, Department of Economics Working Paper 8718.

Romer, C., and Romer, D. 1989. "Does Monetary Policy Matter? A New Test in the Spirit of Friedman and Schwartz." *NBER Macroeconomics Annual 1989*, Cambridge, Mass.: MIT Press, pp. 121–170.

Rush, M. 1985. "Unexpected Monetary Disturbances During the Gold Standard Era." *Journal of Monetary Economics* 15:309–321.

Sargent, T. 1976. "A Classical Macroeconometric Model of the United States." *Journal of Political Economy* 84:207–238.

Sims, C. 1972. "Money Income and Causality." *American Economic Review* 62:540–552.

Sims, C. 1980a. "Comparison of Interwar and Postwar Business Cycles: Monetarism Reconsidered." *American Economic Review* 70:250–257.

Sims, C. 1980b. "Macroeconomics and Reality." *Econometrica* 48:1–48.

Stock, J., and Watson, M. 1989. "Interpreting the Evidence on Money–Income Causality." *Journal of Econometrics* 40:161–181.

Stock, J., and Watson, M. 1990. "Business Cycle Properties of selected U.S. Economic Time Series, 1959–1988." NBER Working Paper No. 3376 (June).

Taylor, J. 1980. "Aggregate Dynamics and Staggered Contracts." *Journal of Political Economy* 88:1–23.

Commentary

by N. Gregory Mankiw

Over the past decade, the debate about monetary policy has taken a surprising and profound turn. Real business cycle theorists like Charles Plosser have challenged some of the central tenets of modern macroeconomics. They have suggested that economic fluctuations reflect the optimal response of the economy to changes in technology and that monetary policy is largely irrelevant to these fluctuations. Most laymen would consider these suggestions ridiculous. And, what is more telling, if we could use a time machine to transport a macroeconomist to the present from almost any point in the past, the macroeconomist would likely agree with the layman's assessment.

To place the current debate in perspective, it is useful to recall briefly the events that began this past decade. In the late 1970s inflation was running about 10%. Paul Volcker, your prototypical tough, inflation-hating central banker was appointed to head the Federal Reserve with the express charge to lower inflation. As in the textbook model—or, I should say, as in the model in *most* textbooks—Volcker lowered money growth and raised interest rates, leading to the deepest postwar recession and, eventually, to lower inflation.

If the general public needed convincing that money matters, Paul Volcker succeeded in convincing them. Volcker was widely cited as the second most powerful person in the United States. A 700-page book on monetary policy made the *New York Times* best-seller list with the subtitle, "How the Federal Reserve Runs the Country."

The irony of this decade is that at the same time that Paul Volcker was removing any doubt in the minds of the public about the potency of monetary policy, the minds of many academic economists were turning to real business cycle theory. Just as Milton Friedman was winning his final victory with the public at large, his intellectual descendants began developing theories by assuming, as a starting point, that money does not matter.

It is impossible to overemphasize how radical this development is. At no time in the history of economic thought has the complete irrelevance of monetary policy been so widely and so seriously debated.

Some of the early Keynesians doubted that monetary policy was sufficient to pull the economy out of a deep depression. They believed that the 1930s might be an example of the famous liquidity trap. But these

Keynesians never doubted that monetary policy could cause a depression if it tried. Perhaps you couldn't push on a string, but surely you could pull on it.

And, although the label "new classical" is often applied to these real business cycle theories, the classical economists themselves never suggested that money was neutral in the short run. David Hume, in his essay "Of Money," wrote:

> In my opinion, it is only the interval or intermediate situation, between the acquisition of money and the rise in prices, that the increasing quantity of gold or silver is favourable to industry.... The farmer or gardener, finding that their commodities are taken off, apply themselves with alacrity to the raising of more....It is easy to trace the money in its progress through the whole commonwealth; where we shall find that it must first quicken the diligence of every individual, before it increases the price of labour.

It is clear that the classical economists like Hume would not have endorsed the complete monetary neutrality of the new classical economists. If we could bring Hume to the present in a time machine, we would likely learn that the old classical economists would rather be new Keynesians than new classicals.

As a matter of the sociology of science, the coincidence of the disinflation of Paul Volcker and the rise of real business cycle theory is a puzzle. Economists are fond of saying that our discipline is not cloistered in an ivory tower, that it is driven by events in the world at large. Surely there are many cases in which this is true, such as the rise of Keynesian economics in the wake of the Great Depression. But the rise of real business cycle theory in the 1980s shows that our profession has its own internal dynamic that is independent of current events in the outside world.

To avoid being misinterpreted, I should emphasize that it would be erroneous to conclude that real business cycle theory must be wrong simply because it departs radically from the long-held views of laymen and economists. Astrology does not become a science merely because many people follow their horoscopes. And whether the earth orbits around the sun, or the sun around the earth, is not a question to be answered by majority rule.

The real business cycle theorists have raised an important scientific question. It they are right—if technology is the driving force of fluctuations and if monetary policy is completely neutral—Plosser will turn out to be the Nicholas Copernicus of macroeconomics. Let me try to outline, however, why I don't expect that outcome.

In assessing why one does or does not believe that money is completely neutral, there are two questions to address. First, how good is the evidence for monetary non-neutrality? Second, how good are the theories of monetary non-neutrality? Plosser surveys both of these questions in his article. When reading it, I found myself agreeing with him surprisingly often. So here I will try only to highlight those key places where my judgements differ from his.

Let me start with the evidence. Plosser emphasizes that the correlation between outside money and real economic activity is quite weak and therefore provides little evidence of monetary non-neutrality. I agree completely, but so what? Surely the absence of a strong correlation provides evidence against the view that exogenous changes in the supply of outside money have been the primary source of economic fluctuations. But the conclusion that the Fed has avoided being the cause of most fluctuations doesn't mean the Fed is impotent. Throughout much of Plosser's sample, the Fed was explicitly trying, in the words of Fed Chairman William McChesney Martin, to "take away the punch bowl just as the party gets going." Even though Plosser might observe little correlation between the quantity of libation and the excitement of a party, he shouldn't conclude that party-goers don't enjoy a good drink.

The key empirical question is whether the Fed could, if it tried, cause a recession merely by reducing the quantity of money. Unfortunately, there is no easy way to answer this question. If the Fed were to run an experiment to test monetary neutrality, it could make the money supply fluctuate randomly for a few decades so we could observe the impact on the economy. Yet what we observe in the data we have are fluctuations in the money supply, even the outside money supply, that are largely endogenous responses to other shocks.

The analysis of historical episodes, such as in the work of Friedman and Schwartz and more recently Romer and Romer, is motivated by the hope that careful attention to history will enable us to identify exogenous movements in money. Such work relies on a heavy dose of judgment. A skeptic can always find some real event to blame for an economic downturn, so he need never be convinced that the downturn constitutes evidence for monetary non-neutrality. But unless we can get the Fed to run an experiment, it is the analysis of particular episodes, rather than the econometric analysis of time series, that must ultimately be used to judge whether monetary policy can influence the real economy.

I should note that even if most shocks causing fluctuations are real rather than monetary, as I am prepared to believe, the question of monetary neutrality is not moot, for two reasons. First, if money is not neutral, then the Fed may be able to use monetary policy to help the economy adjust to real shocks. Second, if money is not neutral, then the economy suffers from some sort of market imperfection that makes money non-neutral—perhaps prices are sticky. If so, then that imperfection is likely to influence how real shocks affect the economy as well. Hence, even if one does not believe that business cycles are monetary in the sense of being caused by fluctuations in money, one might still want a business cycle theory that is monetary in the sense of giving an important role to market imperfections that lead to monetary non-neutrality.

This brings me to the various theories of monetary non-neutrality. As Plosser correctly notes, there is no single theory of monetary non-neutrality accepted by all economists, or even by all economists who believe that money is non-neutral. All the prominent theories rest on some sort of market imperfection that makes the economy depart from the Arrow-Debreu ideal. Some models assume individuals observe prices imperfectly. Other models assume labor transactions are governed by long-term contracts predetermining the nominal wage. Still other models—the ones to which I am partial—assume that prices are set by monopolistically competitive firms who perceive price changes as being costly. Because of these market imperfections, the classical dichotomy breaks down, and money can influence real variables like output and unemployment.

Although Plosser finds each of these models unsatisfactory for some reason, his logic is not compelling. He argues against models with sticky prices by pointing out that prices do change, sometimes quickly. But it is also true that many prices have been documented to change very infrequently, in some cases only every few years. At the microeconomic level, the evidence is clear that some prices are flexible and some prices are sticky. This evidence leads me to prefer macroeconomic models in which some prices are flexible and some prices are sticky. The observation that *some* prices are flexible should not lead one to favor models in which *all* prices are flexible.

Let me close by asking what should one make of the observation that there are now so many theories of monetary non-neutrality in the literature. One might be tempted to conclude that the multitude of theories confirms Plosser's dissatisfaction with each of them. In contrast, my own view is hopelessly eclectic. Each of these theories of monetary non-neutrality has some ring of truth, but none is fully compelling. I am prepared to believe that the world includes all of the market imperfections that underlie these theories and that monetary non-neutrality does not arise from any single imperfection. Including many market imperfections at once makes theorizing messy. But if economic reality is messy, perhaps economic theory can't be otherwise.